he Great Planes/by James Gilbert/with special photography by the author

The Gre

by James Gilbert A Ridge Press Book

at Planes

amlyn, London • New York • Sydney • Toronto

Editor-in-Chief: Jerry Mason
Editor: Adolph Suehsdorf
Art Director: Albert Squillace
Associate Editor: Moira Duggan
Associate Editor: Barbara Hoffbeck
Art Associate: David Namias
Art Assistant: Neil R. Leinwohl
Art Production: Doris Mullane

Published by The Hamlyn Publishing Group Limited
London • New York • Sydney • Toronto
Hamlyn House, Feltham, Middlesex, England
ISBN: 0 600 33855 X

Contents

Introduction

One man's choice is one man's opinion. I must admit to moments of doubt in selecting the Great Planes, but only about those I had to leave out. Of the greatness of the twenty-six included here I am confident. In choosing them I have tried to include something for all tastes, for not everyone is fascinated by the same era of aviation, be it the early days, World War I, the golden twenties and thirties, World War II, or the jet age.

If there seems to be a preponderance of aerobatic types, I am quite unrepentant. Aerobatics has always seemed to me to be the quintessence of flying joy and skill. For those who would have had more warbirds: I do not like war. For my American friends who say there are too many European types, and for my English friends who think I have sold out my native land: one is but the child of one's experience.

Some of these chapters are based on articles that originally appeared in FLYING magazine, and though these few have been extensively revised and expanded for this book, I should like to thank my colleagues at the Ziff-Davis Publishing Company—particularly Mr. Robert B. Parke, FLYING's editor and publisher—for permission to use them here.

Cole Palen, Dave Fox, and Dick King of Old Rhinebeck Aerodrome, New York, gave me unstinting help. Without their fabulous collection of machines, and their extraordinary formation-flying skills in airplanes whose engines are supposed to be unthrottleable, the first few chapters of this book would have been sad, indeed. Bill Rhode allowed me to borrow freely from his enormous aviation library. John W. R. Taylor's eye caught many little errors in the manuscript that mine had missed.

Hawker Siddeley's John Crampton helped with the Sopwith chapter. The Shuttleworth Trust and the Tiger Club in England flew low and slow exactly where my cameras wanted them, as though it were easy. Ray Brandly of the National Waco Club freely taught me all I cared to learn. Mike Murphy put me right on Jungmeister history, and Bill Thomas lent me his Bücker to try for myself, as did Mira Slovak. The late William T. Piper, and his first engineer, Walter Jamouneau, sat to be interviewed on a hot afternoon when I am sure they had better things to do.

Pan American's Captain Ray Jones gladly provided his Staggerwing, Art Yadven his Jungmeister, and Pete Bruschia his Hellcat for me to photograph. Larry Billing eased me in among the production crews of *The Battle of Britain* so smoothly they thought I belonged there. Sergei Yakovlev sought out photos of his designs specially for me. Mrs. Holitscherova of Omnipol kept me up to date on Zlins. Curtiss-Wright, Ryan, Lockheed, Boeing, Grumman and Gates Learjet had all the pictures and information on their products when I needed them. And last but not least, Marty Forscher and his helpers at Professional Camera Repair quickly revived my photographic equipment, rain or shine, even after I'd dropped it.

James Gilbert, New York, 1970

The Wrights Fly

The world is alive with things that fly. Birds flap and soar, bats flitter, bugs buzz, sycamore seeds helicopter down from the branches. Even some flying fish flutter along from one wave crest to another. The question is: With all this as inspiration and example, why did it take man so long to fabricate a set of wings that would enable him to fly as well?

Perhaps it was because for too long he tried to fly by imitating the birds, a natural but misguided notion. Although birds' wings appear to be no more than arms with feathers, something called "scale effect" makes it impossible for man to strap a quiverful of quills to his arms, and thereby to fly. For while a bird's tiny muscles can easily generate enough power to lift it into the air, man's cannot. He is too puny, in relation to the wing surfaces he would have to manipulate to lift his weight. When you double wing size, you must much more than double the power. This "scale effect" is why there are no 200-pound birds. It is why hummingbirds can hover, while eagles only soar. And it is why no more than a few man-powered machines have ever gotten off the ground, despite Herculean physical effort by their pilots.

Beyond scale effect, there are matters of stability and control. A wing alone will always tumble. Bats and birds when flying are mostly wing area and, thus, are inherently unstable. They must make a million tiny corrections to the set or twist of their wings to keep their flight path straight and true. To achieve comparable stability in his flight vehicles, man must have a tailplane, a vertical and a horizontal stabilizer, and movable controls.

There is a third way in which bird-flight is misleading to would-be birdmen, and that is in the actual application of power. Everything that flies in nature flaps its wings to drive itself, a seemingly simple movement that high-speed photography has revealed to be a complex, twisting, warping figure-eight pattern whose actual mechanics man has never yet been able to duplicate successfully. As an alternate source of propulsion, he devised the motor-driven airscrew, or propeller. And yet, it still is odd that man took so long to learn to fly. The fundamentals of flight can be comprehended by any schoolboy who has ever made a paper airplane. Man did cleverer things than fly centuries ago: He made rockets, telescopes, and sailing ships, and he knew astronavigation and the calculus. And as far as constructional techniques are concerned, a simple glider of spruce and cords and fabric would have been easily within the competence of, say, Christopher Columbus's shipwright. But simple or not, the necessary knowledge needed to build a successful flying machine was discovered slowly. Leonardo da Vinci probably came as close as any man to stumbling on the secret of flight by pure reasoning. If only he had deigned to experiment, too! Had he built models and tried to test out his theories he might have made it. But Leonardo was a philosopher, not an artisan, and it needed the classless American society before the gulf between the two was successfully bridged, before thinkers would set to and try to construct what they had thought about.

After Leonardo, little further real progress was made until an Englishman named Sir George Cayley published in 1810 a paper "On aerial navigation . . ." which showed that he, if no one else, had advanced to the point of realizing that flapping wings were no way to go, and that he had stumbled on the importance of proper weight and balance, and the necessity for a stabilizing rear tail. In 1843 Cayley published a description of a sophisticated machine of a type we would now call a convertiplane. It had four lifting rotors (tilted inwards for a stabilizing, dihedral effect) that were to close up to form fixed wings once you were aloft, after which pusher propellers would drive you forward. A bare year before, another Englishman, W. S. Henson, had proposed an aerial steam carriage which was to have a wide, straight wing held up by king posts and wire bracing, a rear tail assembly, and a wheeled undercarriage, and which was to be propeller driven. In all, a device very close to being a real early airplane. Neither, however, was ever built. Cayley experimented throughout his life, and came very close to success. In 1849, he built a machine in which, in his own words, "a boy of about ten years of age was floated off the ground for several yards on a descending hill." A drawing survives of this machine. It was a sort of triplane box kite with rear stabilizing tails, like arrow tails, and underneath a little boat with wheels in which the boy sat. Four years later Sir George coaxed an unwilling coachman into a similar but larger machine which, reported Cayley's granddaughter, "flew across the little valley . . . and came down with a smash." The coachman, shaken but unhurt, emerged saying, "Please, Sir George, I wish to give notice. I was hired to drive, not to fly." Cayley's reply is not recorded.

In the 1890's a German experimenter, Otto Lilienthal, and his Scottish disciple Percy Pilcher, both flew—in a fashion. They built hang-gliders—that is, batwing frameworks of bamboo and fabric, with rudimentary tailplanes, but no power plant. Holding the glider overhead, they ran downhill hoping for a gust of wind to lift them off the ground. In flight they hung from the frame as though it were a trapeze. They never had more than partial stability, so they tried to exercise control by shifting their hanging bodies away from the direction the gliders tilted. But a movable center of gravity is no way to control an airplane, and in 1896 Lilienthal died in a jumble of sticks and string, and a year later Pilcher followed him to that aviator's Valhalla where the too-solid earth never gets in the way. It was probably stall-spin accidents that killed them both. The lift generated by a wing will increase as the angle at which it bites into the air increases, but only up to a certain point. Then the lift begins to decrease and the wing to pitch down. If the machine's distribution of side area is inadequate, so that it approaches stall slightly crabbed, one wing may stall before the other. This causes the unbalanced airplane to spin down. How to get out of a spin was not discovered until the First World War, and stall-spin accidents are still deadly today.

The death of brave men is never much of a deterrent to other brave men, and the year that Pilcher died an elderly American engineer named Octave Chanute took up experimenting with hang-gliders where the others had, so to speak, left off. Chanute learned much, and was luckier as well. Or more discreet. In any event, he quit while he was still alive and unharmed. Among other things, Chanute was the first man to apply the classic bridge-builder's Pratt truss construction to a wing, constructing a biplane braced by struts in compression and wires in tension.

With Chanute and his truss wing,

11

Exploring the feasibility of manned flight in Glider No. 3, 1902. Built by the Wrights in August-September, it was tested at Kill Devil Hills and made nearly one thousand glides. Above: A launching, with Orville as pilot. Below: Wilbur aloft. Right: Rear view of glider about to touch down. No. 3 perfected flight controls: forward elevator for pitch control, wing-warping for roll control, and vertical rudder to compensate for warp drag.

the stage is now set for the entrance of the Wright brothers, Orville and Wilbur. They were two of the five children of a midwestern bishop of the United Brethren Church, all devoutly raised to the old Presbyterian virtues of pertinacity and steady labor for a reasonable reward. Despite a four-year difference in age Wilbur and Orville were extraordinarily close to each other. "Orville and myself lived together . . . worked together and in fact thought together . . ." was how Wilbur later put it. And together they swore never to marry.

As children (by all accounts obedient ones), they had been captivated by a helicopter toy their father had brought home. They had built kites and sold them to other boys for a modest but reasonable profit, had kept a little printing press and done printing jobs for neighboring shopkeepers. They also went into the manufacture of bicycles of their own design. But all the while there smouldered in their minds the spark kindled by that toy helicopter. They read every published word on flying they could find. They learned about Lilienthal and Pilcher. They heard about Octave Chanute, another midwestern resident, and wrote to him, seeking advice and encouragement. This letter, in Wilbur's neat copperplate hand, powerfully conveys the intensity of their passion: "May 13th 1900. Dear Sir, For some years I have been afflicted [sic] that flight is possible to man. My disease has increased in severity and I feel that it will soon cost me an increased amount of money if not my life. I have been trying to arrange my affairs in such a way that I can devote my entire time for a few months to experiments in this field.

"My general ideas on the subject are similar to those held by most practical experimenters, to wit: that what is chiefly needed is skill rather than machinery." Chanute, now growing old, urged them to realize their goal.

Putting aside powered flight for the time being, the Wrights applied their energies to kite and glider flight. Did the neighbors laugh at grown men flying kites? Possibly, for the brothers wrote to the U. S. Weather Bureau seeking a consistently windy and isolated place in which to experiment in privacy. The Weather Bureau suggested Kitty Hawk on the North Carolina coast. The Wrights did not know that Kitty Hawk's fine, official, steady winds were an annual average of gales and calms. There they went, in October, 1900, with a seventeen-foot-span biplane. It was built with Chanute's Pratt trussing, with wings so braced that they could be "warped," or twisted in flight to alter the wing's angle of attack and therefore its lift, and thereby give some control in roll.

Held out in front on four delicate spars was a "horizontal rudder"; we would call it an elevator. The biplane had no rudder proper and, indeed, no laterally stabilizing side area at all. The Wrights flew it mostly as a kite to test the effects of wing-warping; sometimes as a free glider; and once or twice with one of the brothers lying flat on the lower wing. It was really too small to carry a man. So the next year they were back with a bigger, 22-foot glider with a rocking cradle that cupped the pilot's hips as he lay across the lower wing. As the pilot rolled his body in the cradle, connecting cables warped the wings to roll the glider in the same direction. A lever pitched the front elevator up and down to give the pilot control in the pitch axis and "to prevent nosedives."

But the new glider, for all its increased sophistication, flew less well than its predecessor. The principal problem was that while warping the wings did alter the spanwise distribution of lift, it also altered the drag, so that as you warped, one wing hung back and the glider slipped and skidded out of control. At this point the Wrights began increasingly to doubt the theories of previous experimenters. "We saw," they were later to write, "that the

13

calculations upon which all flying machines had been based were unreliable. . . . Truth and error were everywhere so intimately mixed as to be indistinguishable."

Back to Dayton they went, and while bicycles continued to support their enterprise they experimented. They built their own little wind tunnel, and measured and tested airfoils, finding they needed less camber (curve) and a higher aspect ratio (longer, narrower wings). They deduced that another arrangement of spars projecting from the back of the wings could carry a vertical rudder, wired into the warp cradle so that the rudder moved as the wings warped, canceling out differential warp drag. These two obscure midwesterners were finally applying to the problems of manned flight all that had ever been needed to solve them, to wit: a few short years of really persistent, imaginative, and careful experimenting.

Opposite: History is made. Orville
pilots aircraft in world's first powered,
sustained, and controlled flight, at
Kitty Hawk, December 17, 1903.
Below: Another view after epochal
twelve-second, 120-foot flight
across North Carolina sand dunes.

In the fall of 1902 they set out once more for the North Carolina dunes, this time bearing in their baggage the bones of a new 32-foot glider with a new, less curved airfoil and a new vertical rudder. As soon as it was rigged and flown they could see the progress they had made, and within a mere thirty-nine days they made almost a thousand successful flights with it. At last they had real control about all three axes—pitch, roll, and yaw.

They were ready for the final giant step: flight with power. And here they were immediately far ahead of other, lesser experimenters, thanks to that blessed wind tunnel, for they could make real measurements of lift and drag. They didn't have to guess how much power, how much wing area. They knew. That wind tunnel paid off in other ways, too, for the little four-cylinder engine they built for their Flyer was based on the single-cylinder

15

By 1908, Wrights had developed a two-seat military Flyer which Orville demonstrated to Army at Fort Myers, Virginia, in series of flights pictured here. Tests ended disastrously (bottom) when crash ruined plane, injured Orville, and killed his military passenger, Lieutenant T. E. Selfridge.

unit they had put together to drive the tunnel.

The Wrights' first airplane engine was frankly primitive. It was a flat, in-line four, water-cooled by thermo-syphoning, and with a "surface carburettor," whereby fuel was vaporized by allowing it to flow over the hot cylinder jacket. Inlet valves were simply spring-loaded —the suction of the descending piston opened them—while a chain-driven camshaft opened the exhaust valves. The engine had a simple, low-tension magneto, friction-driven from the rim of the flywheel. On a good day it put out about 16 hp at around 1,200 rpm for a few seconds, its power output rapidly falling nearly to 12 hp as it heated up. With its massive flywheel and piston rods it weighed 179 pounds dry, or around 200 pounds with water, oil, and a gallon of fuel. So the power-to-weight ratio was poor. Furthermore, the Wrights, in the wind-tunnel experiments they had used to calculate their power requirements, had underestimated both scale effect and interference effects between their test airfoils and the tunnel walls. Their engine was only barely powerful enough. In only two ways would we have considered it at all modern: It was square, with equal bore and stroke, and it had a five-bearing crankshaft.

Where they did excel themselves was in the design of the propellers the engine was to drive. The Wright brothers seem to have been the first would-be aviators to have realized that a propeller is not a screw or a paddle, but simply a rotating wing, in need of a proper airfoil section just like a wing, and also a spanwise twist, so that it can operate efficiently at a constant (spanwise) angle of attack.

The Wrights' propellers had to be designed for efficiency at very low forward speeds, so they made them big and slow-turning. These propellers were driven, naturally enough, by bicycle chains, one crossed so that the two propellers turned in opposite directions to eliminate torque. The Wrights calculated that their two propellers would produce 100 pounds of thrust at 305 rpm, and it is a measure of their sometimes fantastic precision that later measurements showed the estimate to be within one percent of actuality. These propellers were sixty-six percent efficient in converting torque to thrust, an impressive performance, considering that the best we can achieve in 1970 is only eighty-five percent efficiency. Although neither of the two brothers weighed more than 145 pounds, with 200 pounds of power plant they more than doubled the load their wings had to carry. So the airframe they built to take the engine was their biggest yet, spanning more than forty feet. Their launching technique with the gliders had been to have a helper lifting each wing-tip strut and running with it into the wind until the glider lifted off by itself. But the Flyer and its pilot grossed 750 pounds, so they planned sixty feet of sectioned wooden rail with a wheeled dolly to launch it.

They returned to the Carolina coast again in the fall of 1903, this time taking fully three weeks to assemble their machine. The first time they started up the engine it backfired and wrecked one propeller drive. Power transmission problems delayed flight trials for months. It was not until one bitter breezy morning in December that they were finally ready. By the toss of a coin Wilbur won the right to be pilot on the first trial. With Orville trotting alongside to steady a wing tip, he hurtled down the launch rail and immediately plowed off the end into the sand. Three days later they were ready to try again. This time it was Orville's turn to ride the Flyer. He had better luck, taking off and remaining aloft, a scant few feet off the ground, for some twelve seconds of undulating flight. He covered about 120 feet before pitching gently onto the sand. A similar third flight followed. On the fourth and last flight Wilbur stayed up for fifty-nine seconds, covering 852 feet over the sands and maybe half a mile through the windy air.

Like all their airplanes, this one was desperately unstable and divergent in pitch, which was the cause of that undulating flight path. The end of this flight came when the Flyer dove suddenly and sharply into the sand, snapping one of the front elevator struts. The destruction was completed by a capricious gust that overturned and smashed the machine.

They had lunch, and then sent a cable to the Bishop, that splendid parent who had encouraged them in all they had ever wanted to do: "Success four flights Thursday morning all against twentyone mile wind started from level with engine power alone average speed through air thirtyone miles longest 57 [sic] seconds inform press home Christmas." The press didn't much care.

By the summer of 1904 the brothers had a new Flyer built and no longer felt the need to hide out in North Carolina, but were flying from a meadow near their home in Dayton. By the end of 1905 they could bank, turn, and fly figure-eights with ease, had covered twenty-five miles in one flight, and stayed up more than half an hour at a time. Yet fame still eluded them. Maybe fortune would be kinder? The Wrights were asking $200,000 for all rights to their invention—an immense sum of money, the equivalent of more than a million dollars today. At that price the U. S. Army and Government were not interested. The Wrights went off to England and tried to sell their invention to the British. No takers. Two and a half years were to elapse before they had the least success, two and a half years in which they did no more flying. Finally the U. S. Army agreed to pay $25,000 for a machine that would carry two men and fuel to go 125 miles at 36 mph.

In 1908 Wilbur sailed off to France with a Flyer to give flight demonstrations to would-be French licensees, while Orville stayed home to fly their new two-seater for the Army. France in 1908 was a hotbed of aviators trying to fly, and when on August 8 Wilbur went skittering around a Le Mans racecourse in a two-minute flight it was as though his spectators had seen the Holy Grail. "One of the most exciting spectacles in the history of applied science," wrote one of them. "Good grief!" exclaimed another. "We are beaten! We don't exist!" Orville, meanwhile, dived to disaster with the two-seater, in a fearful crash that put him in the hospital and mortally wounded his military passenger, Lieutenant Selfridge. Yet the contracts were eventually closed, and others, too. Fame, acknowledgement, and a modest reward, all long overdue, were achieved at last.

Today we are seventy years further down the road, and to one trained on modern airplanes it is sometimes difficult to see how the Wright Flyers were so successful. In many ways the Wrights' beliefs led them up blind alleys. In their quest for controllability they made their designs not just unstable, but wildly so. Look closely at their first powered machine: With its droop-winged anhedral, engine and pilot side-by-side, front elevator hinged at close to fifty percent chord, short moment arms to both elevator and rudder, and total lack of fixed side area anywhere—it would be quite unflyable by any modern pilot. Wing warping was a dreadfully inefficient method of roll control, preventing proper bracing of the wing for rigidity, and was soon abandoned in favor of the aileron (already invented and patented before the Wrights ever began experimenting with flying). Nor did their concepts of hinged body cradles operating flight controls, or of launch rails and skid undercarriages, endure long in the flood of aviation activity that their 1908 public demonstrations set off.

What made Wilbur and Orville Wright great was their dogged persistence. They simply kept on at the thing till they made it work. A lesson to us all.

Blériot Crosses the Channel

High drama along the northernmost coastline of France! The London *Daily Mail* has offered the extravagant sum of £1,000, about $5,000, to the first man to fly the English Channel. It is mid-July, 1909. Aviation is far from being an industry, nor yet a science. An art, perhaps. Certainly a passion! A burgeoning miracle, come to set the public's heart aflame and gladden newspaper proprietors.

Here at Wissant is *le Comte* Charles de Lambert, waiting for his army of mechanics to bring one or the other of his two Wright biplanes to perfection. Le Comte is a majestic man, with fine ginger whiskers and steely blue eyes. Will he be the first across? Out at Sangatte an exquisite Antoinette monoplane is being prepared by ten skilled mechanics under the stern if portly presence of its designer, M. Levavasseur. The pilot? He is Hubert Latham, adorned with checked cap, fancy wristwatch, cigarette holder, and all. Mr. Latham is of English descent, although his family seat is now a fine château near Chartres. Mr. Latham speaks several languages and is given to hunting and adventure. Does he have an occupation besides that of aviator and sportsman? "I am a man of the world," was his considered reply when the president of the Republic asked him the same question. Mr. Latham has recently broken the world endurance record for monoplanes and has flown in a measured wind of 16 mph. Now he makes himself comfortable at the Grand Hotel in Calais. Will he be the first to cross the Channel?

At the nearby village of Les Baraques a dirty little monoplane, muddy wings folded back against the oily fuselage, is being unloaded from a farm cart under the instructions of its designer, builder, and pilot, a small, indomitable Frenchman named Louis Blériot, limping heavily from a recent crash. He's a latecomer in the race to be first across, but he still has a chance. He does have family problems: six children and a sobbing wife who has extracted a promise that if he should win he will stay safely on the ground forever. *Elle a raison.* Louis Blériot has smashed more airplanes than any man alive. Latham is ready first. Before dawn on July 13 he is off for a short test flight, which ends in a plowed field and with a bent landing gear. By the nineteenth his machine is fixed and the weather looks good, so at 6:42 A.M. he takes off in earnest. Wireless is being used to cover the great contest, and the news that Latham is off goes out to a waiting world. There is wireless at Dover, too. At 7:23—"Anything yet?" At 7:46—"Nothing in sight, requesting assistance." At 8:06—"Very anxious here. Cannot see escort boat or Latham. Can you?"

He must be down. There must be news soon. At 10:23 it comes: an engine failure seven miles off the French coast. When the rescue boat arrives Latham is sitting on the cockpit coaming trying to keep his feet dry and smoking a damp cigarette.

A new Antoinette, so stable it will almost fly itself, with a large well-padded cockpit and a tremendous 60-hp engine, is rushed to Sangatte for the indefatigable Latham.

The next man to fly, however, is Blériot. On July 25 he is out for an engine run at 3:30 A.M., before it is even light. At 4:00 A.M. he is aloft for a trial flight of fifteen minutes' duration. Excitement mounts among the two thousand spectators who have come to watch even at that early an hour. At 4:40 the sun is well up, and a light breeze is blowing from the southwest. M. Blériot decides to make his bid. He clears the telegraph wires along the edge of the cliff and heads out to sea.

Meanwhile, Latham is sleeping. M. Levavasseur, the designer of Latham's machine, was up briefly at two and again at three to see the state of the weather, but each time he shook his head and returned to bed. At 4:30 A.M. he was up again, and out on the veranda. "Blériot has started," came the cry, and Levavasseur peered out to sea in time to glimpse the tiny drab monoplane disappearing into the mist. Latham is awakened and is sore dismayed, but being a good sport sends a wireless message to Blériot on The Other Side: "Good luck! Hope to follow you soon." But the breeze is rapidly freshening, and Levavasseur forbids him to follow Blériot. Poor Latham! After all the tension of the last fortnight, the forced landing in the sea, to be sleeping while his rival is departing!

But what of Blériot? "I begin my flight, steady and sure, towards the English coast," he told the *Daily Mail's* reporter later that day. "I have no apprehensions, no sensations, *pas du tout.* The Escopette [an escort ship provided by the French Navy] has seen me. . . . She makes 42 kilometres an hour. What matters? I am making at least 68 kilometres. Rapidly I overtake her, travelling at a height of 80 metres. The moment is supreme, yet I surprise myself by feeling no exultation. Below me is the sea, the surface disturbed by the wind, which is now freshening. The motion of the waves beneath me is not pleasant. I drive on. Ten minutes have gone. . . . I am amazed. There is nothing to be seen, neither the torpedo destroyer, nor France, nor England. I am alone. I can see nothing at all—*rien du tout!* For ten minutes I am lost. It is a strange position to be alone, unguided, without a compass, in the air over the middle of the Channel.

"I touch nothing. I let the aeroplane take its own course. I care not whither it goes. For ten minutes I continue, neither rising nor falling, nor turning. And then twenty minutes after I have left the French coast, I see the green cliffs of Dover, the Castle, and away to the West the spot where I had intended to land. What can I do? It is evident that the wind has taken me out of my course. . . .

"Now is the time to attend to the steering. I press the lever with my foot and turn easily towards the west, reversing the direction in which I am travelling. Now indeed I am in difficulties, for the wind here by the cliffs is much stronger, and my speed is reduced as I fight against it. Yet my beautiful aeroplane responds. Still steadily I fly westwards hoping to cross the harbour and reach the Shakespeare cliff. Again the wind blows. I see an opening in the cliff. Although I am confident that I can continue for an hour and a half, that I might indeed return to Calais, I cannot resist the opportunity to make a landing upon this green spot. . . . I attempt a landing, but the wind catches me and whirls me round two or three times. At once I stop my motor, and instantly the machine falls straight upon the land from a height of twenty metres. In two or three seconds I am safe upon your shore. Soldiers in khaki run up, and a policeman. They kiss my cheeks. The conclusion of my flight overwhelms me."

But Blériot, true to form, has crashed again, breaking his propeller and landing gear. To the onrushing greeters he must have been a disheveled figure, drenched with oil and perspiration, his eyes bloodshot, the crutches he needs for his injured foot strapped to the rear fuselage of his broken machine. But he is not too unprepossessing to put off an official of His Majesty's Customs and Excise, who, true to his idiotic calling, later returns to headquarters a form that states: "I certify that I have exam-

GRANDE SEMAINE D'AVIATION DE LA CHAMPAGNE
REIMS DU 22 AU 29 AOÛT 1909

Top row: Blériot model
No. 3 of 1905 (far left). Poster for
world's first aviation meeting,
north of Reims in 1909
(center). Ten different makes of
airplane took part and were
airborne. Blériot's plane
crash-landed and burned, but he
escaped with minor injuries.
Blériot (left) in cockpit of model XI.
Middle row: Blériot No. 4 of 1906
failed to fly in tests on
water (opposite) and land (below).
Bottom row: Blériot (opposite,
fourth from right) at Toury,
France, in 1908, where
No. 8 (below) crashed a month
after successful 17-mile flight.

ined Louis Blériot, master of a vessel 'Monoplane,' lately arrived from Calais, and that it appears by the verbal answers of the said master to the questions put to him that there has not been on board during the voyage any infectious disease demanding detention of the vessel, and that she is free to proceed."

As for Louis Blériot, he later proceeded freely and happily up to London, where a tumultuous welcome continued for days. Multitudes came to inspect his machine when it was put on exhibition in a London store. If the British felt a faintly prophetic unease about being suddenly only thirty-six and a half minutes from the turbulent continent of Europe, they kept it mostly to themselves, happily acknowledging the little Frenchman's feat.

Who was this daring but disheveled aviator, Louis Blériot? He was a manufacturer who had amassed a very sizable fortune making acetylene automobile lamps, then had dissipated most of it recklessly experimenting with flying machines. As you already may have guessed, Blériot's prime purpose in setting out to gain the prize was to build up a market for Blériot airplanes. In this he was wildly successful, for he received orders for more than a hundred in just two days.

Success had come at last. In his nine years of experimenting Blériot had tried every format, every shape of flying machine, and along the way had borrowed every idea, every technique he could from his rivals, and had seen almost every one of his designs end in failure or a wreck. His personality and approach to the problems of flight were completely antithetical to those of the Wright brothers. They—stolid, unemotional midwesterners —had run endless tests, made countless measurements before carefully building their one new Flyer each year. Blériot—emotional, impetuous, impatient—was often involved with three different designs at once, not waiting till he had wrecked one before starting work on the next, while yet dreaming of a third.

His first overpowering inspiration to fly had come in 1900 at the Paris Exhibition, where he had seen a great bat-winged "flying machine" displayed. Weighed down with huge propellers and half a ton of batteries for its electric engines, it was incapable of flight, but quite enough to stir Blériot's imagination. If a real bat's wings would flap, he thought, so should a man-made bat's, so he built himself a flapping wing device that flapped itself furiously into a tangle of junk. Blériot's next project was a giant kite on floats which, while being towed behind a motorboat, turned turtle and half-drowned its would-be pilot, Gabriel Voisin. Then followed a tube-shaped floatplane, with an engine this time, which at least floated well. Next was a tail-first monoplane shaped like a duck, thrust forward by a pusher propeller. This machine also was very quickly reduced to junk. Then came a tandem monoplane, and following this closely there was a neat monoplane, with its engine ahead of the dihedraled wings, a tractor propeller, and a slender fuselage tapering back to a rear-mounted horizontal stabilizer and rudder. It was almost the typical airplane of today, at least in outline. New models followed swiftly, all tractor monoplanes, all moderately capable of flight. With Number Eleven, Blériot really began to make progress as an aviator, progressing from an eight and a half mile flight on May 31 to a twenty-five mile cross-country hop (with one stop) on July 13. It seems that after its fabulous cross-Channel dash the first Blériot Type Eleven never flew again. It exists: You may see it hanging in the Paris Conservatoire des Arts et Métiers. Even for its time it is a tiny airplane, only twenty-five feet six inches in span and with a bare weight of less than five hundred pounds. The fuselage is a simple flimsy box girder of wood with diagonal wire bracing. The wings are equally as simple,

Top left: Blériot XI which crossed English
Channel is unloaded from farm cart prior to flight.
Assembled (top right) and ready to go,
Les Baraques, July, 1909. It was powered by
three-cylinder, 25-hp Anzani engine.
Middle: Another view of RFC Blériot. By 1913,
80-hp Gnome engine was standard.
Above: Blériot XI aloft during international air
race at Hendon, outside London, in 1913.
Left: Plane in poster for 1910 Nice
air show is artist's fanciful conception
of Levavasseur's Antoinette.

with center king posts above and below for the bracing wires and also the warp wires. (Blériot was the first aviator in Europe to make wing-warping for lateral control really work, and he abandoned ailerons, which he had tried on all his previous machines, to do so.) The main landing gear employs a pair of ordinary bicycle wheels, mounted on a trailing axle. An airplane of inelegant simplicity, you might call it. Latham's Antoinette, all agree, was an infinitely more sophisticated and beautiful machine, only kept from success by the really appalling unreliability of its motor. Not that Blériot's engine was much better. It was a three-cylinder semiradial motorcycle engine, the work of an Italian ex-bicycle racer named Alessandro Anzani, who enjoyed a certain notoriety for his foul language. The engine would put out a meager 25 hp before it began to overheat. As far as I know, no one before or since has ever succeeded in getting an Anzani to run for the thirty-seven minutes it took Blériot to reach Dover. The story is that Blériot's motor slowed down so much at one point as to almost put him into the sea, until a chance shower of rain cooled the cylinders. Perhaps. We do know that when the first Gnome rotaries came along soon afterward Blériot bought few more Anzanis, and when the Channel was next flown, on May 21, 1910, by Jacques de Lesseps (grandson of that de Lesseps who dug the Suez Canal), it was a Gnome-Blériot he used.

Simple the Blériot Type Eleven monoplane was; it was also stable and quite easy to fly—no mean virtues when you remember that its designer must have had less than five hours' total flying time when he set off from Calais. Blériot was among the first aviators to adopt the logical system of cockpit controls that is now universal: a foot-operated rudder bar for control in yaw; a central lever that tilts forward and back, left and right, for control in pitch and roll; and a hand throttle.

In his nine years of experimenting, Blériot spent perhaps $150,000. In the fortnight after he crossed the Channel he won prizes totaling $20,000, and got orders for more than $250,000 worth of airplanes.

What of Blériot's promise to his wife to fly no more once he had succeeded in flying the Channel? That brave lady had a change of heart, it seems, for in an interview she said: "Aviation is his very life, and henceforth I shall certainly not ask him to give it up, and if, when my two boys are grown up, they wish to be aviators like their father I shall have no objection."

And what of Hubert Latham, Blériot's rival, whom we left almost in tears, standing on the veranda of his hotel to receive the news that Blériot was off to Dover? It was three days before his new Antoinette was ready and the weather right. This time he had covered perhaps nine-tenths of the distance to Dover before, once more, that treacherous Antoinette engine let him down. His ditching was less smooth this time, with the airplane half-vanishing under the waves, and Latham getting some nasty cuts about the face from his broken goggles. It was his last attempt. Latham went back to his other favorite occupation, big-game hunting (one of his household treasures was the first duck ever shot from an airplane), and in a year or two he was dead, killed by a charging buffalo while on safari. His bravado was not without reason, for he was tubercular and could not have lived long.

And the third contender for the Channel prize, the Comte de Lambert—he packed up quietly and went home, poor chap.

As for the English Channel, it was flown six times in 1910, twenty-eight times in 1911. And we should certainly not overlook the thirty-six balloons that had successfully drifted across its waters even before Louis Blériot's luckiest and most daring adventure.

29

The Fokker Scourge

Anthony Fokker was born in Java, in the then-remote Netherlands East Indies. His father was a more-than-prosperous coffee planter, and young Anthony was more than happy running wild and barefoot with the native boys across the coral sands. In 1897, when he was six, his family returned to Holland, principally so that he could go to school. But young Fokker spent most of his time in the attic, which he converted to a workshop, and where he constructed his own model electric railroad, carefully wiring the doorknob into the high-tension circuit, so he would not be intruded upon. At school he modified his desk so that it contained an aide-memoire remotely operated and invisible to his teachers. He devised a pen that would write four "lines" at once, so that "one hundred lines" could be rattled off as twenty-five. He must have been a poisonous small boy—cocky, arrogant, selfish. After four years of inconclusive battle, he dropped out of school, announcing his intention to develop a new kind of tire in which coil springs replaced air and rubber. It must have been the first and last time the world got the better of Anthony Fokker, for a lawyer, hired with a fair amount of Fokker senior's money, finally announced that such a device was already thoroughly patented by another inventor. Young Fokker was next drafted into the army, but soon malingered his way out.

One day he went to an automobile show in Brussels where Hubert Latham's airplane was one of the exhibits. "You may do as you please," said Fokker senior, with the rich disgust of all rich fathers of problem sons, "but I will never buy you an airplane." Young Anthony retired to his attic and experimented with wood and paper models. Sweepback and

enough dihedral, he found, could confer perfect lateral stability, so that no roll control or wing-warping was required. But downstairs his exasperated parents were planning a career for him. He was to go to an engineering school in Germany. Soon young Fokker was aboard a Rhine steamer and on his way, weeping from homesickness. Next he was badgering his father for the money to transfer to another engineering school twenty miles away. It was not till later that his father found out it was a school of aeronautical engineering. His parents held the widely prevalent view of the time that flying was no more than the shortest route to the cemetery. The school designed and built an airplane as an exercise, and it crashed with the aviation instructor on its first flight. Once more Anthony Fokker wept. Unabashed, he wrote to his father for more money, to build a flying machine of his own. Much to his surprise, back came 1,000 marks without a murmur of protest. It was only the beginning. Poor dad was to shell out no less than 183,000 marks before his son's lust for aviation became profitable. Old Herman, Fokker senior, rather delighted in playing curmudgeon. When his neighbors in Haarlem said, "There's old Mr. Fokker," he would rattle his dentures and growl, "The devil is old, too." Some of his son's begging letters, masterpieces of artifice and youthful conceit, survive, along with his father's choleric annotations of "Nonsense" and "Big words" and "Never" and the like. But he kept right on paying, and in later years allowed that he knew how young men needed capital, and that he himself had been an even worse failure at school than his son. Fokker senior's doubts were confounded in the early war years when his son not only repaid every penny with interest, but declined his patrimony; whatever he might need thereafter, it would never again be money from his father.

Anthony Fokker's first airplane was shared with a partner, who waited till Fokker went off home to visit his parents at Christmas, then took it out alone and wrecked it. It was the last time Fokker encumbered himself with partners.

Fokker's early airplanes were all called "Spin" (Spider), and all embodied the principles of automatic stability he had discovered through his model experiments. There was not much to them: an engine, usually salvaged from the wreck of a previous airplane; a sled-like tripod of skids to which the wheels were attached; tilted, fabric-covered wings; and welded tubes and wires and turnbuckles that ran aft to form the stabilizer, and rose high above the motor to form king posts for the wings. Everything was cut and fitted very much by eye; Fokker had a flair for this kind of improvisation. In those days, if you were an aviator you were all things to all men. Anthony Fokker conceived and built his flying machines, sold them where he could, gave flying lessons, flew for a share of the gate before crowds every weekend, borrowed money, and spent it—and unsuccessfully sought orders for his machines from all the armies of Europe. It was a rough-and-tumble business, where courage counted for more than kindness. The crowds came to see men die, and die they did. Fokker himself had a bracing wire let go one day at 2,400 feet and rode his disintegrating machine down to the tree-tops. He survived almost unhurt, though his passenger died in the smash. Fokker

was also the first man ever to loop an airplane in Germany. "So I set my teeth," he later described it, "and thought, 'Some day you must die. It might as well be now.'"

It was a hand-to-mouth existence to be thus driven to a desperate courage by pride and the promises of air-show promoters. But the devil takes care of his own, and Fokker, who should have been killed ten times over by his own admission, survived. When the tide of his fortunes turned, it caught him by surprise, for he never expected war. It turned dramatically. Within hours those same officers of the German army and navy to whom he had endlessly and fruitlessly demonstrated his machines were bidding for them like crazed collectors at a mad auction. (It mattered not to Fokker who bought his services. He was a neutral, and a businessman, not a moralist.) In a day or two Fokker had sold everything in his shop—whether it flew or not, whether it was his or not, at any price he cared to mention. Everyone was certain the war would be over in three months; one had to seize opportunities as they presented themselves.

But three months came and went, and still there was war. German reconnaissance airplanes began mysteriously to disappear, and on April 15, 1915, when a French Morane-Saulnier monoplane was forced to land behind their lines, the Germans found out why. Strapped to the fuselage top was a Lewis gun, and carefully lined up with it on the propeller blades were heavy steel deflector plates. In this way the airplane had become a flying gun that could be aimed at its target simply by the pilot moving his flying controls. Blinkered by the conservatism of their calling, the commanders of the German air service had no thought but to imitate the Morane's gun, and

33

Above: Dr-1 Triplane taking off. Sturdy construction and absence of bracing wires that could be shot away made Triplane hard to bring down. Right top: Cockpit view forward over twin Spandau machine guns. Bottom: Propeller and rotary engine. Opposite: Von Richthofen (center) and comrades in 1917. Far right: In flight, said the Baron, the Triplane "climbed like a monkey and maneuvered like the devil."

summoned Fokker, whose airplanes they already liked, to do the job. At five o'clock one Tuesday evening he was given a Parabellum machine gun to experiment with.

Fokker had never even handled a gun before, but he knew at once that deflector plates on the propeller were a poor solution to the problem. Two days and two nights later, pale from lack of sleep, he had the answer strapped to his car, and set off for Berlin. The answer was a little Fokker monoplane with a machine gun mounted atop its fuselage just like the French airplane, but with its firing mechanism connected to the propeller by a rod-and-cam arrangement so that fire was interrupted whenever a blade of the propeller turned past the gun's muzzle.

At first the German officers didn't believe it. Fokker started his engine and fired a few shots without one catching the propeller. There must be some trick to it, they thought. Would Herr Fokker care to fire a belt of one hundred bullets from the air? A target was set up on the turf and Fokker dived on it with his guns blazing. To his contemptuous delight the bullets ricocheted everywhere, as did the German officers, rushing madly for cover and throwing themselves flat on the earth. When they had picked themselves up and dusted off their uniforms their minds at last were clear on what they must do. They must pass the buck. Would Herr Fokker care to demonstrate his invention to the officers at the front? So Fokker once more lashed the little monoplane to the back of his car and set off for the front. There the offi-

cers didn't believe his synchronizing device, either. Perhaps he would care to demonstrate it to the Crown Prince, who was in residence only a few miles away? Fokker performed a few of his favorite aerobatics, then dived on the field and fired a burst into the stream that bordered it. Even he did not have the gall to make the Crown Prince of Germany run for cover. Very interesting, said the Crown Prince. It was perhaps Herr Fokker's father who invented the device? For Fokker was only a boyish twenty-four. People were always asking him for Herr Direktor or the *real* Herr Fokker. "You seem to be a real Flying Dutchman," the Crown Prince admitted, asking Fokker back for lunch and some of his special sherry. But Fokker did not drink. His only weakness was candy.

Still no one would make a decision. Perhaps Herr Fokker would care to shoot down a Frenchman to prove that his synchronized gun really works in combat: So for several weeks Fokker, uncomfortable in a German uniform, patrolled the skies of northeastern France till he stumbled upon a lumbering two-seater Farman observation biplane. He crawled up behind it, took aim, and decided suddenly that the whole job could go to hell. Let them do their own killing! He returned to the German field at Douai. There was an argument, but in the end it was agreed Lieutenant Oswald Boelcke would take on the job. On his third flight Boelcke, who was later to become the first German ace, scored. The entire German air corps was at once convinced that Fokker was a genius. He was deluged with orders for the gun-synchronizing device and for his monoplane. Lieutenant Max Immelmann received the second Fokker that was ready, and he too scored at once. Within a week or two, half a dozen Fokkers were in action with devastating effect. The ponderous Allied observation airplanes went down like ninepines.

It was the beginning of the "Fokker Scourge," the "Fokker Terror," the excuse with which the British press, ever alert for incompetence in high places, was to belabor the Allied authorities in general and the Royal Aircraft Factory at Farnborough in particular. With some justification. Fokker's gun gear remained a secret from the Allies for five months, and it was a full year before the first Allied fighter sported an interrupter gear.

These E-type Fokker monoplanes were a far cry from the early Spider series. Fokker had realized the moment he first watched the French pilot Pégoud loop-the-loop that instability was no longer aviation's supreme problem. More powerful engines and more effective controls had almost taken care of that. His inherently stable Spiders were inherently unsuitable for such flip-flops. So in 1913 he had gone to Paris and picked up a battered old Morane-Saulnier monoplane, a light, strong, and agile design popular with French stunt pilots, and had first rebuilt it and later evolved his own variants of it. Such, essentially, was the E-I. The engine, an 80-hp Oberursel, was also a German copy of the French Gnome rotary. The E-I had a welded steel-tube fuselage of box section, fabric covered, with a welded steel undercarriage below and king post above. Out from the king post a cat's cradle of bracing wires stretched to the wooden wings, whose ash spars and poplar ribs were deliberately flexible, since the entire wing was warped by the pilot for roll control. The pilot sat on a wooden bench, behind his machine gun, and he sat high above the wings, with no protection from bullets or the propeller's icy blast. Cockpit fittings were vestigial and rudimentary: on the left, a fuel-tank selector and a barometer to show altitude; on the right, fuel indicators and valves. The control column carried the gun button and a "blip switch," an ignition cutoff that was used to reduce power, since these early rotaries ran only at full power. No airspeed indication; the wind in the wires had to serve that purpose. This was by any standard a most primitive airplane. The top speed was around 80 mph. The engines regularly failed, the gun jammed, and even Fokker's famous interrupter gear would occasionally malfunction, so that the luckless pilot shot off his own propeller. (This happened to both Boelcke and Immelmann in combat.)

Along came the E-II, and the E-III with a more powerful engine and twin guns, and the E-IV with a big 160-hp, twin-row Oberursel that was so heavy it was almost a flying gyroscope.

No weapon lasts forever. While the E Fokkers had things all their own for a full year, the Allies in the end began to develop better scouts of their own. When Immelmann's Fokker monoplane came apart in the air it was the end of the E-type on the western front. From here on these planes were flown only in the east or for training.

Anthony Fokker was by now living a weird dual life. A self-made millionaire still in his mid-twenties, he lived modestly in a little German boarding house, his sole amusements outside his work being a pet monkey that stole things and a dog that would sit on the couch however often it was told not to. To his workmen he was *der Alte*—"the old man"—though he was still a fresh-faced youth. To his rival German aircraft manufacturers he was simply the enemy. Half his life Fokker spent at the front, visiting the squadrons that flew his aircraft, becoming the intimate friend of every German ace. As these men respected his ability as a designer and pilot, so he adored them. "They were as different as men of the same breed can be," he wrote. "One by one I saw them die as I knew they must die, for they were in a contest not with a human opponent but with Time, the cruelest foe in the world. Judging their bravery by my own, I reckoned them supreme." Back in Berlin Fokker kept open house for the pilots, surrounding them with all the champagne and pretty girls they wanted. (So did every airplane manufacturer.) And while the pilots relaxed, in or out of their cups, Fokker listened avidly to every word they had to say about his designs, those of his rivals, and those of the Allies.

When the days of his E-types began to be numbered he came out with several biplane fighters, with only indifferent success. He was stuck with the damnable Oberursel engine; he'd even bought the Oberursel factory. There was a vastly better engine: the 160-hp, water-cooled, in-line Mercedes. Fokker thought it a better engine than either the Rolls-Royce or the Hispano-Suiza, but he couldn't get any. The Albatros factory, by jealous intrigue, had secured the entire Mercedes output to use in their own airplanes.

Greater power was out for the moment and so, therefore, was speed. Fokker decided to go hell-bent for rate of climb and maneuverability. The Fokker Triplane was the result. With its triple bank of wings, its clean lines, and almost total absence of wires and struts, it seemed almost to float in the air, and in Richthofen's words "climbed like a monkey and maneuvered like the devil." The Fokker Triplane was the vehicle of von Richthofen's immortality and also his death, but it was in fact used by few units and built in quite small numbers. Yet in the hands of a master pilot it was supreme. You could even make a flat turn in it, reversing your direction in four seconds without banking the wings. So maneuverable was it that Allied pilots never found out how slow it was and how short its range.

Fokker's Triplane was the first fighting airplane to use a thick airfoil section, which conferred upon it a gentle stall and excellent behavior at low speeds. It was in every way a cut above the E-type, having cantilevered wooden wings, cable-operated ailerons, balanced controls, and twin Spandau machine guns. It would hit 115 mph at low level. Its climb rate was spectacular: under two minutes to 1,000 meters (3,280 feet) and only ten minutes to 4,000 meters, with a ceiling of almost 20,000 feet. Landing speed was a gentle 30 mph, but the airplane was almost impossible to keep straight on the rollout, and ground loops were normal. The airplane was extremely strong and would absorb a considerable amount of enemy fire, notably through having no bracing wires that could be shot away.

Still Fokker smarted under the successful machinations of his rival manufacturers, while the army acceptance board remained hopelessly obtuse to the advantages of his designs. He had to have that marvelous Mercedes engine. But how to break the Albatros people's stranglehold on its production? The pilots, Fokker knew, were ever his friends and allies. Could they help him? After all, their own necks depended on the quality of the planes they flew. He confided his problems to von Richthofen's technical officer and proposed a contest among all the manufacturers, whereby a delegation of crack fighting pilots would choose the best airplane—the one to be built in quantity. Quickly the idea was approved and accepted. And part of the contest rules was that every contestant should use the Mercedes engine, to make things fair. At last Fokker got his hands on one!

The trials began on January 18, 1918, a good day for flying, surprisingly mild for the time of year, and almost clear, with but a thin cover of cloud at 13,000 feet against which the darting machines would show to advantage. Fokker came determined to win, bringing eight different designs with him. The competing manufacturers vied with each other in lavishly entertaining the pilots. Many of the younger pilots were so hung over they could hardly fly, and numerous valuable prototypes were casually wrecked in landing and taxiing accidents. From this sad and disreputable scene one proud figure stood out, his integrity and conduct above reproach: von Richthofen.

Yet when the Bloody Baron chose to test one of the Dutchman's designs first, word went quickly around that he was "sold on Fokker." He was not. The airplane, he reported, was maneuverable and performed well, but it was directionally unstable and altogether vicious at the stall. Fokker, who was if nothing else a test pilot of pure genius, knew in his

heart that von Richthofen was right. "A slight landing accident," Fokker announced, wheeling the machine into a hangar and secretly summoning two of the best welders from his factory. As with the interrupter gear, they worked through the night and over the weekend, laboring like gnomes in the cavernous darkness of the hangar, lit only by the violet glitter of the welding torches, cutting the fuselage in half to weld in another two-foot bay, and enlarging the fin. Thus was an airplane "designed" in those happy days. In truth the fuselage Fokker had started with was an almost standard one off the Triplane production line. The longer span of the biplane wings was simply too much for it.

Some adjustments had been made to the control gearing, he hinted, when Monday came. Would Herr Rittmeister care to try it again? He would find it much easier to fly, though its special quickness on turns was still a

Very few Fokker D-VII's still
fly. Here are three views of one of them
restored and painted in the
colors of German ace Willi Gabriel,
a member of von Richthofen's
Jasta 11 who scored eleven victories.
As a fighter, the D-VII was not
so maneuverable as the Triplane, but like
all Fokkers it had few bad habits
and was easy to fly. With either of
two engines, the D-VII
could reach a top speed of 120 mph.
This one still will do 100.

notable feature of the ship. Von Richthofen was very amazed that mere 'adjustment' could so improve an airplane. It was now quite free of vices and a delight to fly. The Baron's colleagues agreed with him. General von Hoeppner, chief of the German air service, took Fokker to one side. "How many planes could you build at once, Herr Fokker?" he asked. Fokker answered irritably that his works were filled with some wretched A.E.G. training planes he had been ordered to build. "Let us not waste time quarreling," said the general forcefully. "What would your price be for four hundred of the new planes?" Fokker could hardly believe his ears! It was an order of staggering size. He named his price, 10,000,000 marks, and got it. But even more joyful news was to come. His hated rivals, Albatros and A.E.G., were ordered to build his design and to pay him a royalty on each and and every one! Thus did their greed in gobbling up all the Mercedes engine production backfire. Fokker had hoped to stage a comeback, but never anything like this.

No time was lost in starting production. Fokker, of course, had no formal plans for his new design, which he named the D-VII, and he had to lend the prototype to the rival factories so they could copy it. (Production quality and control were never Fokker's strong point. An Albatros-built D-VII was always a better airplane than ever came out of Fokker's own ramshackle works.)

The first combat D-VII was delivered to von Richthofen's unit a bare two months after the trials at which it had been chosen. While the Baron was seen flying it when visiting nearby units, for combat he stuck to his legendary blood-red Triplane in which he died. Yet news of this latest Fokker scourge spread swiftly among Allied pilots. Here was a seemingly magical airplane, with strange thick wings and almost no struts, which seemed to be able to stand still in mid-air while spitting a deadly stream of lead from its twin Spandaus into the soft and unprotected underbelly of its victims as they sought to climb out of its range.

Somewhere around a thousand D-VII's had been built by the time of the armistice, and many famous pilots flew them, not least Hermann Goering, that sorry successor to von Richthofen as commander of JG-1, and a figure who was to achieve a wider fame before his ignominious death from a cyanide pill in a Nuremberg cell twenty-seven years later.

In all the world perhaps two original Fokker D-VII's are still flying. The one depicted here is the proud property of Cole Palen, of Old Rhinebeck Aerodrome, New York. We asked him how it flies. "Like a puff of warm air," was his graphic answer. "It'll break ground for no reason at all, without nosing up or you making any real effort. It just floats away. I would say it's very sensitive on the elevators—so many of the early machines were. And it's a rudder airplane. Give it rudder and automatically you're going to get the right angle of bank to make your turn. The ailerons are there just to keep the angle of bank where you want it.

"The stalling speed I would guess to be about 40 to 45 mph. It stalls pretty much straight ahead, without undue wing-dropping.

"It will definitely ground-loop, though it's not so bad as the Triplane. But you do have to land into wind; this applies to almost any of the early airplanes. But I would say it is the easiest-flying of the World War I fighters. I think it would compare favorably with a Piper Cub, except for that damn rollout.

"From my machine I don't think it was as fast as Fokker claimed. I don't think it ever could go more than 100 mph. Like the Triplane, it was the kind of airplane you couldn't very well run away from a fight in, but its exceptional characteristic is its rapid rate of turn. It will out-turn anything else I've flown. And that story of D-VII's being able to hang on the propeller and still fly is absolutely true. It will hang at about forty-five degrees and still be in full flight and very controllable. The vertical reversement and the Immelmann are very nice, and the Lufbery circle is very rapid.

"The engine is reliable, though I think mine is turning unusually slowly. It isn't giving quite the power these days that it used to. I get about 1,270 rpm when I should get 1,400.

"The engine is a high-compression straight-six in-line. The carburetor air is crankcase warmed, and it has a dual ignition—and in a sense dual carburetion—for there are two bowls and jets each feeding three cylinders. You can almost fly on three cylinders. . . . Well, you can't really, but you can make a very long glide.

"The engine starts itself, without a starter, and you don't have to crank it. You just pull the propeller through a few times with the engine on low compression, and you can hear the carburetor drawing, sucking gas, and then you turn it over a few times till you know you've got a good mixture in the cylinders. Then you wind the old Bosch hand crank to make a spark, which goes through the distributor and into a cylinder. It may kick backwards at first, but it's got sense and eventually it will settle down and run properly. It will idle very slowly. We can keep it running at 150 rpm.

"Would you believe I am still using original World War I spark plugs?"

Fokker's D-VII was paid the signal honor of being the only German airplane named as booty by the Allies in the Armistice surrender terms, Article IV singling out *In erster Linie alle Apparate D.VII* ("especially all machines of the D-VII type"). Wonderful advertising of the worth of his plane, noted Fokker, but the cost ran too high. It was a challenge too obvious to ignore. The entire contents of his factory were quickly hidden in barns and lofts for miles around. Then he devised the pre-posterous, unholy, impossible plot of smuggling all these airplanes over the border into his native and neutral Holland. More than 400 engines and 220 complete airframes, including 120 D-VII's were loaded into six trains, each one made deliberately too long for any sidings, and spirited across the border. How was it done? With bribes—20,000 guilders' worth. It is a curious thing that if you take as cynical a view of the world as Anthony Fokker did, the world has an uncanny habit of proving you right.

Fokker, still only twenty-eight, had also built up a cash fortune of some 30,000,000 marks (about $7,000,000), and he was able to smuggle out most of this by converting it to foreign currency and packing it in old suitcases or aboard his yacht.

The D-VII's were sold to many countries: Holland, Belgium, Poland, Sweden, Denmark, Italy, Spain—some of them by Goering, now Fokker's sales agent. (Goering's new job did not last long. His expenses proved far too lavish for Fokker.) Of those plundered by the Allies no fewer than 142 were shipped to the U. S. Army designers were urged to study the type, and the wonderful performance of the Mercedes engine was praised.

D-VII's served with the U. S. military for several years, and they were preferred by their pilots to the SE-5a's also in use. Eventually lack of spare parts forced them off the inventory in the mid-twenties, though D-VII's continued to fly in Holland until 1939.

But was that even the end of it? Ghostly galleons are still sometimes seen sailing the misty seas; phantom highwaymen are still midnight-galloping across their windy heaths; and embattled armies are still somehow heard, when the wind is right, clear across the centuries. In the cloudy skies of eastern France, above fields where trenches once snaked like open wounds, might not the clatter of a Mercedes and the chatter of twin Spandaus be heard? Perhaps.

Tommy Sopwith's Scouts

Even as a young man Tommy Sopwith (Thomas Octave Murdoch Sopwith, now Sir Thomas, C.B.E.) was hardly strapped for cash to support his taste in spectacular transportation. When he put into Dover harbor that summer afternoon in 1910 it was in his own 166-foot schooner. (Well, half his, for he shared it with a chum.) All Dover was buzzing with the news that a Blériot flown by an American had just landed nearby after the first Channel crossing by airplane with a passenger. A fat passenger, too: the American's French mechanic. What a super wheeze, thought Tommy Sopwith, and he and his friends went off to view the American aviator's Blériot. Sopwith was enchanted, and a day or two later there he was at Brooklands plonking down a fiver for a passenger ride in someone's Henri Farman. Soon he was the owner of a little 40-hp monoplane. But when he took off in it before a crowd of interested spectators on October 22, it was not only the airplane's first flight, but Sopwith's first go at piloting. He crashed, but you often did in those days. Tommy Sopwith wasn't hurt at all, and still pretty keen, so he went on to take his Royal Aero Club Aviator's Certificate—it was No. 31—a month later, this time on a biplane. And a bare five weeks after that ignominious first flip, or flop, he was thinking that his extravagances in the matter of flying might be offset if he won the Baron de Forest's £4,000 competition for the longest all-British flight from England across to the Conti-

nent before the end of 1910. Tommy Sopwith covered 169 miles from Eastchurch to Thirimont in France in three and a half hours to win the prize, a good show all round. On February 1, 1911, he was off once more, from Brooklands to Windsor Castle to be received by King George and give a royal command performance of this new science of flying. That summer he sailed to America, where, says one chronicler, "he carried all before him." Back home in 1912, he founded the Sopwith Aviation Company.

At first it built one or two rather ordinary biplanes, then a couple of modestly successful flying boats, the Sopwith Bat Boats. The first intimations of Tommy Sopwith's true genius came to an unsuspecting crowd at Hendon Aerodrome one November afternoon in 1913, when a strange, compact little biplane swept down all unannounced from a wintry sky and proceeded to do two laps of the Hendon racing course at simply phenomenal speed. This was the first Tabloid, flown by Sopwith's colleague Harry Hawker, and that very morning at Farnborough, in official tests by the Army, it had shown a measured speed of 92½ mph and a climb, with pilot, passenger, and fuel for two and a half hours, of 1,200 feet in one minute. And this, mark you, on the rather uncertain 80 hp of its Gnome rotary engine. No wonder the little airplane was almost instantly ordered by both the Royal Flying Corps and the Royal Naval Air Service.

In 1914, Sopwith built a special Tabloid floatplane with a 100-hp Gnome Monosoupape for the Schneider Trophy contest. This Tabloid had a single big float under the fuselage and was launched into the Hamble River with Howard Pixton, another of Sopwith's chums, in the cockpit. Pixton opened the throttle and the Tabloid promptly turned upside down and sank. Willing hands rescued Pixton almost at once and the Tabloid an hour or two later. The answer, it was decided—once the excitement had subsided

Opening pages and opposite:
Sopwith Pup was quick and light on controls,
is considered by some to be
nicest-flying airplane ever made. Below:
Rudder of Sopwith Snipe, with
horn-balance configuration to compensate
for power of plane's engine.

and Howard Pixton had put on dry clothes—was that you probably needed two floats for stability. So they cut the one float carefully down the middle, filled in the openings, and remounted it as two floats. It worked, and to the astonishment of the French pilots this ridiculous biplane was 23 mph faster than their own best monoplane. Picky Pixton won the Schneider Trophy at a breathtaking 86.75 mph. The splendid Picky was, in Sopwith's own words, "a very simple sort of chap, with a slight impediment in his speech," and when Jacques Schneider himself invited the winner to the very grand Monte Carlo Sporting Club for some champagne, all Picky could stammer out was, "Thank you very much. Mine's a small Bass."

The Sopwith Tabloid was perhaps the very first single-seat scouting plane to see service, for there were one or two—unarmed of course, as were all scouts at first—in France after war broke out in 1914. Two Royal Navy Tabloids were rigged as bombers and on October 8 were sent off with orders to find and bomb some German Zeppelin sheds. It was a misty autumn day and one pilot missed the target altogether, but the other dropped his eggs accurately from 600 feet on a shed at Düsseldorf and was rewarded with a great explosion and fire that nearly engulfed his little Sopwith. He found out later that he had destroyed a new Zeppelin.

The first of Sopwith's airplanes to make a really resounding name for itself, however, was the Type 9700, unofficially known as the Sopwith 1½-Strutter by virtue of its W-shaped arrangement of struts joining the upper wing to the fuselage. The 1½-Strutter was the first British airplane to go into service with a gun-synchronizing gear. This used a basically Russian principle developed into hardware by a Royal Navy warrant officer named Scarff, who also won immortality as the inventor of the Scarff Ring rotating machine-gun mount for rear-cockpit gunners, which the 1½-Strutter also pioneered. In fact, the 1½-Strutter was the first real two-seat fighter, and its forward-firing Vickers gun and movable Lewis gun for the rear-cockpit gunner together packed considerable wallop. The 1½-Strutter also helped pioneer both the variable-incidence tailplane and dive brakes, both features of all jet airplanes today.

The Admiralty got in first with orders for the new Sopwith, but when the RFC suddenly woke up, just before the opening of the first Battle of the Somme, and found itself twelve squadrons short of what it needed for that operation, the Royal Navy gallantly handed over seventy-two Sopwiths to its sister service. The 1½-Strutters served in large numbers with both services, and also were manufactured under license by the French, who supplied five hundred and fourteen to the Americans in 1918.

Designs followed one another with great rapidity in the Great War. Hardly was the 1½-Strutter out of Sopwith's experimental department when its place was taken by a new single-seater, smaller than the 1½-Strutter, but clearly similar to it. The service pilots who first flew it christened the little newcomer the Pup. It was always gentle and docile to fly, quick and light on the controls, ever obedient to the commands of its pilot. There are those who say the Pup was the nicest-flying airplane ever made. Again the Admiralty got Pups first, and by the end of 1916, No. 8 (Naval) Squadron had shot down twenty German airplanes with them. Naval Eight by all accounts must have been a splendid bunch of chaps. The squadron was formed expressly to lend a helping hand to the poor old RFC over the Somme.

Throughout the battles of Ypres, Messines, and Cambrai, the Pups were right in the thick of it, and they were about the only British airplanes that could keep up with the German Albatros. A certain ace named Lieutenant McCudden wrote: "When it came to maneuvering the Sopwith Scout would turn twice to an Albatros' once. In fact, very many Pup pilots have blessed their machine for its handiness when they have been a long way behind the Hun lines and have been at a disadvantage in other ways." On January 4, 1917, a Pup even had the audacity to attack von Richthofen, who wrote later, "We saw at once that the enemy airplane was superior to ours." Richthofen got his Pup, but only, he noted "because we were three against one."

With only 80 hp, the Pup may have been a little short on power, but it was certainly long on those two great engineering virtues, simplicity and lightness. Its fuselage was a simple box girder of ash longerons and spruce spacers with crisscross wire bracing. Behind the fire-resistant engine bulkhead were ash struts and aluminum covering sheet, while the rest of the fuselage was fabric-covered. The wings were constructed of spruce spars spindled out carefully for lightness, and spruce ribs. The wing tips and trailing edges were formed simply of steel tube. The covering was fabric. The landing gear was a V-shaped steel tube for each wheel, and had the same split-axle wheel attachment as the 1½-Strutter. The power plant was the quite reliable 80-hp Le Rhône rotary engine, neatly cowled in a circular piece of aluminum. Armament was a single Vickers machine gun mounted on top of the fuselage just ahead of the pilot, with a small windshield at its rear end, carefully padded in case the pilot should strike his head on it. Empty, a Sopwith Pup weighed only 800 pounds, and although not overburdened with power it was noted for retaining its maneuverability at altitudes where other scouts began to wallow.

Did you think that Anthony Fokker invented the triplane? Tommy Sopwith's Triplane was effectively the first. It is even whispered that Fokker resorted to subterfuge, to chicanery, to get the mangled remains of the first Sopwith Triplane that was shot down delivered to his works, so he could examine it and see what made it tick. For tick it did. One unit equipped with Sopwith Triplanes, "B" Flight of Naval Ten squadron, shot down eighty-seven Germans in three months of 1917. This was the sinister "Black Flight," with all Canadian pilots and all-black airplanes with gloriously sinister names: *Black Death, Black Maria, Black Roger, Black Prince,* and, rather lamely, *Black Sheep.* Black Flight's commander was the great Flight Sub-Lieutenant Raymond Collishaw, who in one period of twenty-seven days downed sixteen German airplanes.

Cecil Lewis wrote of the Sopwith Triplane in *Sagittarius Rising:* "Of all machines, the Triplane remains in my memory as the best—for the actual pleasure of flying—that I ever took up. It was so beautifully balanced, so well-mannered, so feather-light on the stick, and so comfortable and warm . . . for its docility, the lack of all effort needed to fly it, and yet its instantaneous response to the lightest touch, it remains my favourite. Other machines were faster, stronger, had better climb or vision; but none was so friendly as the Tripe." If you think about it, the triplane layout has such obvious advantages it is puzzling that more designers did not make use of it. The arrangement gives the pilot superb visibility. All three wings are of very narrow chord, while top and bottom wings are far above and below his line of sight, and the center wing right in line with it, so it obscures little of the sky. The short wing span means a quick rate of roll, and the narrow chord means only the smallest travel of the center of pressure with changing speed;

Young Tommy Sopwith, at controls
of early pusher biplane (left), formed his own
company to produce modestly
capable Bat Boat (below) in 1912 and
the extraordinarily successful
Tabloid in 1913 (bottom). In Army
tests, Tabloid attained measured speed of 92½
mph and a 1,200-feet-per-minute rate of
climb, although powered by slight
and uncertain 80-hp Gnome rotary engine.

Color photographs show replica of
Pup flying in all its World War I glory.
Pup was powered by 80-hp Le Rhône
rotary engine and armed
with single Vickers machine gun
mounted on fuselage. It weighed only
800 pounds empty and was noted
for maneuverability at altitudes where
other scouts began to flounder.
Von Richthofen considered it superior
in some respects to German planes.
At bottom left is pranged
Camel, which came softly to rest with
minimal damage to prop and landing
gear at Noyelles-sur-L'Escaut
near end of war in 1918.

51

Type 9700, more familiarly known as 1½-Strutter, was made in two versions, single-seat bomber (below) and two-seat fighter. Compartment behind pilot had room for 12 bombs. These were first British planes with gun-synchronizing gear. Right: Contemporary Pup buzzes field.

so a triplane can have a short fuselage, which does marvelous things for maneuverability in the pitch and yaw planes. About the only inherent disadvantage is the interference drag of the triple wing. Do not make the mistake of looking on the design of First World War airplanes as backward. Given the power plants then available, and the lack of light alloys, it is doubtful any modern designer could do much better. Even the power plants were very good. While a modern piston engine is appreciably more reliable than those old rotaries, its power-to-weight ratio is not notably better.

Maneuverability was ever the great virtue of any of Sopwith's various scout designs, and none had this quality in greater abundance than his masterpiece, the Camel. It was once more a biplane, but a biplane with double ailerons (ailerons on both upper and lower mainplanes), a humpbacked, stocky biplane with more power—130, 150, or even 180 hp—and an airframe of great strength. In the hands of an expert, the Sopwith Camel was one of the great fighting weapons of all time. It was the first British airplane to carry twin Vickers guns, with a high rate of fire and belt-loading, so that they did not require constant reloading, like the drum-fed Lewis guns. Well over five thousand Camels were built, and they shot down, according to official records, 1,294

enemy aircraft. I do not know how many Camels were in turn shot down, but I suspect that far more were wrecked in training accidents, for like the animal after which it was named the Camel could turn and bite you. It could be a beast. It was fast and heavy, and the main elements of that weight—engine, guns, pilot, and petrol tanks—were concentrated in a short length of fuselage, so that the airplane had little angular inertia. Its heavy rotary engine acted as a giant gyroscope, so that, due to precession, the nose wanted to drop in a right-hand turn and rise in a left-hand turn. There were similar effects if you tried to raise or lower the nose which required great amounts of rudder to cor-

rect, and we all know what great amounts of rudder can lead to at low airspeeds: instant spin. Nor was that all. You must remember that those old rotary engines did not have a simple power lever, but two engine controls, one for air and one for petrol, and both had to be set exactly right. And what was exactly right for takeoff might not be quite right for climbing away, for the Clerget engine would choke at about two hundred feet if the mixture was not slightly leaned off. The Camel also was notably tail-heavy at full power, and did not have an adjust-able tailplane. All these little features could gang up on a low-time pilot, and they usually did so just after takeoff, when you were short of both altitude and airspeed. And you spun in. The RFC made up its own version of a popular music-hall song of the day about just such a prang:

"I was testing a Camel on last Friday night,
For the purpose of passing her out.
And before fifteen seconds of flight
*   had elapsed*
I was filled with a horrible doubt,
As to whether intact I should land
*   from my flight.*
I half thought I'd crash—and I half thought
*   quite right.*
*   The machine it seemed to lack coagulation,*
*   The struts and sockets didn't rendezvous,*
*   The wings had lost their super-imposition,*
*   Their stagger and their incidental, too!*
*   The fuselage developed undulations,*
*   The circumjacent fabric came unstitched,*
*   Instanter was reduction to components,*
*   In other words—she's pitched!"*

But in the hands of a master there was nothing a Camel wouldn't do. There was a certain celebrated Captain Armstrong of 44 Squadron who would loop a Camel on takeoff and who specialized in snap rolls done at fifteen feet, or even, on one occasion, with the wing tip brushing the grass as he rolled. But there are old pilots, as the saying goes, and bold pilots, but no old bold pilots, and even Captain Armstrong spun in eventually, just two weeks before the war ended.

An inexperienced Camel pilot was not much use to anybody, as Second Lieutenant W. R. May found out when he was posted to No. 209 Squadron early in 1918. May was doubly inexperienced. When the great German offensive began he had been pulled out of air-gunnery school and sent on active service. And he was doubly unwelcome at 209 Squadron, being two days late on arrival through having got caught up in a party en route. The squadron commander of 209 simply wasn't going to have him in the unit, but while May was stepping out of the C.O.'s office in disgrace he ran into a Captain Brown, who was one of 209's flight commanders and an old friend from May's home town of Edmonton, Alberta. Brown persuaded the C.O. to relent, and took the young whippersnapper on his own flight and under his own wing, so to speak, ordering him firmly to stay out of combat till he was more experienced.

But keeping out of things was not one of May's specialties. When, on April 21, 1918, Brown's flight got involved in a tremendous scrap with some Fokker Triplanes, May began sensibly enough by circling above it at 12,000 feet. A Fokker went by just below him and he let it go. But when another did the same, it was too much for him and he dived after it. "The flight was at close quarters," he wrote afterward. "Enemy aircraft were coming at me from all sides. I seemed to be missing some of them by inches, and there seemed to be so many of them that I thought the best thing to do was to go into a tight vertical turn, hold my guns open, and spray as many of them as I could." Hold a Vickers gun open and sooner or later it will jam, and May's did—both of them. He spun out of the melee and headed for home, "feeling pretty good," he remembered, "until the next thing I knew, I was being fired at from behind!" Glued to May's tail was a blood-red Fokker Triplane.

By all accounts it should have been all over for May in the next second. But as they weaved across the fields, in and out of the trees, the German's guns also jammed, and as he tried to clear them he flew into a hail of machine-gun fire from an Australian unit on the ground, and also took a burst from May's own flight commander Captain Brown, who had miraculously seen his fledgling wing man's predicament and came howling down to his rescue. The little German Fokker soared briefly,

then crunched down into a pile of turnips. The Aussies came running to inspect their prize. Imagine their astonishment to discover that its dead pilot was the legendary, seemingly immortal Manfred von Richthofen. Thus the Red Baron's end, the outcome of a young Camel pilot's foolhardiness. To this day nobody knows who got Richthofen—Brown or one of the Aussies.

Toward the end of the war every manufacturer was producing airplanes in a fine frenzy, and with new designs, too. Most were soon forgotten. Who today remembers the Sopwith Bulldog, or the Rhino, the Hippo, Sparrow, or Snail? The Salamander, the Scooter, the Swallow, the Buffalo, the Dragon, or the Snark? The Snapper or the Cobham? One very fine and memorable Sopwith Scout did follow the Camel, and although barely a hundred Snipes had been delivered to the squadrons by the time of the armistice, the type is remembered as potentially one of the finest fighters of the whole war. The Snipe was the Camel's offspring and looked it. Later Camels had been fitted with 150-hp rotary engines designed by W. O. Bentley, whose name also attaches to the automobile, and when he went on to make a 230-hp engine, Sopwith eagerly matched it with a new airframe. The actual Snipe was hardly faster than a Camel, but it did climb. The Snipe managed to be maneuverable without the trickiness of the Camel. It was not nearly so vicious.

The Snipe was just in time to take part in a battle so extraordinary that it reads today like a dream. On October 27, 1918, one Major Billy Barker was patrolling at 21,000 feet in a Snipe when he encountered a Hun two-seater and shot it down. He then was attacked by a Fokker D-VII and wounded in the leg. Barker spun down, recovering to find himself surrounded by fifteen more Fokkers. He fired at two of them, which spun away, and got on the tail of yet another, which he sent down in flames. At this instant, he was wounded in the other leg and fainted, his Snipe falling out of control. Groggily he came to, once more surrounded by a dozen or more German airplanes. He shot still one more down in flames, and was wounded a third time—one elbow was shattered by a bullet. All now seemed lost, and Barker was preparing to ram a final Fokker, so both would crash to their deaths together, but at the last minute, while perhaps ten feet from the German airplane, Barker fired his guns once more and this German too went down. Barker dived for the Allied lines, only to meet a new formation of eight Germans. He got away from these and crash-landed near a British balloon. For his bravery and fighting dash in this fantastic battle, Major Barker was awarded the Victoria Cross, England's highest award.

Governments are ever ungrateful creatures, prone to turn and bite the hand that lately worked so desperately to feed them. Tommy Sopwith struggled on, doing very little business, till in 1920 he was confronted with a huge and excessive demand for the return of excess war profits. He chose to go out of business. A full twenty shillings on the pound was paid to all shareholders.

Sopwith and his partners founded a new company, H. G. Hawker Engineering, persevering at first with contracts for refurbishing the Snipes of the tiny peacetime RAF. In 1936 a marriage was arranged between Hawker and the Armstrong Siddeley Company. Among the offspring was the Hawker Hurricane. Later lean times led to more amoeba-like corporate grapplings and swallowings, and that giant octopus of British engineering today, the Hawker Siddeley Group, is a direct descendant of the original Sopwith Aviation Company. The Hawker Siddeley Group is proud of its ancestry. To this day it keeps, neatly filed away, many of the plans and engineering drawings of those famous Sopwith Scouts.

SPAD: the Favorite of Aces

"I hurried to the field," Eddie Rickenbacker remembers, "and there they were, three beauties. They were more impressive by far than any other airplane, any other automobile, any other piece of equipment I had ever seen. This new SPAD would mean the difference between life and death. With it, a little luck and continuing aid from above, perhaps I could attain fame in the skies and join the great aces of the war—Lufbery, René Fonck, Billy Bishop, the Canadian, even the great Red Baron himself, Manfred von Richthofen. Well, at least I could dream. For the SPAD was the ultimate aircraft in the war in which aviation was developed."

The dream came true. Rickenbacker, son of Swiss immigrant parents, had survived a bruising childhood (he once affixed a large umbrella to his bicycle and sailed off a barn roof) and had graduated to the smashing life of a racing driver. Then he had struggled through a miasma of official incompetence and accusations that he was a German spy to become a pilot with Uncle Sam's Hat-in-the-Ring Squadron, the 94th Aero Pursuit, the first ever to be composed entirely of Americans. "There has never been a closer fraternity than the one existing among the pilots of a squadron fighting together high in the sky, and no group of fighters had a greater spirit than those of the 94th Squadron," Rickenbacker has written. At first they flew Nieuports cast off by the French, Rickenbacker flying wing man to the great Raoul Lufbery, learning all he could and fighting through the miseries of air sickness. Then one day they got their SPADs. "The best ship I ever flew," Rickenbacker always insisted, "was the SPAD, built by the *Société pour Aviation et ses Dérives,* whence it took its name. The final SPAD could do 130 miles an hour, climb to 22,000 feet and stay together no matter what maneuvers you put it through." The Nieuport was notable in that it didn't. If you pulled at all steeply from a dive in this lightly built little machine, you could lose the fabric covering from the top wing, and often the wing's leading edge, too, and for most pilots that would be that. But Rickenbacker seems to have had some private arrangement with fate. "I pulled the stick back into my lap," he says, describing how it happened to him during a scrap with two Albatros, "and a rippling, tearing crash shook the plane. The entire spread of linen over the right wing was stripped off . . . I manipulated the controls but it did no good. . . . The ship was in a tailspin. . . . It was death. I had not lost my willingness to fight to live, but in that situation there was not much that I could do. Even birds need two wings to fly." All else having failed, he then pulled open the throttle, and found a combination of power and control application that barely held the Nieuport out of a spin. From 2,000 feet he made the two miles to the nearest American aerodrome, and came in for a landing at full throttle, slithering to a crooked stop in a cloud of dust.

The SPAD grew out of the aviation ambitions of a wealthy silk merchant named Armand Deperdussin, who did not design his own machines but employed one Louis Bechereau to do it for him. The clean and slender monoplanes that Bechereau designed had some splendid racing successes in the years before the war: Deperdussins won both the Gordon Bennett and the Schneider trophies in 1913. But in 1914 came a financial scandal, with tales of fraud and stock manipulations, that upset the Deperdussin firm and saw Louis Blériot, the rival air manufacturer—of all people—put in charge of it. The first thing Blériot did was to change the company's name from *Société pour les Appareils Deperdussin* to *Société pour Aviation et ses Dérives,* a neat touch of merchandising that contrived to retain the initials SPAD, yet reveal also that things were under a new management. The second thing he did was to persuade Louis Bechereau to stay on. By this

Opening pages and below: Type XIII SPAD
entered World War I in April, 1917. It had
200-hp Hispano-Suiza engine, top
speed of 130 mph, and two Vickers machine guns.
More than 8,400 of them were built.
Survivor shown here has been extensively
restored, still flies capably.

time it was 1915, and the more farsighted air-plane designers, Bechereau among them, were already beginning to realize that the days of the rotary aero engine were numbered. The trouble with the rotary was that to get more power you had to build a bigger engine, and the bigger rotaries got the more impossible the centrifugal forces within the engine and the gyroscopic effects on the air-plane's handling became. The future be-longed to the stationary engine. Bechereau heard about a young Swiss engineer working in Spain, named Mark Birkigt, who had designed a water-cooled, V-eight power plant for the Hispano-Suiza automobile company. Hispano-Suiza had a factory in France, and here Beche-reau found one of the new engines on test. This Hisso was a curiously advanced conception for its time, embodying concepts that still seem modern today: overhead cams, a one-piece aluminum block with screwed-in cylinder liners, dual ignition with cam-driven magnetos, forced lubrication even to the con-rod little-ends and gudgeon pins.

The Hispano-Suiza seems to have been just what Bechereau needed, for until it came along he had been floundering, turning out fourteen military designs in the first twelve months of the war alone, all of them dreadful. One was even built in small quantities: the A2, a wretched notion which perched a gunner all alone in a separate nacelle ahead of the tractor propeller. Mark Birkigt's new engine, and the gun-synchronizing gear he developed for it, did away with such abominations.

With neither dihedral nor wash-out to the wing, a SPAD was not stable—al-though this was no great disadvantage in a fighter—and it did drop a wing smartly at the stall. Due to the very thin airfoil, the airplane had a high rate of sink at slow speeds and was best brought in under power. And it did ground-

loop. (What First World War airplane didn't?) To reduce the risk of nosing-over, the SPAD's landing gear was put unusually far forward, which made it most unstable on the ground—"like a big fat guy on a toboggan going down a hill," was how one SPAD pilot described it. The SPAD was so prone to biting its tail on the ground that it would even quite happily ground-loop on takeoff. But once you were in the air, and had started to gain speed, it became less touchy. It flew "like a Venetian blind going down the sky."

Bechereau's first Hisso SPAD was the Type V. His first winner was the Type VII, the prototype of which took the air at Vil-lacoublay in April, 1916. It was a handsome machine with straight flat wings, a fish-shaped fuselage with a 140-hp Hisso and associated Vickers gun up front. It was immediately or-dered into production and, ultimately, no less than 5,600 were built, as the type progressed through the 180-hp Hisso to the 200-hp engine. When the 200-hp geared Hisso came along, Bechereau enlarged his now famous design the better to carry the bigger engine and added an additional Vickers gun; thus Type XIII was born. This first flew in April, 1917, and 8,472 SPAD Thirteens were built by an armada of airplane factories in every Allied country. There was another two-seat SPAD, the Type XI, with its wings slightly backswept to keep the center of gravity within limits. The final SPAD was the XVII, a 300-hp monster that first appeared in June, 1918. Only twenty of these ever were delivered, "for which," observed one French captain, "let the Boches be thankful."

The SPAD would never outmaneuver, say, a Nieuport or a Fokker Triplane, but it was stable and a very steady gun platform, was fast both in level flight and on the climb, and could be relied upon to stay together whatever you did to it. Its construction used the standard techniques of the day: wooden, wire-braced, fabric-covered fuselage; hollow wooden box-section spars; and wing ribs of spruce-capped ply, again with wire bracing. The trailing edges were of wire, pulled into curves by the tightening doped fabric to give the familiar scalloped look.

If ever there was a plane the aces loved, it was the SPAD. In the first six months after they got SPADs, *Les Cigognes,* the famous French Stork Squadron, shot down more than two hundred enemy aircraft, a record never equaled by any other squadron in the war. France's ace of aces, René Fonck, that extraordinary braggart, went marauding alone in a SPAD. Fonck, the highest-scoring Allied ace with seventy-five victories, survived the war and lived to a ripe old age. On at least two occasions in his fantastic career he shot down six Germans in one day. Once he dispatched a formation of three Huns in ten seconds, so quickly their wreckage was all found within a circle of four hundred yards.

The SPAD was Georges Guynemer's "flying machine gun," and he even had one built with a huge 37mm Hotchkiss cannon fitted into the V of the Hisso's cylinders, firing through the hollow boss of the gear-driven propeller. The classic Vickers provided a sighting burst before you let go with the Hotchkiss.

Ernst Udet, the second highest-scoring German ace, had a weird encounter with Guynemer, whom he recognized from his SPAD's marking, in May, 1917. He wrote an account of this fabulous fight twenty years later: "We rushed towards each other at the same altitude, whistling a hair's breadth apart. My opponent's machine glistened light brown in the sun. Then began the ring-around-the-rosy. From beneath, we looked like two big birds of prey in a love game, but up here it was a game of death. . . . I half-looped to dive on him from above. He at once comprehended and hung on to me, likewise looping. I tried a turn. Guynemer followed me. Once, on the turn, he fastened on me for a second. Metal hailstones rattled through my right wing hitting the struts. I tried sharp turns, curves, sideslips, but with lightning speed he anticipated my every movement. . . .

"Not only the machine above me is better, but the man sitting in it can do more than I. But I struggle on. Again a turn. In the wink of an eye he appears in my sights. I hit the firing mechanism—the machine gun is silent—jammed! With my left hand I grasp the stick so as to hammer with the right hand and try to reload. No good—the jam persists. . . . For eight minutes we turn with each other, the longest eight minutes of my life. . . . Now he whistles over me lying on his back. I have a moment to let go the stick and hammer the gun with both fists. Guynemer observes the movement from above and he knows I am helpless in his trap. Back he dashes lying almost on his back; he lifts his hand and nods pleasantly, and dips into a long dive westward towards his own front. I fly home benumbed. The people say Guynemer had a jam himself. Others maintain he was afraid I would ram him in the air. But I believe not. I believe that, even today, a vestige of old-time knightly chivalry still remains."

It was in a SPAD that Guynemer, with fifty-four victories, vanished without trace. So loved and respected was he by the French people, and so terrible his loss, that the French government withheld the news for a week, fear-

ful of the effect it would have on the country's morale. (Said President Clemenceau: "He was our pride and our protection. His loss is the most cruel of all. . . . He will remain the model hero, a living legend, the greatest in all history.")

And, of course, the Americans flew SPADs. For the Americans, led by a general staff so inane that their first command when war came was that aviators should wear spurs on their boots at all times, had no fighting planes of their own. "Despite the enormous sums expended on aircraft," said General Dunwoody, director of aviation supply, "we never had a single plane [of American design] that was fit for use." So the American Expeditionary Force acquired 893 SPADs, took off its spurs, and went to work. Eighty-eight Ameri-

can pilots qualified as aces (five or more victories) in that war to end wars. Rickenbacker's own 94th Aero Pursuit Squadron had been the first AEF unit into battle, but when he was named to command it on September 24, 1918, the 94th was six victories behind the 27th. Rickenbacker resolved to put his unit back on top and called his pilots together for a pep talk. "Baby your engines," he told them. "Do not run all out when it is not necessary. Save that reserve for when you need it." No time was to be wasted in saluting, or other military folderol. There would be no drinking twenty-four hours before a mission. Each man was to give his best for America, for the Allied cause, and for the best squadron ever to fly the skies—the 94th!

Nor was their leader ever any-

where but out in front. One day he returned from a close battle to count more than a dozen bullet holes around the middle of the airplane, one right through the windshield.

On November 10, 1918, the 94th got its sixty-ninth and last Hun. The Hat-in-the-Ring Squadron had shot down more Boches than any other U. S. unit, and its commanding officer, with twenty-six victories, was the American ace-of-aces. The 94th, which had been the first U. S. air unit in action, was also the last, for the next day Rickenbacker stole off alone into the fog for one last flight. "I was the only audience for the greatest show ever presented," he later wrote in his autobiography. "On both sides of no-man's land, the trenches erupted. Brown-uniformed men poured out of the Amer-

ican trenches, gray-green uniforms out of the German. From my observer's seat overhead I watched them throw their helmets in the air, discard their guns, wave their hands. Then all up and down the front the two groups of men began edging towards each other across no-man's land.

"Suddenly gray uniforms mixed with brown. I could see them hugging each other, dancing, jumping. . . . I flew up to the French sector. There it was even more incredible. After four years of slaughter and hatred, they were not only hugging each other but kissing each other on both cheeks as well.

"Star shells, rockets and flares began to go up, and I turned my SPAD toward the field. The war was over."

Barnstorming in the Jenny

Behold, in all its khaki, wide-winged glory, the bird that began it all, the machine that for maybe a million Americans was their introduction to the brave new world of flight.

It began with a beelike hum overhead, and maybe a buzz job on your little community. Then, with a slow wiggle of those long wings, the Jenny would miraculously land in some nearby cow pasture and await your pleasure, and your five bucks. (For five minutes, and your little sister could go, too.) You stood in line, crushing the clover, and trying not to ogle too obviously the tall, lanky fellow in the crumpled leathers and baggy whipcord busy about his machine, feeding it oil from one dented can and gasoline from another. Did he call you "kid"? He was hardly more than one himself.

You waited in an agony of anticipation, torn between terror and delight till your turn came. Eventually your slim hero (it just might have been Slim Lindbergh himself) helped you up on the wing and over the sill into the front cockpit, and he lifted your little sister in after and strapped you both down. The oily OX clattered into a roar and you bumped and bounced and suddenly you didn't. You had left the ground, in spirit perhaps forever. The trees shrank to mere bushes and fell below. Big fields joined in a patchwork quilt of green and brown. The slipstream slapped at your face, and your little sister screamed and hid; you didn't care, for you were high, high on exhaust fumes, the extravagant odor of castor oil, and flying. (Was it your house you could just make out over the woods?) Then the crazy assembly of struts and wires you were riding wobbled and tilted, and began to descend, till you were bumping and slowing through the grass, and it was someone else's turn. Was any other five minutes in your life ever so short, or any other five dollars so well-spent?

The Jenny, officially the JN-4D, was America's first mass-produced, commercially successful airplane. Its conception came from the U. S. Army's disgust with the accident record of the completely open-to-the-wind pusher airplanes used as trainers in 1914. Europe had progressed to tractor airplanes with enclosed fuselages, and the Army wished American airplane builders would, too. So Glenn Curtiss, their leader, hired designer B. Douglas Thomas away from Sopwith, over in England, and soon had the Jenny in full swing. The English powers-that-be soon returned the compliment, and bought several hundred Jennies for use as training planes with the RFC and RNAS. At home, the Jenny remained the standard military trainer throughout World War I and for five years thereafter.

But it was the barnstormers who earned the lady her immortality. War can give you a powerful taste for wandering, and in 1919, for $600 or so, you could pick up a surplus Jenny still snugly packed in its crate, and be in business. (This price, by the way, represented a considerable loss for Curtiss, who had paid the Army twice that much per airframe to buy back unneeded production after the armistice.) You were a barnstormer, a "gypsy pilot." You almost certainly had trained in the military on the Jenny, anyway, and were immediately at home in the bird. No matter that you had never seen combat. "A pilot is as good as he talks," the saying went, and some of the gypsies were first-rate talkers. Every one became an instant ace, just returned from shooting down the Boche.

The pull was that it sure beat working for a living. At first you could ask and get $25 for a ride, even more with a few flip-flops thrown in, and there were barnstormers who saved $10,000 in their first year. By 1925 prices had steadied at $5 for five minutes, and you were lucky to earn $5,000 in twelve months. In the end the gypsies simply bled their market dry. Almost every place you landed you'd find that some other barnstormer had been there before. So you developed a technique for testing a town's interest in aviation. You buzzed it a time or two. If the folks continued about their business, so did you. But if the cows and the chickens fled in all directions and every kid in the place tried to follow you, you'd pick a likely looking field, buzz the place once more just to be sure, and land. You gave the farmer a free ride for the use of his meadow, and picked two stalwart youths from the crowd as helpers for the same payment. Some barnstormers carried a mechanic with them, while others were their own engineers. Gas? You walked into town with your cans and had them filled at the gas station. Accommodations? The farmer or his neighbor would be happy to oblige the "Major" or the "Colonel." You moved south in winter, back up north in the spring. You owned nothing but your airplane and the clothes on your back, plus a too-small roll of bills in your back pocket. You were young, footloose and fearless, always broke, always hopeful. Your airplane was slightly less well-off, what with living its life always in the open, and your somewhat limited knowledge of maintenance. The Jenny's lower wing was always snagging on something or other, and you fixed it yourself with some dope and a patch of canvas or a piece from some young lady's petticoat. If a flying wire twanged, you replaced it with the top strand from the farmer's fence, and hoped to be miles away before he noticed his loss.

The one trial of your carefree existence (other than the risk of starving to death) was your Jenny's OX5 engine. Also a Curtiss product, the OX5 has been nicely de-scribed as a failure looking for somewhere to happen. One old-timer used to call his "Galloping Dominoes," because if he didn't have a forced landing in seven hours, he sure would in eleven. There were dozens of things that would go wrong with an OX. It was single-ignition, so one fouled plug could bring you downhill. The single-pushrod, arm-and-stirrup valve mechanism employed three springs per valve in an era when spring manufacture was neither exact nor a science. The overhead-valve mechanism was open to dirt and weather, bugs and grit. But the biggest weakness of the engine was its cooling system. It was water-cooled, one reason for its excessive, 390-pound weight. In summer the thing overheated and spewed water through cracks in the water jacket, thus fouling the ignition system. In winter dripping water froze on the carburetor, stopping its vents and sticking its valves. To make sure of trouble, the OX's ever-leaking water pump was mounted just above the carburetor, so that water in the gas was a certainty. You could even have an engine failure with an OX and never know what caused it, for as soon as you stopped twitching after your forced landing and got out to prop the danged thing, off she'd go, sweet as a bird.

Fortunately, the old OX was designed to be repaired. You thought little of yanking off a cylinder in some remote pasture and dropping it over a fence post to hold the valves in place while you repaired a busted part with a spare. You carried in your head a catalogue of all the automotive and marine parts that fitted an OX. Even a cracked water jacket could be plugged with pitch till you found a blacksmith with a brazing outfit.

The OX5's vast weight and girth also explained the Jenny's huge wingspread. It took a wire-braced cathedral to get such weight aloft on such meager power. In Texas they used to say that on a good day a Jenny could just about keep up with a jackrabbit. But that fan-

69

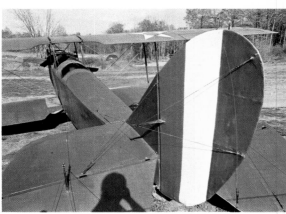

Top and right: A rare flying Jenny,
one of some 6,000 built and of perhaps a dozen
that survive—mostly in museums.
Color scheme is post-World War I U.S.
Army. Left: Jenny's monstrous 390-pound
OX5 engine that produced a mere 90 hp and was
described as "a failure looking for
somewhere to happen." Above: Tail assembly.

Cat's cradle of struts and bracing wires
that held Jenny together was a wingwalker's
delight. Curved skids under lower
wing and king posts above upper wing enabled
stunt men of Hollywood and
flying circuses to clamber over plane while
aloft with relative ease.

tastic birdcage of a wing was just made for the wingwalker's unlikely art, for not only did you have serried ranks of struts and wires between the mainplanes themselves to hang on to, but king posts and bracing wires rising clear above the top wing, plus a stout, curved skid under the lower wing tip and a good old-fashioned spreader bar between the wheels. You could roam almost at will over the whole airplane, or even transfer to another.

Wingwalking is popularly attributed to the imagination of one Ormer Locklear, a Texan, of course, who in 1917 found himself training to be a Signal Corps flying officer. Legend has it that he threw out a trailing antenna only to have it snag in the tail-control wires. So he hopped out of the cockpit and squirreled along the turtleback, untangling the radio antenna just in time to receive the mes-

sage "Locklear, U R grounded." But not for long. Soon he became so nimble that while aloft with a student he clambered down to the spreader bar and sat there admiring the view, which must have given his students confidence, once they got over their shock.

As business became more competitive, barnstorming alone became no way to make a living, and the gypsy pilots took to hunting in packs, as it were. Thus evolved the idea of the air circus—the stunting and wing-walking and parachuting which drew crowds of people hoping to see some silly fellow break his neck. Once out, they could be persuaded to cough up five bucks for a ride. But it was certainly more than sheer commerce that motivated the stunt men. That old human intoxication with the roar of the crowd had a lot to do with it. (Slim Lindbergh got his newspaper

nickname, "The Flyin' Fool," in his barnstorming days.) You'd start with aerobatics—loops, barrel rolls, falling leafs, and spins. Then maybe a car-to-plane transfer, using a dangling rope ladder. When mere wingwalking palled, the idea of a transfer from one Jenny to another in flight was evolved, maybe with a can of gas under your arm as an early demonstration of Strategic Air Command's old standby, in-flight refueling. One of Lindbergh's specialties was to open his chute while standing out on a wing, so that it pulled him off and into a gentle descent. Soon the stunt men began to ham things up: dropping dummies that looked like falling bodies, falling off a wing tip while a rope still attached them securely to the airplane, seeming to hang by their teeth from the spreader bar while a stout harness actually held them, dressing up as a little old grandmother and pretend-

ing to steal a Jenny. Bridges fascinated all barnstormers. When merely flying under them no longer provided a thrill, they flew a loop around them, then did it again with the prettiest blonde they could find for a passenger. You had to have your wits about you to live long at this sort of game. A lot of men didn't, and a lot of men died. The Aircraft Year Book for 1923 noted 179 serious accidents barnstorming, with 85 people killed and 162 hurt. Curiously it wasn't wingwalking that was the biggest killer, but parachuting, followed by low-level aerobatics and in-flight structural failures. But when the Federal government introduced the first civil air regulations in 1927 it was no more than a final blow to the barnstormers, for by that time their airplanes were beat and barnstorming was just about played out with the public. The era of glory—for barnstormers and for Jennies—lasted a long ten years. Of the twelve hundred private airplanes flying in the United States in the early twenties, probably half were barnstorming, and they must have hopped a million people.

Today, of the six thousand or so Jennies built, maybe a dozen survive, mostly in museums. Maybe a handful are still flying, and the best of these are modern replicas, like Cole Palen's Hisso-engined, somber-hued beauty shown here in postwar U. S. Army colors. It was one just like this that Lindbergh soloed on at Brooks Field, when he grew tired of the uncertainties of barnstorming and joined the Army Air Service. His own Jenny was so battered and tattered from a thousand close shaves that he was ordered to get it off the Army's field.

Now, fifty years later, we have landed on the moon, but it all had to start somewhere, and maybe that day in Farmer Jones' pasture was where it did. For make no mistake about it, it was the Jenny that first got Americans into the skies.

73

Lindbergh & the Ryans

Dusk, one fall day in 1926, and a young mail pilot is droning across the Midwest in an old DH, his head full of daydreams. How far, he wonders, *could* an airplane fly, say, if its fuselage were completely filled with gas tanks? There's a new, clean-limbed monoplane he's heard of, designed by an Italian immigrant named Bellanca, that has been lifting some unheard-of payloads on test flights. It has a marvelous new engine, named the Wright Whirlwind, which is light, powerful, and phenomenally reliable.

"In a Bellanca filled with fuel tanks," he thinks, "I could fly on all night, like the moon. With the engine throttled down it could stay aloft for days. Possibly—my mind is startled at the thought—I could fly nonstop between New York and Paris. If one could carry fuel enough (and the Bellanca might)—if the engine didn't stop (and those new Wright Whirlwinds seldom do stop; they aren't like our old Liberties)—if one just held to the right course for long enough, one should arrive in Europe. The flying couldn't be more dangerous or the weather worse than the night mail in the winter."

New York to Paris—some dream! For, since the end of the war to this year of 1926, aviation has hardly advanced. Perilous mail services and barnstorming are about the size of it. New York to Paris. A prize of $25,000 has been offered by a New York hotel magnate for just such a flight. And while a new Wright Bellanca would probably cost $10,000 or $15,000, the pilot who won the prize might show a profit. "Why shouldn't I fly from New York to Paris?" he wonders. "I'm almost twenty-five. I have almost four years of aviation behind me, and close to two thousand hours in the air." Two thousand hours of every kind of flying. In truth, this lad, Charles A. Lindbergh, is perhaps as likely as anybody to bring off such an incredible feat.

Ten or fifteen thousand dollars. He has $2,000 saved, but he knows several businessmen in his home city, St. Louis, who are very much interested in aviation. Lindbergh goes to see them, and expounds his wild plan. They are so impressed with his competence that they say, simply, go find a plane and leave the financing to us.

Lindbergh's first choice, the Bellanca, turns out not for sale. A Fokker? A trimotor would cost him $100,000 and they will not sell him a single-engined design for such a hazardous venture. A Travel Air monoplane? Travel Air is not interested. But there is a tiny California outfit named Ryan that is building a monoplane mailplane of unusually good performance. Lindbergh telegraphs his requirements, and back comes a speedy reply: Ryan will build him a special plane in ninety days for $6,000, or around $10,000 with the Wright engine. Lindbergh is all set to go to California when a telegram arrives from Bellanca, reopening negotiations. Lindbergh goes at once to New York to find that one Charles Levine has bought the Bellanca and is willing to sell it to him for $15,000.

"We will sell our plane," Levine explains, "but of course we reserve the right to select the crew that flies it." Lindbergh is dumbfounded. "You understand we cannot let just anybody pilot our airplane across the ocean," Levine continues. Lindbergh picks up the $15,000 check he has just put on Levine's desk. "You are making a mistake," Levine argues. "The Bellanca is the only airplane that is capable of flying between New York and Paris." But Lindbergh is determined to make the flight his way, and he still has the offer from Ryan. Lindbergh doubts that Ryan has understood what it is letting itself in for, but Ryan is his only remaining chance.

When the unknown mail pilot and the officers of the Ryan company meet on February 23, 1927, Lindbergh's first surprise is that Claude Ryan himself is not among them. A short month before, Ryan had sold out to his partner, B. F. Mahoney. But Lindbergh is most impressed to discover that the Ryan company's one engineer, Donald Hall, has already been doing homework on the project.

Many changes to the standard Ryan mailplane will be needed to make it into a transatlantic machine. First the wing area has to be increased to carry the enormous fuel load. A bigger wing means moving the tail surfaces aft and the engine forward; thus an almost completely new fuselage is needed, and a new landing gear, as well. Hall proposes to put the main tank under the wing, around the center of gravity. Where, he asks, does Lindbergh want the cockpits for himself and his navigator? But Lindbergh is proposing to go alone. It takes Hall a while to digest and accept this, but good designer that he is, his reaction is to start estimating how much fuel the missing navigator will allow Lindbergh to carry. He calculates fifty gallons. By the way, he asks Lindbergh, just exactly how far is it from New York to Paris? Lindbergh simply doesn't know. They drive to the San Diego Public Library and, stretching a piece of string between the two cities on a globe, they find the distance to be 3,600 statute miles. That means Lindbergh needs a still-air range of about 4,000 miles. Back at the factory, Hall's boss Mahoney reaffirms the price of $6,000 to build Lindbergh a transatlantic airplane, with delivery in sixty days. The total with engines and instruments will be $10,580. Lindbergh's backers approve, and work begins, with Hall's enthusiasm a match for Lindbergh's.

From this point, when all became committed to the flight, the ship evolved quickly. It was a flying fuel tank, with ten feet more span than a regular Ryan. Only absolutely essential equipment was installed. There was no parachute, no night-flying equipment save a hand-held flashlight, and no gas gauges. There was no forward visibility either, with that huge tank in front of the cockpit. Lindbergh was able to see only sideways and above. For takeoff and landing he would squint sideways through the open window. There was neither radio nor sextant. Dead reckoning and estimates of drift from wave observations would have to do. Range was the thing. Range was even more important than navigational accuracy in crossing the Atlantic.

The plane that Hall designed and the Ryan company built for Lindbergh remains to this day an enduring masterpiece of pure performance. It was intended to carry 425 gallons of fuel; in reality the tanks were built a little oversize, and their real capacity was nearer 450 gallons. Empty, the plane weighed just over a ton. Carrying pilot Lindbergh and completely fueled, the *Spirit of St. Louis* weighed 5,250 pounds. In effect, the *Spirit's* useful load was one and a half times its empty weight! With 223 hp, maximum speed was 124 mph, and the takeoff run at gross weight was 2,500 feet. Maximum still-air range was an astonishing 4,210 miles. After test flying the plane, and planning his transatlantic flight on charts bought from a ship's chandler, Lindbergh flew to New York in two stages. First

PT-20A low-wing monoplane (below) was one of several trainers Ryan developed for military during World War II. Better known, but less beautiful, was PT-22 with five-cylinder Kinner radial engine. S-T-A (opposite) was sport trainer of 1935 with 125-hp Menasco engine.

came a magnificent fourteen-and-a-half-hour flight nonstop from San Diego to St. Louis, clear across the Rockies by night. From St. Louis he made New York in seven hours flat. In New York, the long wait for a favorable weather forecast began. On his way to the theater one night, Lindbergh stopped to telephone the weather bureau, and learned that, suddenly, the weather clear across the north Atlantic was improving. Thoughts of the theater vanished. Early in the muddy next morning, after a sleepless night, Lindbergh made a perilous takeoff, clearing telephone wires at the end of the field by a mere twenty feet, and was on his way. His next thirty-three and a half hours comprise one of the epic endurance feats of human history, a long battle with exhaustion so intense that once it seemed to fill the plane around him with phantoms.

There were tangible enemies stalking his tracks as well: ice that formed a paralyzing coating all over the plane, and thunderheads in the night. He even faced the possibility of loss of control while still awake, for he was flying an unstable airplane by reference to needle, ball, and airspeed alone.

His landfall in the south of Ireland was, unbelievably, within five miles of his plotted course. His welcome at Paris's Le Bourget field was both a triumph and a torment—a triumph of recognition by the world of his feat, and a torment to his basic shyness and desire for privacy. But the world was happy, for the world had a new hero of the kind it loved best: young, handsome, brave, and modest.

After Lindbergh's marvelous flight, the Mahoney-Ryan Aircraft Corporation quickly forgot about mailplanes and began manufacturing a fine six-seat version of Lindy's *Spirit of St. Louis,* called the B-5 Brougham.

In 1929 the corporation was merged with the Detroit Aircraft Corporation, which was owned by Lindbergh's backers, and two years later the whole edifice tumbled, a victim of the Depression.

But that was not the end of Ryan airplanes, for within a year or two Claude Ryan himself formed a new company, Ryan Aeronautical, and began to build one of the most exquisitely beautiful airplanes of all time. The Ryan S-T (the designation stands, prosaically, for "Sport Trainer") has an almost sculptured appearance—superbly streamlined, with a delicacy of form that makes it the epitome of the high-performance monoplane, circa 1934. Somehow there is harmony between the straight wings and curved tail, between the closely cowled engine and deep but narrow oval fuselage, between the windshielded open cockpits and the cat's-paw landing gear reaching down for the ground, that no other design of open-cockpit monoplane has ever quite achieved.

The S-T had an all-metal fuselage, with a skin made of the new aluminum alloy, Alclad—a thick skin that did away with the need for stiffening stringers. The wings were an odd mixture of ancient and modern, with alloy ribs and steel compression members allied to traditional spruce spars and fabric covering. The spreading fingers of bracing wires and struts may seem anachronistic in a monoplane, but they were very much part of the speed scene in the early thirties, when most every racing airplane sported them.

The Ryan S-T, tagged $3,985 at the factory, was a winner from the start. There was some criticism that the machine could use more power, so Claude Ryan came out with the S-T-A, with a 125-hp Menasco, instead of the 95-hp engine in the regular S-T. In 1936, he offered the S-T-A Special, with a 150-hp blown Menasco, absolutely the last word in grace and pace, with a claimed maximum speed of 160 mph—a magical performance of better than one mph per horsepower. An S-T-A Special sold new for $5,185, which is perhaps half what you might be asked for one today. Every sportsman-pilot in America wanted one.

The U. S. military ordered a handful of Ryans as an experiment, a version Ryan called the STA-1, and the army the XPT-16. The plane won approval, and as the country drifted toward war, orders for Ryans grew larger and larger, mostly to supply the Civilian Pilot Training Program. Most Air Corps Ryans were the less beautiful ST3-KR, or PT-22, version, with the five-cylinder Kinner radial (the Menasco having proved unamenable to military life), with a larger cockpit opening, and with completely uncowled landing gear allowing easier maintenance.

The Ryan airframe has always been rugged. The airspeed indicator on Ryans is redlined at 156 mph, but there were many wartime instructors who saw well over 200 indicated when nervous pupils decided to "pull through" halfway round a slow roll. One S-T-A owner of my acquaintance bravely pushed his bird up to 210 one day. "The wings flapped a bit," he admitted, "and the wires were singing like banshees, and the wind whistled, but there was no vibration or buffeting, and she coasted out easily to a more comfortable speed."

The singing wires during aerobatics are one of the endearing things about Ryans. The flat wires were set to be stream-

lined to the airflow in level flight, and the moment you get the airplane upside down, of course, the angle of attack is completely changed, and the wires are no longer edge-on to the wind. The sound they make is the loveliest whine imaginable.

The Ryan has had something of a reputation as a "hot ship." It has always had rather a high accident rate, and still does. The truth is, in the hands of a pilot who knows what he is about, it is as safe a bird as you could want, but it does have characteristics that can bite the unwary. With badly crossed controls, a Ryan—particularly the swept-wing PT-22—will snap on you. And with that rather narrow-track and stilty gear, coupled with slippery heel pedals for the brakes, you can easily ground-loop the beast if your footwork is the least bit sloppy. My friend with the S-T-A recommends that Ryan pilots be "accomplished mambo dancers." Most Ryan owners will insist that the airplane is no problem to handle, but at the same time they will be very happy if you let *them* do the landing.

In round numbers, maybe a hundred of the Kinner Ryans, the PT-22, are still flying today, and about thirty STs. To my mind, the S-T-A remains Claude Ryan's enduring masterpiece. If there is ever a museum of the airplane designer's art, there is one bird that surely belongs.

NC-10

WINNIE MAE

M-SOL

Lockheed's Plywood Bullets

Preceding pages: Replica of "Winnie Mae,"
Lockheed Vega which set round-the-world speed
record in 1931. Pilot Wiley Post
(opposite) later flew it to altitude record
of 55,000 feet. Ground speed of 340 mph at
that height suggests that he
was first aviator to fly a jet stream.

They were three brothers, born Loughead, an Irish name which is properly pronounced something like Lockheed. (After half a lifetime of being miscalled Log-head, they bowed to the inevitable and decided to spell it like it is.) Their mother, Mrs. Loughead, was on her own, maintaining a modest place on the shores of San Francisco Bay. She supported her four children (there was a sister, too) by selling feature articles to the San Francisco *Chronicle,* and grapes and prunes from her groves to all comers. But fruit held no fascination for her sons, nor feature writing, either. They all wanted to be engineers. Victor, the eldest, departed first, migrating to Chicago to be an automobile engineer. Malcolm got a job in 1904 as a mechanic for White steam cars. The youngest, Allan, was still a kid when he was hired as a solderer in a repair shop. Before long Allan followed Victor to Chicago to work as a mechanic for Victor's boss, a truck and automobile distributor who dabbled in aviation on the side. Allan was fascinated. In 1910 his boss bought a Curtiss Pusher, but neither of the two appointed pilots could get it airborne. Allan did by then have a few minutes of copilot time, and talked his way into being allowed a try. "I've got a twenty-dollar gold piece that says I'll make it fly," he boldly announced, but such was his confidence that there were no takers, even at three to one. He did indeed get the Curtiss up and down, whole and in one piece. "Now I was an aviator," he later announced. Aviation in 1910 meant barnstorming, and that was how Allan Loughead aviated until one wet September day in 1911, when he tried to take off in a Curtiss that was sodden with rain. AVIATOR IN GREAT PERIL was how the local paper headlined the crash. "Aviator Loughead has miraculous escape from death" was the newspaper's opinion.

Aviator Loughead evidently agreed, for he returned home to San Francisco with a midwestern bride, and became once more a mechanic. But that was not all; on the side, together with brother Malcolm, he designed and built a small seaplane. It was called the Model G, for no better reason than that the Loughead brothers wished the purchasing public to think that all the previous experience of building models A through F had gone into it. For eighteen months they planed and glued and stitched away at their creation, a conventional biplane of its era, with a cruciform tail hinged on a universal joint, and an 80-hp Curtiss OX driving a tractor propeller. The Model G first flew (Allan piloting, recovered from his previous funk) on June 15, 1913, and it flew well, in spite of grossly oversensitive controls due to that all-moving tail.

In 1915, when the Panama-Pacific Exposition opened in San Francisco, the Loughead brothers finally saw a chance to make some money with their own seaplane. In fifty days of hopping passengers they made $6,000. Emboldened by success, they next formed the Loughead Aircraft Manufacturing Company, and set to designing and building a monster twin-engined ten-seat flying boat. They hired a likely lad who was always in and out of their shop—a garage mechanic named Jack Northrop—to do some stress analysis and help with shaping the hull. This new seaplane flew strongly, and the Lougheads had hopes of selling it to the Navy. But when America entered the war, the Navy decided on a policy of standardization, and the Loughead F-1 seaplane wasn't to be the standard. The Curtiss seaplane was.

The Lougheads next rigged the F-1 as a land plane, and tried flying it to Washington as a demonstration of its excellence. After it ended up on its nose in Arizona, they took it back to California where they flew passengers, and also movie cameramen who gladly paid $150 an hour for flying time whenever aerial footage was needed.

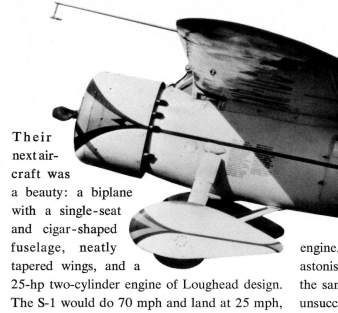

Their next aircraft was a beauty: a biplane with a single-seat and cigar-shaped fuselage, neatly tapered wings, and a 25-hp two-cylinder engine of Loughead design. The S-1 would do 70 mph and land at 25 mph, and it had folding wings so it would fit in any garage. For 1919 it was an advanced design, but, with that fleet of cheap surplus Jennies available, nobody wanted it. The S-1 cost $30,000 to develop, and not one was ever sold.

Malcolm Loughead had long held the idea that he could build a four-wheel hydraulic brake system for automobiles. "Keep at it," Allan told him, with classic understatement. "It's a million-dollar idea." So, in 1921, they liquidated Loughead Aircraft. Malcolm went off to Detroit to develop hydraulic brakes—using for the first time the phonetic name Lockheed. Allan, meanwhile, sold real estate in Los Angeles and later became a regional distributor for Lockheed brakes. But in spare moments he and Jack Northrop, now working for Donald Douglas, would meet to work on the design of an all-plywood monoplane. In 1926, they drew up a stock prospectus for a new company and showed it to a wealthy brick and tile manufacturer named Kenneth Jay. Jay took one look at the drawings of their streamlined monoplane and offered to put up all the $25,000 they were asking, in return for fifty-one percent of the common stock and all of the preferred. But he insisted the company be called Lockheed, to capitalize on the growing success of brother Malcolm's brakes.

They called the plane the Vega, a simple name that connoted astronomical speed and distance. They built the first Vega for a grand total of $17,500, including machine tools. The biggest cost was the Wright Whirlwind engine. For 1926, the Vega was an astonishingly futuristic airplane. It had the same cigar-shaped plywood fuselage as the unsuccessful S-1, but this fuselage was hung from a beautiful, one-piece tapered wing which was so clean it didn't even have a bracing strut.

The Vega's timing was uncannily good, too. Just as the factory was putting the finishing touches to it came the furor over Lindbergh's flight to Paris and the wild boom in aviation that followed.

Lockheed's first Vega made its maiden flight on July 4, 1927. Before the month was out the company had a purchaser for the airplane—George Hearst of the newspaper empire. A pineapple millionaire from Hawaii named Jim Dole had put up $35,000 in prize money for an air race from California to Hawaii and Hearst wanted to enter the Vega. Dubbed the *Golden Eagle*, and carrying two pilots, it was one of four entrants to set off from Oakland on August 16, 1927. It was never seen again. However, in its brief lifetime the *Golden Eagle* had made a profound impression on many people, notably on an Australian adventurer named Hubert Wilkins, who'd seen its slippery lines flash past the window of his hotel room in San Francisco.

Wilkins was a man obsessed by polar exploration. He dreamed of flying clear across the Arctic Sea and had wrecked several lesser airplanes trying. Wilkins bought the second Vega, had it fitted with extra tanks, set on skis, and flown to Alaska by his friend Ben Eilson. On April 15, 1928, they left Point Barrow for Spitzbergen, 2,200 miles away across a wilderness of ice. After more than twenty hours of flying they put down in a blizzard and sat for five days in the plane, shivering and hoping their emergency rations would last. Then, with Wilkins pushing and heaving to free the stuck skis, they tried to take off. Each time Wilkins would lose his hold on the Vega, so that Eilson was forced to put down again. Finally, down to ten gallons of gas, they were airborne together and in only five miles they came to the Norwegian settlement they had been aiming for.

The flight of Wilkins and Eilson was a miraculous combination of navigational skill, bravado, and plain luck, and it made the Vega. The company was deluged with orders. The backlog soon totaled more than a quarter of a million dollars. This was not enough to hold Jack Northrop, who wanted to move on to metal construction. He left and was replaced as chief engineer by Gerry Vultee (who was also to start his own airplane company in time).

Among the customers who came knocking, early in 1928, were officials of Western Air Express, who wondered whether Lockheed could increase the Vega's power and speed. Oh, and one other thing: Everybody knew no airline pilot could do a proper job without the wind on his cheek. Could Lockheed please give its plane an open cockpit?

Lockheed met the first request by substituting a 450-hp Pratt & Whitney Wasp for the old 220 Whirlwind. Because of the Wasp's powerful slipstream, fulfilling the second request meant moving the pilot from his usual position in a Vega, right behind the engine, to a newly fashioned cockpit in the rear fuselage, just ahead of the vertical stabilizer. To allow the poor goggled pilot to see anything forward, the wing had to be jacked up on stilts above the fuselage. The resulting airplane, called the Air Express, was ugly but it did go. With a 150-mph cruise it outran the Vega by 35 mph.

Lockheed had rolled out just three airplanes in 1927. Production the next year was sixty-four planes and sales were over

$750,000. "It takes a Lockheed to beat a Lockheed" was the upcoming company's slogan; "Lockheed aircraft will carry the same payload farther, faster, and with less fuel expenditure," which about summed it up. The airlines became major customers for the planes and almost every speed king of the day flew Lockheed.

One Lockheed pilot who earned undying fame was the one-eyed oil field roustabout Wiley Post. Post flew a splendid blue and white Vega named the *Winnie Mae* in honor of the daughter of his boss, F. C. Hall. In 1931, Post, who had never crossed any body of water larger than Long Island Sound, set off on a flight around the world. He took with him a navigator named Harold Gatty who, like Hubert Wilkins, was an Australian. Gatty's six-month intensive preparation for the flight played a large part in its successful completion. Their time for the trip was under nine days. Two years later, Post was off again, solo this time, but with one of Lawrence Sperry's first autopilots to help him. He began the trip by flying nonstop from New York to Berlin in 25 hours, 45 minutes, and went through some notable adventures, including having the autopilot twice go out on him. He achieved the almost unbelievable feat of beating by 21 hours *solo* the around-the-world record he had previously made with a navigator along for aid and assistance.

Later, Wiley Post was fascinated by the prospects of flight in the stratosphere, and had Goodrich build him a pressure suit. Post added supercharging and a droppable landing gear to the *Winnie Mae* and achieved an altitude of 55,000 feet and speeds of up to 340 mph. High-flying Wiley was perhaps the first pilot to chance upon a jet stream. Another extravagantly colorful Lockheed pilot was Roscoe Turner, a dandy who often flew with a lion cub (with its own parachute) for passenger.

Lockheed made several low-wing variants on the same basic design. There was the

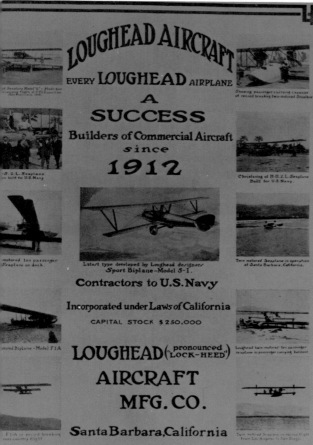

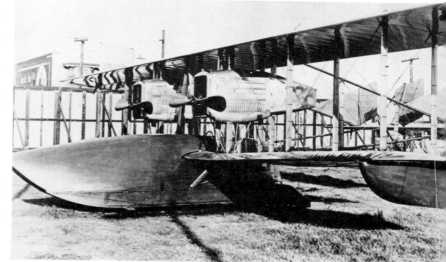

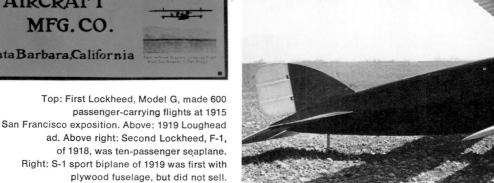

Top: First Lockheed, Model G, made 600
passenger-carrying flights at 1915
San Francisco exposition. Above: 1919 Loughead
ad. Above right: Second Lockheed, F-1,
of 1918, was ten-passenger seaplane.
Right: S-1 sport biplane of 1919 was first with
plywood fuselage, but did not sell.

Explorer, which evolved into the Sirius, an open-cockpit airplane designed by Gerry Vultee to Charles Lindbergh's specifications. Lindbergh spent all his time in the Lockheed factory while the plane was a-building, much as he had done earlier at Ryan. He and his bride Anne Morrow flew the equivalent of several times around the world in this Sirius, prospecting air routes for Pan American, before the airplane was wrecked while being loaded onto a ship in China.

After the Sirius came the Altair, which had a hand-wound retractable gear and the same 450-hp Wasp that powered most of its predecessors; it could hit 230 mph. The last of the wooden Lockheeds was the Orion, which featured the first successful hydraulic retractable landing gear. With a 650-hp Wright Cyclone engine, it could cruise, with six passengers, at 200 mph. Prices varied from $13,500 in 1928 for a regular Vega, to $25,000 for a 1931 Orion. Far more Vegas were built than any of the other variants. Less than two hundred of

all models were ever built.

The structure of these Lockheeds was a true masterpiece of the cabinetmaker's art. The fuselage was built in two halves inside a concrete mold which was first lined with gore-shaped, tapered strips of veneer. The inner surface was then liberally sloshed with casein glue, every man jack in the factory being called in to wield a pot and a brush. Then a cross-layer of birch veneer was laid on, followed by more glue, and another longitudinal layer to form the third ply. A rubber air bag was placed on top, a cover was bolted on, and the air bag inflated to apply an even pressure of twenty pounds per square inch while the glue cured. The fuselage design was never pure monocoque, for a sturdy wooden skeleton of longerons and ring formers was built, to which the two outer half-shells were later tacked and glued. Cutouts for doors, windows, and cockpits were easily made, and the piece of three-ply sawed for the door was later made into the door itself. The beautiful, thick,

Top: Sleek design of "Golden Eagle," first of Vega series, seemed futuristic when airplane appeared in 1926. Above: Air Express was Vega modified to accept 450-hp Pratt & Whitney Wasp engine. Opposite: Charles Lindbergh climbing aboard Sirius designed to his specs.

tapered wings were more orthodox, with long tapered spars, and ribs built up of strips, with a kind of Pratt truss used to maintain the airfoil. The whole wing was covered with birch veneer plywood.

The Lockheed company proved weaker than the airplanes it built. In 1929, the company was sold to that ill-timed and ill-conceived corporation, Detroit Aircraft, which was meant to be a General Motors of the air. Allan Lockheed warned against the deal. "Out of the group that ultimately made up the Detroit Aircraft family," he said, "our company alone had any degree of financial stability. I was certain only tragedy could come out of the proposed sale." But he didn't own a controlling interest and he was outvoted. He resigned, and sold his shares for $23 each. Detroit Aircraft lost $733,000 that year, and its own shares went from $15 to 12½ cents in two years. In 1932, the Lockheed company was sold, for $40,000, to the only bidders, a group headed by Robert E. Gross,

which still runs Lockheed today.

Of the 197 wooden Lockheeds that were built, only about a dozen survive. Most of the others were simply cracked up at one time or another. In the mid-thirties, as the airlines modernized, they sold their old wooden planes off to little transport companies in places like Mexico and Alaska, where short runways and the difficult climate or topography got them in the end. The retractable-gear Orions and Altairs often perished when the gear jammed in the up or half-up position. After 1936, large numbers of Lockheeds were smuggled across to Spain by the Republicans and later vanished in the debris of the civil war. One Vega is still privately owned, having been put out to grass after years of use in experiments by the military to see if a wooden airplane could be made transparent to radar. Lindbergh's *Tingmissartoq* is in Washington, and Wiley Post's *Winnie Mae*, the most magnificent Lockheed of them all, hangs regally in the Smithsonian Institution.

87

Ford's Tri-Motor: the Tin Goose

Watch one on finals and you'll see at once why they call her the Tin Goose. She does look like some huge, mythical, big-bellied bird, wings spread for touchdown. And it takes only an ounce of imagination to see the nose as a bird's head, with the cockpit windows for eyes. Under closer inspection you see the tin: acres and acres of corrugated Alclad, like finely grooved tin roofing, covering her bones.

A ride in one is an extraordinary experience. The Ford is perhaps the noisiest airplane ever built. That famous skin oilcans and washboards, while the three open radial engines roar like lions, and the control cables flap and slap against the fuselage. In the cockpit, the noise is still worse. One pilot must cup his hands around the other's ear and YELL to make himself heard. The cockpit is lovely, though. The windshield is raked forward and forms a big V. At its point an ancient compass is mounted on rubber cords, so the vibration doesn't shake its alcohol filling to a froth. There seem to be almost no instruments, except for a cluster of moving-coil ammeters down by the pilot's knees. There are two great wood-spoked steering wheels that look as though they came off a Model T. They did; commonality came early to Ford. You wind the wheels to move the ailerons, and swing the whole control column back and forth to move the elevators. An enormous gearshift lever between the two pilots' seats operates the wheel brakes, both together. This is the famous Johnson bar brake system. The starter buttons, three in a row, would also be instantly familiar to any Model T owner. (The old joke was, you can tell a Ford pilot by his three arms. . . .) Yet for her day, which began in 1926, the Ford Tri-Motor was a lot of airplane. It was big: fifty feet long and seventy-four

feet in span, with a sixteen-foot passenger cabin you could stand up in. It carried twelve passengers. The Ford was an all-metal monoplane in an era of wood and fabric biplanes, and a multi-engined machine at that. The Ford was quite desperately slow, with a cruising speed of under a hundred miles an hour. But what else in 1926 went faster? Only racers. She would carry a ton of load, and float off the ground in only a few times her own length and float back onto it just as easily. She had no tendency to ground-loop, thanks to her enormously wide-track main wheels, and quite moderate angle of attack in the three-point attitude. There are Ford Tri-Motors still flying in scheduled airline service today, forty years on. This is a design that endures.

The origins of the Ford Tri-Motor go back to an eccentric inventor named William Bushnell Stout. He was a skinny fellow with heavy spectacles and a Groucho Marx moustache, who claimed to be incorrigibly lazy. As a college kid he got a job taking care of furnaces and, since he loathed getting up early to feed them, he devised a splendid Rube Goldberg arrangement of pulleys and cords and coal-laden buckets which would do the job while he slept. "There must be a better way" was the keystone to his thinking. "Simplicate and add more lightness" was his formula for better airplanes.

After his college days, Bill Stout first covered aviation for the Chicago *Tribune*, then founded and edited his own aviation magazine, *Aerial Age*. During the First World War he worked for Packard, which was building Liberty aero engines, and later he became an adviser to the wartime Aircraft Production Board. In this job, Stout got to look over a host of different airplane designs whose engineering left him generally unimpressed. There had to be a better way. He was very taken with the structures that Junkers

Opening pages and below: Ford 5-AT
Tri-Motor with 420-hp Wasp engine. First model,
4-AT, made its appearance
in 1926. Tri-Motors were big and slow
(under 100 mph), but some 200 were built and
a few of them still are flying
in regularly scheduled air service.

in Germany had been developing—with great thick monoplane wings, internally braced, and corrugated metal skins.

Soon after the armistice, Stout designed and had built his first airplane. He called it the Batwing, a thick-winged monoplane whose wing tapered so acutely that at its root it merged with the tailplane. The design owed much to Junkers, and much to Deperdussin's prewar racers. Stout promoted himself an old wartime Hispano-Suiza engine and got the Batwing airborne. On the strength of that hop Stout was able to get financial backing and built a second, improved Batwing. Ex-journalist Stout saw to it that the new machine was richly publicized, and soon acquired a contract to build a twin-engined torpedo-bomber for the Navy. He came up with a twin-tailed machine that resembled the military bombers of, say, ten or fifteen years later. Its potential was never established, for the Navy's hotshot test pilot cracked the thing up on his first flight. The Navy then canceled the contract.

Stout, after this failure, was broke and discredited, but it was at this point that he had the most inspired idea of his life. He contacted all the prominent Detroit industrialists who showed an interest in aviation, simply asking each to contribute a thousand dollars toward the founding of a new aviation company. "The chances are," he freely admitted to them, "that you'll never get your money back, but you'll have fun." Sixty-two went along with the idea, and some anted up more than the requested $1,000. In consequence Stout found himself suddenly in charge of $125,000. Among the donors was old man Henry Ford, persuaded by his son Edsel, who had been fascinated by airplanes since his childhood.

The new Stout Metal Airplane Company's first design was made of wood and fabric; I know not why. It was something like a pregnant Batwing, a four-seat, deep-bellied monoplane much underpowered by an OX engine. This plane was called the Air Sedan. A subsequent version, made of corrugated metal and powered by a Hisso engine, was demonstrated to the Army Air Service at Selfridge Field. Here the Fords, father and son, came to see it one day. "I think this fellow is on the right track," whispered Henry to Edsel. "Mister Ford," said Stout, who had heard the remark, "this thing isn't worth a damn! I need more horsepower. To get it I need more money—" Old Henry Ford grumpily interrupted him. "You don't need more money, son. You need more airplane!" And the Fords gave Stout more money to build more airplane. Even the tubby little Air Sedan had been an obvious progenitor of the eventual Tin Goose. Stout's "more airplane," the Air Pullman, and its development, the Air Transport, were very close indeed to the final Tin Goose, except for being single-engined. In the summer of 1924 the Fords, who had continued to feed money into Stout's company till they had a majority interest in it, announced that they would build a proper factory for production of the Air Transport and at the same time they ordered five airplanes with which to start their own private airline between various Ford factories around the area. The service ran like clockwork. Once Edsel Ford missed the Ford flight by twenty minutes. "This is an airline, not a yacht," was his father's comment.

On July 31, 1925, Henry Ford bought out all the other shareholders. He put his chief engineer in charge of the new acquisition, although Stout was still on the payroll. Ford wasn't satisfied with the Air Pullman, and told Stout to design a bigger, multiengined transport. Stout stuck three Whirlwinds onto a Pullman airframe. It looked ugly and flew worse. The pilot hired to test it told Ford succinctly to "forget it." Ford's problem of what to do next was neatly if mysteriously solved when the Stout factory burned to the ground one winter night.

Henry Ford was by now somewhat disenchanted with Bill Stout. What was needed,

91

Streamlined Italian tri-motor was Savoia-Marchetti SM-79 bomber (right). Junkers JU-52 passenger plane (opposite) was put into Berlin-Rome-London service by Lufthansa in 1932. Below: Fokker C-2, in U.S. Army colors, and other wood-bodied tri-motors were never so popular as Alclad Fords.

he decided, was less promotion and more engineering, so while a new factory was being built he sent Stout off on a lecture tour and put in another designer. He also hired three young graduates of the Massachusetts Institute of Technology, one of whom was James McDonnell, later to be head of McDonnell-Douglas, and set them to work turning the Air Pullman into a successful tri-motor. The result was the 4-AT—the first Tin Goose. The plane's maiden flight was on June 11, 1926, and in no time at all the new Ford Tri-Motors were coming down the assembly line as though they were automobiles. Nearby, Ford built a six-hundred-acre airport with two paved runways—the first in the United States—complete with radio beacons, a passenger terminal and weather station, a pilot training school, and a mooring mast for dirigibles.

Between 1926 and 1933, 198 pro-duction model Tri-Motors were built. All sorts of customers bought them—airlines, oil companies, wealthy sportsmen. Ford made much of the airplane's all-metal construction, particularly after a competitive wood-wing Fokker tri-motor came apart in a thunderstorm in 1931. (The accident was widely publicized because it killed the famous football coach Knute Rockne.) The Ford was one of the first airplanes to employ Alclad, high-strength sheet duralumin thinly coated with pure aluminum to prevent corrosion. The tri-motor concept was an attractive safety factor; engine failure meant the loss of only one-third the power. In fact, a lightly-loaded Ford could stay aloft on one engine only.

Perhaps the most famous Ford was *The Floyd Bennett,* which Bernt Balchen flew over the South Pole with Commander Richard E. Byrd in November, 1929. The plane was later

buried in the snow by Byrd, who returned to Little America with another expedition twenty years later, dug out the old Tin Goose, warmed it up, and flew it again.

Ford developed the 4-AT into the 5-AT model, which had three 420-hp Wasps, and a bigger cabin seating up to fifteen. The 5-AT could carry almost its own weight—nearly two tons—in load, and it cruised at just over 100 mph, an inconsiderable speed. This lack of speed was what retired the Ford Tri-Motors in the end. The Boeing 247 and the Douglas DC-2 which appeared in the early thirties were clearly superior aircraft. Perhaps the real truth of it is that Henry Ford simply lost his enthusiasm for manufacturing airplanes; he'd never had any for flying itself. He always thought it far too dangerous, and only flew once in his whole life, when Lindbergh coaxed him into one of his own Tri-Motors for a short hop. Three of Ford's young test pilots had died in crashes. One, a close friend, was killed in a little single-seater prototype of a "Flying Flivver" in which Ford had placed high hopes. It was when Henry Ford heard this news that he ordered the airplane factory to be closed.

The Ford was not the first trimotor, nor yet the last. Many transports of that era followed the layout. At a time when engines were not so powerful it was a sound format. The Germans had their Ju-52; the Italians their SM-79 bomber; and there was even a Russian trimotor that was more like the Ford than you would believe. Yet the three-motored airplane all but vanished from the skies for decades—until the sixties, when Boeing brought the concept up to date in its 727, a splendid jet descendant of the old Tin Goose.

93

Moth:

A Light Aeroplane for All

As a young man of twenty-seven, Geoffrey de Havilland had a good job with a firm of automobile engineers. *Reputable* automobile engineers, the record is careful to state, a rare institution then and not a common one now. Forty-five shillings a week, he made—say, $11—almost a fortune, but it was not enough for de Havilland, who burned with the dream of building his own airplane. He knew nothing of aerodynamics and little of structures, but in those days few people did. Young de Havilland had a grandfather who must have had a stronger faith in the inheritability of talent than most grandfathers, for he lent his young grandson £500 for his project. De Havilland resigned his job, found a room that was spare near Bedford Square, took on his friend Frank Hearle as assistant, and was in business.

The plane the two lads built followed the classic layout of the Wright brothers: biplane wings, twin pusher propellers, a forward elevator, and a rear rudder. By midwinter it was ready. For taxiing tests they chose a site on Salisbury Plain, every bit as windy and as shivery as the Wright's own Kitty Hawk, and they huddled over a coke-burning brazier to fight the chill. The tests began; on one, feeling himself almost airborne, de Havilland heaved back on the elevator, bounced briefly into the air, and then collapsed in a tangle of white pine and oiled silk. It was the end of the D.H. 1. De Havilland, as if to reassure the little knot of spectators already running toward the wreckage, but perhaps more to convince himself he was still breathing, thrust an arm up from the jumbled wreckage, only to collect a sound clout on the wrist from the still whirling propeller—fortunately his only injury.

No job, no money, no airplane, and one arm in a sling: what next? It seems de Havilland must have enjoyed tempting providence, for at this juncture in his life he chose to get married. Once more that splendid grandparent came to his aid. Announcing that he had intended leaving Geoffrey another £500 anyway, he said the lad might as well have it now.

So, after the honeymoon, de Havilland started on airplane No. 2. This time it flew properly and caught the attention of the British government, which bought it for £400 and hired de Havilland as an aircraft designer to work at the Royal Aircraft Factory. Just like that, for the Great War was coming on and aircraft designers were scarce. Aircraft designers who had built airplanes that actually flew were very scarce indeed.

When the war came, de Havilland was briefly with the Royal Flying Corps, then was seconded to the Aircraft Manufacturing Co., just north of London, again as designer. Here he toiled for the duration of hostilities, with no mean success, for his designs flew strongly (when the engines allowed) and were built in enormous numbers. Even the U. S. Army Air Corps flew de Havillands. Almost five thousand D.H. 4's were built under license in the United States.

By war's end, de Havilland had made his name with the public and was able to raise £20,000 to start his own company. Not much work came along at first, but one wealthy sportsman ordered a large private touring airplane, and when it was delivered casually inquired if de Havilland would like any additional financing. He would, and with it he bought the aerodrome at Stag Lane, where his factory was.

In 1923 the famous Lympne trials were organized by the Air Ministry to encourage the development of light airplanes suitable for private ownership. De Havilland came up with a tiny low-wing monoplane, a single-seater powered by a two-cylinder motorcycle engine, named the D.H. 53 Hummingbird. The Air Ministry ordered a few for the RAF, and

Opening pages: Inverted Author
Gilbert halfway around loop in D.H. 82A
Tiger Moth. Remote-control camera was mounted
on top wing. Below: Very early Cirrus
Moth, dating to 1925, had modest
60-hp engine. Bump at middle of top wing
is gravity-feed fuel tank.

one was used in experiments in air-launching small airplanes from a dirigible. One RAF test pilot evolved what he felt was a splendid game with the D.H. 53. He would cruise the wide-open spaces of Salisbury Plain till he found a motorcyclist on a lonely road. He then descended till he was flying just behind the cyclist, who hearing the motorcycle engine in his ear would think it was another motorcyclist seeking to overtake and would wave the pilot on. At which the RAF man opened the throttle and sailed right on by.

The Lympne trials had been based on the erroneous premise that a successful light airplane, when it was achieved, would be as low-powered as the automobiles of its day, and entries had been limited to power plants of no more than 1,150 cc, which meant they barely flew at all, let alone well. The D.H. 53

was a rotten airplane, and the final indignity was when, in completing a demonstration flight across the English Channel, one was overtaken by a Belgian goods train of the slowest kind. In retrospect, it was a lucky thing that the D.H. 53 was so poor, for it set de Havilland thinking that this ultralight approach to aviation for everyman was unsound. His next design was the D.H. 51, which employed a 90-hp war-surplus engine that de Havilland bought in bulk for less than a pound each, but there were grave certification problems with this engine, so de Havilland went to a big 120-hp power plant built by his old wartime employers, and which was licensed. But it was far too expensive. So he thought again.

Engine problems had plagued his work throughout the war. Engines were never available when promised and couldn't be relied

on to work when they were eventually delivered. One of the few good ones had been the Airdisco in his D.H. 51's, a V-8 developed from a French Renault engine by de Havilland's friend Frank Halford. Halford was now following the uncertain profession of free-lance engine designer, so de Havilland stripped down an Airdisco and invited Halford to look at it. Could he make a four-cylinder engine of 60-hp out of one bank of the Airdisco's eight cylinders? The idea must have seemed somewhat harebrained to Halford, whose mind was in any case busy on a new engine for Aston Martin cars, but he reluctantly agreed to try. They would use Airdisco (Renault) pistons, cylinders, and valves in a new crankcase, with automotive carburetors and magnetos to keep costs down. It was a wispy, tenuous kind of beginning, so they called the new engine the Cirrus. With a suitable engine on its way, de Havilland, a glutton for work, started on the design of D.H. 60. For all the greatness it was to achieve, the D.H. 60 was in appearance just another de Havilland biplane, deriving from a pattern that went back to D.H. 4. It had straight, squarish wings set one above the other, wood-strutted and wire-braced, and attached to an all-wooden fuselage of simple square section with a curved top decking. The fin and rudder were shaped by two curves coming to a point, a feature that was to mark just about every de Havilland airplane until they began to enter the transonic speed range in the late 1940's. D.H. 60 boasted an airfoil-shaped fuel tank (capacity fifteen imperial gallons) amidships on the top wing, and an undercarriage that used rubber in compression, rather than the then-usual arrangement of stretched rubber cords. The two occupants sat in open cockpits, one behind the other. Almost the only novelty in No. 60's design was the ailerons. Captain de Havilland's patent ailerons were an attempt, only partly successful, to

97

Above: D.H. 1 was not
de Havilland's first plane, but
first military model, built in 1914.
Left & right: 1929 two-seater,
one of last Cirrus Moths
built. With improved 115-hp Hermes
engine, it had 105-mph speed
and 700 feet/minute rate
of climb. Two curves coming to
point were distinctive
design feature of de Havilland fin
and rudder till 1940's. Below:
D.H. 60 Hermes Moth displays
typical straight wings, one above
other. It still has bulging
fuel tank atop wing.

eliminate adverse yaw by limiting the travel of the downgoing aileron. Unfortunately, the downgoing aileron not only provides most of the yaw, but much of the roll movement, too, and the Captain's patent ailerons have a sloppy feel that has endured. This lack of aileron effectiveness was not helped by their installation on the lower wing only.

Captain de Havilland had other interests than aviation, and one of them was insects, notably butterflies and moths. Moths, or most of them, fold their wings back along their bodies when at rest, and de Havilland arranged for his D.H. 60 to do the same, so you could tow it on the road behind a car, and keep it in an ordinary garage. All the D.H. 60 then lacked was the dignity of a name. But surely there was one ready-made! The Moth.

The Captain made the Moth's first flight on February 22, 1925, and even he seems to have been surprised at how nicely it flew. As was a remarkable gentleman, Sir Sefton Brancker, not long after. Sir Sefton was director of Civil Aviation, and he took the powerful step of starting five government-sponsored flying clubs and ordering a grand total of ninety Moths to equip them. It was the beginning of private flying on any appreciable scale in Britain or, indeed, the world. (The Taylor/Piper Cub was still ten years in the future.)

The prototype Moth had (I think) a blue-painted fuselage and clear-doped, gauzy, dragonfly-like wings, and so did the first few turned out thereafter, but soon silver was adopted as the standard finish, Moth-silver being a kind of British parallel to Cub-yellow. The exhaust pipe, which ran along the left side of the cockpit and burned your left wrist if you weren't careful, was moved to the right side—I know not why—where it burned your right wrist. A little of the vertical fin was taken away and given to the rudder to lighten the load on your feet, and the luggage locker was moved to behind the rear cockpit, and that was all. The Moth was now perfect.

Its performance might seem modest enough by today's standards, but for a private airplane in the 1920's it was progress. The Cirrus Moth cruised at about 80 mph, with a rate of climb of maybe 500 feet per minute, and a fuel consumption of four and a half gallons per hour. All this was a giant step forward from the pitiful flutterings of the ultralight airplanes of the Lympne trials. The Moth in flight was very quiet and not uncomfortable, and the purchase price of £830, while far from being within the reach of all, was certainly within the reach of many. You could operate a Moth for under a pound an hour, and this modest expenditure, further reduced by the Government's generous and enlightened subsidies to the flying clubs, made flying intensely popular in no time at all. The Moth was an extremely practical airplane and, more important, it was quite reliable.

Its development continued steadily. Soon there was the Cirrus II Moth with the engine lowered an inch or two to improve the pilot's rotten forward view; and the Genet Moth, with a rather uncertain 75-hp radial engine of that name; and the Hermes Moth, with a new kind of Cirrus uprated to a tremendous, breathtaking 105 horsepower.

But soon there came a problem. Owing to the Moth's very success, the supply of war surplus Airdisco engines and, therefore, of the Cirruses that were made from them began to dwindle. Further, the company making the conversions found the work not notably profitable and began to lose interest. The Cirrus was a cornerstone of the Moth's success; what was Captain de Havilland to do? Nothing for it but to make his own engine, with Halford's help.

Although General Motors might disagree, one of the quickest ways to develop an engine, both mechanically and in the public's eye, is through racing, and this was the

route de Havilland chose to follow. After his racing engine had established itself, while putting out some 135 hp, he planned to manufacture it in a form derated to nearer 100 hp. A racing airplane would be needed. Quickly de Havilland came up with D.H. 71, named Tiger Moth, but no relation to our later heroine of the same name. Two D.H. 71's were built in the traditional great secrecy. They were low-wing monoplanes of the sleekest lines designed to have the smallest possible cross section that could enclose de Havilland's test pilot Hubert Broad, who fortunately was fairly narrow.

Halford's new engine was a pippin. For its 135-hp output it weighed, at three hundred pounds, only fourteen pounds more than the old Cirrus. The handling of the D.H. 71 kept Hubert Broad busy, and it was not a notable racing success, although one did capture a world speed record in its weight class at 186.47 mph. And it did prove out the new engine. De Havilland chose for the new power

plant the name Gipsy, and the airplane thus powered became the Gipsy Moth.

With the 100-mph Gipsy Moth, the high tide of success for de Havilland began to be a flood. His company, which in 1924 employed but a few hundred people and was capitalized at under £49,000, grew by 1930 to a business worth almost half a million pounds and employing fifteen hundred people. Production rose from less than one airplane a week to better than three a day. The Moth was making de Havilland rich, and he was able to reduce the machine's price progressively. By 1929 it was down to a mere £650. Eighty-five out of a hundred private airplanes in Great Britain were Moths of one persuasion or another. When His Royal Highness the Prince of Wales (now the Duke of Windsor) purchased one, a Moth became absolutely the thing to have, and the society glossies were full of pictures of Sporting Characters and Bright Young Lady Pilots setting off for weekends in the country in their

Moths. Any kind of private airplane in England became, in general parlance, "a Moth," in the same way that, later in the decade, any small airplane in America was "a Cub."

The things people did in their Moths! In the United States the fair and intrepid Laura Ingalls looped a Moth 344 times in succession to set some dubious kind of record. People flew all over the world in them. But surely the boldest Moth adventurer of all was Francis Chichester, in whose life the Gipsy Moth has played a big part. A native Englishman who proved troublesome in his youth, Chichester was shipped off to the Dominions, New Zealand to be exact, where in quite a short time he made a small fortune in the timber business. Returning to England, his pockets jingling, he took flying lessons and, once he had a license, bought a Moth. After a shakedown cruise around Europe, but still with less than a hundred hours of flying time, he set off on a solo flight for Australia. At this date (1929) only one other pilot had ever flown solo to Australia. Chichester made it after some terrifying adventures, which so little daunted him he next set off to be first across the Tasman Sea that separates Australia from New Zealand. For this adventure his Moth was set on floats, and Chichester had to devise a new technique of astro-navigation to find the two tiny islands which were to be his stepping-stones. In the lagoon at one of them his Moth sank, but he fished it up and over the course of a year or so rebuilt it, unaided by professional hands. It was his intention to continue on around the world. He got as far as Japan, where a wire stretched between two hilltops plucked his Moth from the skies and almost sent Chichester to his grave. For his recent circumnavigation of the world he chose a sailing boat, but was faithful enough to his earlier love to christen her *Gipsy Moth III*. She was met, sailing into Plymouth Harbor at the end of her fantastic voyage in 1968, by a Gipsy Moth airplane, flying low over the waves. One wonders how Sir Francis felt at the sight.

Where Chichester had led, others followed. In 1930 an ex-secretary named Amy Johnson flew another Gipsy Moth to Australia. Her airplane, registered G-AAAH and named *Jason,* is to this day hanging from the ceiling of the National Aeronautical Collection in London. By the end of 1930 nearly two thousand Moths had been sold and delivered. The success of the species was such that de Havilland was to some extent hoist with his own petard, and obliged to call everything he designed a Moth. There was the Giant Moth (more of a Giant Myth really), a big 500-hp biplane transport seating eight in a cabin plus the chauffeur in a breezy cockpit behind them; the Hawk Moth, a high-wing monoplane intended for air taxi work and superficially resembling Lindbergh's immortal Ryan; and a host of others.

It was soon time to develop the Gipsy Moth further. The first improvement had been a welded steel-tube fuselage variant, the Metal Moth, manufactured side-by-side with the spruce and three-ply structure. Then came wider let-down cockpit doors and a luggage locker enlarged to hold a set of golf clubs, for the Moth could land and take off easily from almost any fairway. An enclosed coupé top was a popular option on Moths going to Canada. So equipped, one flew the first air mail into Newfoundland. The Gipsy Two engine, pulling 120 hp, came along, and so did a strengthened Metal Moth called the Moth Trainer, intended to whet the interest of the military.

The area most needing improvement in Moth design—forward visibility—remained. Just where you wanted to look, while taxiing and during the short takeoff run, and especially on landing, the sky was filled with the Gipsy's cylinders and clattering valve gear. Nor could the engine be lowered without bring-

Canadian-built Tiger Moth
was primary trainer for Commonwealth
pilots. It varied from British
version in important details, notably the
provision of a detachable cockpit
canopy to protect fliers from winter cold,
and use of tailwheel instead of skid.

Canadian-built Tiger Moth was primary trainer for Commonwealth pilots. It varied from British version in important details, notably the provision of a detachable cockpit canopy to protect fliers from winter cold, and use of tailwheel instead of skid.

ing the propeller tips too near the ground. The solution was to invert the engine, and this was done in 1930 with the engine called Gipsy Three, which first powered a new high-wing monoplane, D.H. 80, soon named the Puss Moth. Upped to 130-hp output, the Gipsy later became the Gipsy Major, and the Metal Moth, powered by it, became the Moth Major.

The Tiger Moth, the most massively successful Moth of all, came about because the Royal Air Force, while nibbling at the Moth Trainer, was unhappy about the poor accessibility of the front cockpit. Service crews all wore parachutes as a matter of course, and getting into or out of the front, or instructor's, cockpit of a Moth meant clambering under the top wing and through the cat's cradle of supporting struts and wires. Difficult enough on the ground while you were wearing a parachute, but quite impracticable if you had to bail out quickly in the air. Could de Havilland do something about this? De Havilland, with prospects of a big RAF order in mind, found that he could. No abstruse calculations in a design office took place, though. Instead, a Moth was

dismantled in a small shed and jury-rigged as needed. The top wing was moved forward eighteen inches, then four inches more. Fine, you could get in and out of the front cockpit even with a chute strapped to your bottom. But the center of gravity was now behind the center of pressure. So all four wings were swept back nine inches at the interplane struts, the rear spars were shortened, and new struts fitted. Pencils flew furiously across the backs of old envelopes. Still not quite enough was the verdict, and so the upper wings were angled back an additional two inches. That was it.

After the first few Tiger Moths had flown (the name was borrowed from the earlier D.H. 70 racing airplane), it was found that this sweepback had brought the lower wing tips too near the ground, and so to raise them the interplane struts were shortened. Which explains why to this day the lower wings of a Moth have more dihedral than the upper pair.

Thus cut and fitted, an already sweet-handling design was rendered sweeter, for the increased dihedral and wing sweep added to the Moth's lateral stability, as well as vastly improving the pilot's view.

The excellent inverted Gipsy was installed in other designs, as well: the Leopard Moth (which had a sad history of structural failures), the Fox Moth, the Hornet Moth, the twin-engined Dragon, and so on. (There never was a small aero engine as reliable as the Gipsy Major. Certainly it is more so than the modern flat opposed power plants.)

The RAF's order for a new basic trainer would be large, and de Havillands had plenty of competition from such now-forgotten machines as the Blackburn Bluebird and B.2, the Avro Cadet and Tutor, the Robinson Redwing, and the Hawker Tomtit. Trials were held, supported by a great deal of advertising from the competing manufacturers in the aviation press, at the Aeroplane and Armament Experimental Establishment at Martlesham Heath. Thirty-five D.H. 82 Tiger Moths were ordered as a result. In retrospect it seems that one point in the Tiger's favor was that it was not so easy to fly as some of its competitors, and in truth it does a creditable job in magnifying many kinds of sloppiness in piloting technique without allowing them to become dangerous. The airplane had and still has some obvious faults. "The shaking and juddering while ticking over," one RAF instructor noted, "the dreadful aileron control, the effort required to put up an inverted formation at the Hendon Display, the difficulty in operating in any sort of wind; no brakes and the tail skid tearing up great chunks of grass field!" He might also have commented on the extraordinary draftiness of the cockpits, but being no doubt a rugged, outdoors Englishman he probably didn't even notice.

The clubs wanted Tiger Moths, too, but most of them had to wait until 1937, such was the rush of service and export orders. One exception was Sir Alan Cobham's National Aviation Days air circus. In 1926, Cobham had flown to Australia and back in a D.H. 50 float-plane, landing on the River Thames alongside the Houses of Parliament to receive his hard-earned knighthood. (He was also the D.H. 53 pilot who was overtaken by the train.) De Havilland saw that he got two Tiger Moths for his circus fleet, modified, like several of the RAF's machines, so the engine would run throughout inverted aerobatics. One of Cobham's circus pilots, C. Turner-Hughes, kept records of his days with the show, and recorded 788 hours on the Tiger Moths, including 2,328 loops, 2,190 rolls, 567 bunts (forward loops), 522 upward rolls, 40 inverted falling leaves, and 5 inverted loops. He survives to this day, hale and hearty, proof that aerobatics are good for you. His successor, Geoffrey Tyson, flew inverted all the way across the English Channel on the twenty-fifth anniversary of Blériot's first crossing, and became the hero of the hour. Like Turner-Hughes, he went on to become a test pilot, never losing his aerobatic skill, as those who watched his eerie demonstrations in the huge 140-ton Princess flying boats at Farnborough during the fifties will well remember.

The Tiger Moth had entered what might be called its Middle Period, the era of its mass production. Almost nine thousand were built in all, and from the mid-thirties till long after the end of the war there can hardly have been a British or Commonwealth pilot, military or civil, who was not trained, at least in part, on the type. The peaceful Tiger even came close to going to war, when plans were made to fit it with small bomb racks, and when a small unit of them sought German submarines around the Scottish Islands, its pilots mercilessly frozen by sea spray and tormented by droppings from the carrier-pigeon communications system in the front cockpit. (One Tiger did, in fact, find a submarine and manage with Very lights to summon Royal Navy units which sank it.)

The clubs, the very British flying clubs, were revived soon after the war and

Moth's Offspring (from top): Two-seat cabin-model Hornet Moth had unusual range; three-seat D.H. 80 Puss Moth was efficient monoplane; low-wing Moth Minor had promise, but its career was cut short by World War II. All three were powered by variants of Gipsy engine.

equipped with Tiger Moths. I was taught to fly at the West London Aero Club in 1952 on Tiger Moths, my instructor a mere slip of a girl pilot who needed a heap of cushions to see over the Tiger's coaming, and was only occasionally exasperated by my ineptness at the controls. You talked, as ever in most Moths, at full bellow through tubes connected to earphones, a system called Gosport Tubes, only one degree more effective than telepathy, but I can still hear her pretty girlish voice, distorted like distant bath water, gurgling to me: "No, no, no, Gilbert. Like THIS." Yet somehow I learned, and went on to win an aerobatic contest for Tiger Moths, the Esso Voltige Trophy, twelve years later. She would have been proud of me, and not a little amazed.

In its old age the Tiger turned adventurous once more and inspired its own club, the Tiger Club, sponsored by a wealthy paper manufacturer named Norman Jones, who raced in Tigers whenever possible and revived Cobham's old air circus idea with tremendous success. The Tiger Club also developed the Super Tiger, a much modified lightweight aerobatic special with a more powerful brand of Gipsy engine, smoke systems, inverted fuel supply, and fuel tank moved from midwing to where the front cockpit had been. But the Tiger's flat-bottomed airfoil was against it. The Super Tiger was unhappy on its back, and no match in contests for the continental aces in their Stampes and Jungmeisters. The first Super Tiger was named the Bishop, for that was the name of the club's instructor; the next two the Deacon and the Archbishop. Fervently one hoped for a fourth to be called the Actress, for obvious if disreputable reasons, but it never happened. But on the fiftieth anniversary of M. Blériot's journey, one of the club's aces did once more fly the Bishop across the Channel inverted (only to kill himself practicing inverted flight a year or two later). Generally, however, the old Tiger is

a good choice of mount if you're going to have a prang, as the Tiger Club more than once found out. They've pranged a few, often to the rich emotional satisfaction of an interested crowd at an air show. But usually with less tragic results. The Sutton harness holds you firm in your seat, and there's a deal of matchwood to be made of the structure before the solid earth can smite you. In one London newspaper's files there is an insane photograph of Lewis Benjamin in a Deacon, absolutely vertical, a foot above the grass, after an unwonted spin. His pride was hurt and so was his nose, but that was all. The Deacon was indisposed for longer.

The Super Tiger is draftier than ever, and even more helpless than a standard Moth when taxiing on a windy day. But she does do the most beautiful hammerhead stalls of any type of airplane in the world, and is also an excellent glider tug. But the ailerons are still, after thirty-five years, dreadful; no other word is appropriate to describe them.

Maybe five hundred Moths of all sorts still fly, mostly in England and Commonwealth countries. De Havilland's name was buried with some haste by the Midland combine that took over his company and would have you talk of the Hawker Siddeley Tiger Moth (though no one does). The Tiger Moth has lately gained an FAA-type certificate, and several are proudly flown by collectors on a standard certificate of airworthiness, while the handful of Cirrus and Gipsy Moths qualify as antiques. Most of the Tiger Moths flying in the U.S. or Canada are the Canadian-built variant with a canopy, brakes, and a tailwheel, for you cannot just get out and push and heave away throughout the North American winter without real suffering. Whatever the type of Moth, if you get the chance to ride in one, take it. This was the machine that taught Winston Churchill's famous Few to fly, not to mention the hordes that came after them. A great airplane.

"What Waco

is that, Mister?"

I have a friend from Waco, Texas, who has a Bücker Jungmeister that he has re-engined with a 200 Lycoming. It is an odd-looking beast, it's true, with this modern flat engine instead of the old Siemens radial. "Hey, mister," people are forever running up to him and asking, "what kind of Waco is that?" Well, it's understandable. There aren't many Bückers around the U.S.A., but there are still, happily, any number of Wacos. And, good grief, the number of different models of Wacos there are! It almost seems as though no two airplanes the company ever turned out of exactly the same type. And the nomenclature is impossible, with most models needing three letters and a number as well to define them. To help dispel confusion this chapter concludes with a chart (the first of its kind, as far as I know) which explains the particulars of Waco model numbers. The general idea is this: Where there are three letters, the first letter simply denotes which engine the airplane has; the second letter denotes which set of factory plans was used in building the plane; the third letter designates the type of over-all design. The number that follows the three letters in many Waco designators merely means that the model itself has been improved upon.

In the case of the commonest Waco, the UPF-7, it works out this way: U means it is powered by a 220-hp Continental; P denotes which kind of Waco wing it has; F shows it to be the famous open-cockpit model; and the -7 means it is the seventh slightly improved version of this basic type. (All F-model Wacos had two cockpits, with the pilot in the rear, and two passengers sitting side-by-side in the front. But the UPF-7 was the PT-14, a military pilot trainer, and in the front cockpit it had a bucket seat for only one. So the table, you see, only establishes general principles for identification.) One more thing: the name, Waco, isn't pronounced like the Texas town, *way*-co, but rather, *wah*-co or *whoc*-ko. Nothing to do with Texas, for Waco was ever an Ohio enterprise. The Waco emerged, phoenix-like, from the corpse of the expired Jenny—as was true of so many airplanes. As long as you could buy a surplus Jenny for five or six hundred dollars, it didn't pay anybody to manufacture new airplanes. But by the mid-twenties the surviving Jennies were becoming extremely weary, and very slowly there began to develop a market for newer and better designs. Waiting for this moment were Clayton Brukner and Elwood "Sam" Junkin, who had been friends since high-school days and amateur airplane constructors since the First World War. They set up shop first in Lorain, Ohio, taking into partnership a well-known local barnstormer named Buck Weaver, who very shortly found better employment in Wichita, and who wouldn't be in this story at all had his partners not borrowed his name for their Weaver Airplane Company, whence WACO.

I suppose the first proper Waco was the Seven, a neat wooden biplane that Clayt Brukner and Sam Junkin (now in Troy, Ohio) built in 1923. They sold five that year, no mean feat. The next year they got all carried away with themselves and built an eight-passenger cabin biplane powered by a Liberty Six, but hard as they tried they could sell only two of them. But they did get rid of fifteen Waco Sevens, and thus emboldened they re-engineered the design with a steel-tube welded fuselage, and watched sales of this Waco Nine hit

Right: Early Taperwing warms up Wright Whirlwind engine. Disappearance of treacherous OX5's after 1928 was beginning of high performance in aircraft. Opposite: Waco Ten was adapted for service as Northwest Airlines mailplane on skis.

47 in 1925 and 164 in 1926.

This Waco Nine was a stout-hearted, resolute sort of bird; some survive to this day. Nineteen twenty-six was the year the Federal government began issuing type certificates of approval for an airplane's design, and when the Waco Nine was sent to the Air Corps engineering laboratories it was found to have a better-than-9G structure, when 6G was all that was required.

Like other contemporary designs, the Nine labored under the necessity of being propelled by an OX5 engine, for if Jennies were beginning to be all used up, the OX5's unhappily weren't. As war surplus they were so plentiful and cheap (at fifty dollars apiece) that you didn't even bother to overhaul one; you threw it in a ditch and installed another. Besides, in the mid-twenties there were almost no other engines except the very much larger Liberty. So the OX5 was almost inevitable, and the big wing area of many of those early airplanes was dictated by this engine's poor power-to-weight ratio.

But if nothing much could be done with the engine, at least the airframe could advance. So in 1927 the Waco was improved still further, gaining ailerons on the lower wings as well as the upper, plus a hydraulic shock-absorbing landing gear, an aeronautical first for a small plane. This new Waco Ten promptly won the Transcontinental Air Race. These early Wacos were all three-seaters, with an odd layout in which the pilot sat behind, and two passengers were squeezed cozily side-by-side in the front cockpit, while the en-gine radiator under the top wing leaked hot, rusty water indiscriminately over everybody.

In 1928 Waco Tens won races galore and also took the famous Ford Reliability Tour by a handsome margin. There began at last to be some customers for Wacos with the more modern Wright Whirlwind engines.

With the Whirlwind came whirlwind progress. In 1929 there first appeared the famous aerobatic Waco model, the Taperwing, with a new wing that had been designed to use the Whirlwind's great power to full advantage. Fearless Freddie Lund flew a red, white, and blue Taperwing equipped with perhaps the first-ever smoke generator used for aerobatic shows. Joe Mackey and Tex Rankin were two other famous Taperwing pilots of the day. The Taperwing was absolutely one of the strongest aerobatic airplanes ever made. As far as I know, nobody ever broke one, though even today, forty years on, one Bob Lyjak, who flies a Taperwing at the Experimental Aircraft Association air shows every summer, is still trying valiantly and unsuccessfully.

The Taperwing was the beginning of that plethora of Waco models that so confuses people today. Waco weathered out the lean years by every means it could, including offering fully fifteen different models. Every Waco model remained in production as long as even one customer could be found for it—although this was no great feat when airplanes were still largely custom-made. The price, too, could be easily adjusted to suit the customer's pocket. A Waco Nine was $2,385, a Ten $2,050, and a military Taperwing 300TA could

run a Latin American government $15,200.

In 1929 Waco was the biggest manufacturer of what we would now call general aviation airplanes in the United States, producing more units than any two of its rivals together. New models came thick and fast. In 1930 the F was introduced. It still was an open-cockpit three-seater, but smaller and neater and more economical than its predecessors. At the same time, Waco had the prescience to see that as aviation became more general, people would expect from it the same kind of easy comfort they got in their automobiles. A seat right out there in the rush of the slipstream, for instance, was bound to lose appeal eventually. In 1931, therefore, in the depths of the Depression, Waco brought out a four-seat airplane with an entirely enclosed cabin. It also hedged its bet by producing an open, side-by-side two-seater, the A Waco.

In 1934 came the D model, an exquisitely streamlined Waco intended for Latin American air forces, but also available to any civilian who could afford it. In 1935 they cleaned up the lines of the cabin Waco, and enlarged it slightly to seat five, gaining 20 mph in the process. This became the "Custom" Waco, but if you couldn't afford one you could still buy the "Standard" cabin Waco. No other significant changes were made until 1939, when the fat Waco cabin was given another going-over. The result was the E model; with a 450 Pratt & Whitney it could cruise at 200 mph for eight hundred miles, while still landing at a modest 55 mph. Performance, indeed!

There was an additional prewar Waco: the N, which pioneered the tricycle landing gear. From then on Waco had all the military business it could handle, first churning out UPF-7's for the civilian pilot training program, then building the famous Waco troop gliders, which served their purpose, I suppose, although it is hard to wax enthusiastic about them.

For a full fifteen years Wacos steadily outsold all competition. Their formula was a peculiarly American one: the big, overpowered, radial-engined biplane—no great delicacy of line, but a structure as sturdy as a bridge. And if you wanted more performance you simply bought the model with the bigger engine. Those Wacos weren't for the faint-hearted. You moved blindly forward on takeoff until you were going fast enough to dare to lower the nose, and you were equally blind at touchdown on landing. But you carried a good load, and you got off in a hurry. In a ZPF, for example, you could start your takeoff run 400 feet from the line of trees and be sure to clear the topmost boughs.

Examples of almost every Waco model survive, but by far the commonest is the UPF-7, simply because it was built in such numbers for use as a wartime trainer. Waco built six hundred UPF-7's before being ordered in 1942 to turn its energies to troop gliders. (One wonders what on earth happened to all those gliders; the records show that over-all some fifteen thousand were built.)

With the war's end, airplane manufacture slumped. Waco played around for a while with a weird high-wing pusher named the Aristocraft, which had a long drive shaft

113

Top & right: Waco 9 first appeared
in 1925, was burdened with OX5 engine,
but had first Waco steel-tube
welded fuselage. "Miss Pittsburgh" shows
vulnerable OX5's exposed radiator
and valve gear. Above: UPF-7
seats two passengers side by side
in front cockpit (one in military model),
and pilot in rear. Left: ZKS-7
biplane has 285-hp Jacobs L-5MB engine.
K is wing design, S the post-1935
designation for four-seat
standard cabin model.

Evolution of cabin Waco (from top):
UIC was standard cabin model in 1933. VKS-7F
was four-place standard cabin
airplane of 1942. ARE was 200-mph
five-passenger model of 1939. AVN-8 was
1939 custom cabin model
with tricycle landing gear.

running back to a propeller mounted on the central one of three fins. It worked not too well, and was clearly going to cost a deal of money to get certificated, so Waco, which by then was convinced that the great postwar boom in private airplanes was a figment of somebody's imagination, took its wartime profits and departed the arena.

In fact, the Waco company continued to exist for some years manufacturing hydraulic log-splitters, until it caught the eye of Alexandre Berger, the businessman who was known in aviation as "the junk man" for his propensity for accumulating aviation properties no one else wanted. He bought the old Waco company just for the name, and later advertised several European light planes for which he had the United States sales rights as "Wacos." Well, they weren't, and nobody was fooled. Mr. Berger and his empire are no longer with us. Let us hope the name Waco henceforth will be allowed to rest in peace.

Waco Model Designators

MODEL DESIGNATORS TO 1930

Model	Introduced	Type
Seven	1923	All-wood, three-place, OX5 engine
Eight	1924	Six in cabin, two in open cockpit, 250-hp Liberty engine
Nine	1925	Improved Seven with steel-tube fuselage
Ten	1927	Improved Nine with four ailerons and shock absorbers
GXE	1927	Improved Ten with brakes
O	1928	Evolved from Ten. SO is straightwing, TO is taperwing.

THIRD-LETTER MODEL DESIGNATORS USED AFTER 1930

A	1932	Open cockpit; two side-by-side seats
C	1931	Pre-1935: regular Standard-model cabin Waco
		Post-1935: Custom-model Waco, seating four or five. 20 mph faster than Standard model
D	1934	Export military Waco, seating two in tandem, open or enclosed cockpit
E	1939	200-mph five-seat cabin Waco
F	1930	Seats three in two open cockpits: two passengers in front, pilot in back. (UPF-7 trainer sat only two.)
G	1930	Single-seater with special landing gear. (CG was Waco troop glider.)
M	1931	Mailplane version: Taperwing with lengthened fuselage
N	1939	Similar to C, but with tricycle landing gear
C-S	1935	1935 designation for Standard model
S	1935	Post-1935 designation for Standard cabin model, with four seats

WACO MONOPLANES

RPT	1941	Prototype of 125-hp low-wing trainer
W	1947	Final Waco: The Aristocraft, a high-wing pusher cabin monoplane

FIRST-LETTER ENGINE DESIGNATORS USED AFTER 1930 (all radial engines except M)

A	330-hp Jacobs L-6MB	I	125-hp Kinner B-5	R	110-125-hp Warner Scarab
B	165-hp Wright R-540 (five-cylinder Whirlwind)	J	365-hp Wright R-975-E1 (nine-cylinder Whirlwind)	S	420-450-hp Pratt & Whitney R-985 Wasp Jnr.
C	250-hp Wright R-760 (seven-cylinder Whirlwind)	K	100-hp Kinner K-5	U	220-hp Continental R-670
		M	125-hp Menasco C-4	V	240-hp Continental W-670M
D	285-hp Wright R-760-E1	O	210-hp Kinner C-5	W	450-hp Wright R-975-E3
E	350-hp Wright R-760-E2	P	170-hp Jacobs LA-1	Y	225-hp Jacobs L-4MB
H	300-hp Lycoming R-680-E3	Q	165-hp Continental A-70	Z	285-hp Jacobs L-5MB

The Incredibly Agile Jungmeister

There can be few more wondrous and astonishing events than the first time you see a Jungmeister properly flown. The moment is impossible to forget. For me it came in England twenty years ago at the little country airfield, bumbling with bees, where we were cadets learning to fly. An air show had been arranged to break up the midsummer calm, and the great Cantacuzeno was coming all the way from Spain to perform. He flew a Jungmeister and he was, our elders and betters had told us, something to see, so we lay on our backs in the clover and chewed on grass stems and waited. We flew Tiger Moths, so biplanes and, we liked to think, aerobatics were our business, too.

When Cantacuzeno flew in on the misty, warm morning of the show, we were astonished at how tiny his Jungmeister was. Its narrow, backswept wings seemed no larger than those of the model airplanes we so laboriously made and so quickly broke. As he touched down on the turf, those tiny balloon wheels on that ridiculous, forward-jutting undercarriage seemed to reach down for the earth like the paws of a jumping cat. Yet it was clearly a thoroughbred airplane. Its lines had a classic racehorse grace that set it apart from our clumsy, maternal Moths.

Cantacuzeno was a royal prince of Rumania, and woe betide anyone who forgot his rank and title. With the capture of his native land by the communist ideal he became an exile, living in Spain, whence he would occasionally venture forth (for a princely fee) to demonstrate his fantastic aerobatic prowess. It was the amazing precision and almost impossible audacity of his flying that made it so enthralling to watch. For no more than an infinitesimal instant was he ever in level flight. Mad, insane maneuvers followed each other with effortless ease. At no time was he ever more than five hundred feet above us, and every maneuver seemed to finish with the little biplane inverted, its cat's feet stretching up to the clouds, its hanging rudder almost parting the daisies.

We were quite unprepared for his finale. We thought he had finished and was coming in to land. Motor throttled back, he glided down in front of the crowd till his wheels lightly but firmly touched the grass. Then, without warning, we heard the throttle advanced and saw the nose rear up into the summer sky; everything let loose as he entered the wildest snap roll, and we gasped in shock, for he was only twenty feet above the grass. As suddenly as it had started, as soon as the Jungmeister was right way up, the roll stopped. The throttle closed and he landed, for all the world as though that crazy gyration had never happened.

It was, we later learned, a specialty of Cantacuzeno, this landing flick, and probably could only be done in a Jungmeister, for only in a Jungmeister could you be absolutely certain that it would snap perfectly every time and, more important, stop snapping the instant you told it to stop. A year or two later I watched him perform this for a bigger crowd, three or four times in one pass. He was so low between snaps that you couldn't see him at all behind the heads of the onlookers. Suddenly he'd rear up, spinning, like a man on a trampoline, then disappear out of sight again. Cantacuzeno, against everybody's prognostications, died conventionally in his own bed.

The Jungmeister's roots run deep into aviation's history. Carl Bücker had been a pilot in the German navy in the First World War, flying mostly the primitive seaplanes of those days. The Versailles Treaty forbade the manufacture of aircraft in postwar Germany, so he moved to Sweden, and for more than ten years was managing director of the Svenska Aero A.B., a small concern that at first specialized in producing Heinkel designs under license, later developing its own airplanes and making good use of high-quality Swedish steels in their

"You think about it and it happens,"
thus the aerobatical responsiveness of the
superbly finished Jungmeister on the
opening pages and below, as described by
its American owner, an airline pilot. "It
never resists you," says another enthusiast.
"It's smiling all the time."

fuselage construction. With the rise of National Socialism the restrictions of the Versailles Treaty began to crumble, and in 1932 Bücker sold out in Sweden and moved back to Germany, taking with him a quite extraordinarily talented young Swedish engineer named Lars Andersson.

In 1933 Bücker set up his own company, Bücker Flugzeugbau, backed by an automobile coachbuilder in whose shops the new concern was housed. In under six months their first design was ready to fly: a light but very sturdy biplane trainer named the Jungmann, whose narrow wings were sharply backswept and whose fuselage was a masterpiece of welded steel-tube design. The Jungmann was an immediate success, from the first flight of the prototype in April, 1934, and it was quickly chosen to equip the *Luftsportverband*, the civil flying organization that trained the nucleus of Hitler's Luftwaffe. The Jungmann was powered by a slim in-line Hirth engine of 80, later 105, horsepower.

It was immediately apparent to anyone who flew a Jungmann that it was highly, even unusually, aerobatic. The only snag is that even with a 105-hp Jungmann you do lose a lot of height doing aerobatics. It just doesn't have enough power. So the idea of a super-Jungmann began to germinate in the minds of Bücker and Andersson. Militarily, its justification was to develop control harmonization and coordination in budding fighter pilots.

In 1935 the Bücker concern moved out of its parent automobile body shop into its own premises at Rangsdorf Aerodrome. Here production of the Jungmann really got along, and here work began in earnest on the super-Jungmann. First, Andersson carefully recalculated every load path through the structure, seeking to combine unrestricted aerobatic load strength with the lightest possible structural weight. He went through the design of the control system again, rebalancing and reposi-

tioning hinge points, drawing on fast-accumulating flight experience with the Jungmann. What began to appear from all his figuring was a very slightly scaled-down Jungmann, something that could withstand a terminal-velocity dive, yet that weighed, dry, only 925 pounds. Youth was very big in Germany in those days, and as the Bü-131 had been called the Jungmann (Young Man), so this new design, the Bü-133, was named Jungmeister (Young Master). The prototype was powered by the latest in-line Hirth motor, but all subsequent Jungmeisters had a 160-hp Siemens Halske radial.

In 1935, the Luftwaffe also came out from underground, and when the higher-powered 105-hp Jungmann was introduced in 1936 the Luftwaffe adopted it as the standard basic trainer, and the new Jungmeister as an advanced trainer and aerobatic show plane.

Every sporting pilot in Europe lusted after a Jungmeister in 1936. The sport of aerobatics had a brief but bright moment of glory in that year, being included in the program of the Olympic Games for which Germany was host country. The contest, at Tempelhof airdrome near Berlin, was won by the German Graf von Hagenburg flying, of course, one of the brand-new Jungmeisters. Another of the fortunate few to get their hands on the type this early in its history was the noted Rumanian pilot, Captain Alex Papana. His airplane, registered **YR-PAX**, was the first Jungmeister to visit the United States. With its pilot, it arrived in the most spectacular possible style— in the belly of the dirigible *Hindenburg.*

121

Bü-131 Jungmann was light but sturdy
pilot trainer with narrow, sharply sweptback
wings. Planes below & opposite have been
re-engined with modern American power plants,
which alters their appearance
but increases their desirability because
of superior aerobatic performance.

No sooner was the little biplane unloaded from the giant airship and reassembled at Lakehurst, New Jersey, than Papana was off across the continent to Los Angeles, where the National Air Races were about to start. His demonstrations of acrobatic flight before that throng were a revelation to all and especially to the native American stunt fliers used to struggling with vastly heavier and less agile machinery. "Awed" and "inspired" are two words one of them uses to this day to describe his feelings toward the little biplane.

Papana was still around in the spring of 1937, in time to fly in competition in the U.S. for the first time. In a big air meeting at St. Louis he faced the best aerobatic pilots of the nation. Tex Rankin flying a Ryan ST was first, but Papana, close behind him, was second.

In hardly more than a year the Jungmeister had become generally accepted as the finest aerobatic machine in the entire world. At the international contest in Zurich in late July, 1937, no less than nine out of thirteen competitors flew Jungmeisters, winning the first three places. Over-all winner of the contest was again the Graf von Hagenburg, who in conse-

quence was invited to the United States to perform at the Cleveland Air Races. Papana was there, too, and to the delighted spectators it seemed there was an unofficial contest between the two, with each trying to outdo the other in daring. According to the air-show promoter, Bill Sweet, who watched their every flight, Papana's specialties were multiple snap rolls and the first hesitation, or point, rolls seen in the U.S., while von Hagenburg was noted for his quite desperately low inverted flying. A photo survives of him practicing this for the Zurich contest. He is sailing by a little knot of disbelieving spectators with the lowest part of the airplane, the vertical stabilizer, certainly no more than a yard above the turf. (You must remember that in the Jungmeister, as in every biplane, the top wing seriously obscures forward and downward vision when you are inverted.)

So you might say it was only a matter of time, and that time was up even before the Cleveland meet was over. Von Hagenburg, rolling over for an inverted flypast, failed to push the stick forward hard enough, and sank earthward till his rudder touched the ground. He plowed to a halt in a vast cloud of

122

dust. The crowd leaped to its feet in horror, for the Jungmeister was destroyed. But von Hagenburg was luckier—luckier than anybody else who has ever been caught the same way, for his only injury was a cut on the head. Thirty minutes later he was paraded joyfully up and down for everybody to see—seated like a king, his bandages for a crown—on the back of one of those beautiful Cord convertibles. The crowd, as they say, went wild. An hour after the crash he was airborne again to finish his act, this time in Papana's Jungmeister. (See photographs on page 127.) Afterwards he commented rudely that it did not perform so well as his own Jungmeister, seeming to be "loose." But it was noticeable that he did not get so close to the ground, then or ever thereafter. Both he and Papana flew again at Cleveland in 1938.

Papana's airplane lasted longer, in fact until some weekend warrior landed a Boeing P-12 on top of it in 1940. The wreckage was quickly bought by Mike Murphy, a senior figure in American aerobatics, who had coveted a Jungmeister ever since seeing Papana's newly arrived airplane on its way to Los Angeles. Murphy had repeatedly tried to buy the wreck-age of Hagenburg's machine, but it was crated up and shipped back to Germany. With Papana's he was more successful. He rebuilt the airplane, and at the time he sold it to another famous U.S. aerobatic pilot, Beverly (Bevo) Howard, in 1946, he had never been beaten in any contest while flying it. Bevo Howard replaced the Siemens with an American 185-hp Warner radial, and still has the airplane today. It is almost certainly the oldest and best-known Jungmeister in the world, and has probably won more contests than any other machine. It is destined for eventual retirement to the Smithsonian Institution, an honor it richly deserves.

Jungmeisters went on winning. Rudolf Lochner won the German National Championships at Dortmund in 1937, with six out of twenty competitors flying Jungmeisters. Von Hagenburg won the contest at Saint-Germain-en-Laye outside Paris in 1938, and Albert Falderbaum was German national champion in 1938 and 1939. In 1938 Bücker sent his fabulous test pilot Arthur Benitz on an extended Jungmeister tour of South America, with gratifying sales results. At least one Jungmeister is still airworthy in Brazil today. Jung-

Bü-133 Jungmeister: Characteristic
blistered cowling (opposite) covers seven
cylinders of 160-hp Siemens-Halske
radial engine. Extensively strutted and
braced wings (bottom) are sharply swept back.
Tail unit (left & below) is welded
steel tube, airfoil in cross section.

meisters were also built outside Germany: under license by Swiss Dornier at Altenrhein, and (with in-line 160-hp Hirth motors) by CASA in Spain. Jungmanns were manufactured by Tatra in Czechoslovakia and, later, in considerable numbers in Japan.

Never one to sit still for long, Bücker moved on to other designs: a high-wing design called the Bü-134 that was an outstanding flop; the ultralight low-wing Bü-180 Student; the cabin low-wing Bü-181 Bestmann, which inspired the Zlin in Czechoslovakia and the SAAB Safir in Sweden; and the Bü-182 Kornett, another failure. The Bestmann was commercially quite successful, and more than a few are still flying. Bücker's airplane manufacturing ended when the Russians took over his Rangsdorf factory at the war's end. Lars Andersson is today with SAAB in Sweden, while Carl Bücker still lives in Germany.

The Jungmeister is undoubtedly Bücker's enduring masterpiece. The airplane was never numerous. Probably not more than six hundred ever were built. Of these, perhaps thirty survive, a dozen of them in the U.S. The structure was perhaps too perfect, too intricate to allow plebeian mass production, and its purpose was in any case too limited in scope.

Jungmanns were built in thousands, and survive in some abundance. Some have been repowered with modern American engines of 180- or 200-hp by aficionados who sought but could not find a real Jungmeister. Jungmanns perform well enough, but all that extra weight up front does make itself felt.

The superbly finished Jungmeister photographed for this book is the property of Art Yadven, by trade a DC-8 captain with Trans Caribbean Airways. It was the property of a Swiss aero club when he came across it. So jealously do the Swiss guard their remaining Bückers that by law those owned by aero clubs may only be sold to a Swiss citizen. Yadven's airplane belonged to an accommodating Swiss citizen for perhaps five minutes, after which it was crated and on its way to the United States.

Once here, the fabric was torn off and the airplane carefully inspected. The fuselage tubes were repoured with linseed oil—the classic anticorrosion treatment—and one longeron in the turtledeck that was cracked and some formers at the bottom of the fuselage that had become oil-soaked were replaced. After twenty-five years that was all that could be found wrong with it. The airplane was then covered with Ceconite, and extensive use made of Ray Stits' famous filler. That fantastic finish that so catches the eye in the photographs was achieved by months of loving work and more than twenty coats of dope. Yadven, who paid $8,000 for the airplane in Switzerland, reckons that he has spent more than $22,000 on refurbishing it since.

What makes the Jungmeister so special that otherwise sane men are prepared to go to such fantastic lengths to acquire, restore, and preserve one? Says Mike Murphy: "It's the airplane you don't fly—you wear it. It fits you. Now, thirty years later, it's still the nicest airplane to do aerobatics in. It never resists you. It's smiling all the time. The airplane will snap roll at 70 mph or 170.

"The only reason it isn't winning world contests today is it doesn't have the yo-yo capability the rules require. It won't go straight up and straight down forever.

"It's just a beautiful-flying airplane. I never was beaten in a Bücker," he says, with a hint of nostalgia in his voice.

Says Art Yadven: "You know the feeling you have when you sit in an airplane for the first time, how you feel strange for a few hours? I think within minutes of getting in the Jungmeister I felt we belonged together. That's the best way I can put it. And I've never met anything else with such lightness of the con-

Below: Graf von Hagenburg, noted for incredibly low-level inverted flying, practices specialty in Jungmeister at Rangsdorf airdrome, 1937. Bottom: At Cleveland Air Races, von Hagenburg crashed (left), but escaped with minor injuries, waved to crowd from Cord (right), and went up again.

trols. It feels that you don't consciously *do* a maneuver—you just think about it and it happens. And it's certainly an easy airplane to fly, though I think it might get a little tricky in crosswind." (In 1935, European airfields were circular. The crosswind wasn't invented till later, for you always landed into wind.)

Other Jungmeister owners include Ray Woody, past president of the Aerobatic Club of America and a vice-president of National Airlines; Pappy Spinks, the new president of the Aerobatic Club of America; and the Texan Frank Price, who has two and for $350

will sell you a set of plans to build your own Jungmeister replica.

The structure of a Jungmeister is sufficiently conventional to belie the care with which it was designed. The fuselage is welded steel tube, with a high wooden turtledeck above. It is this very high but narrow fuselage that enables the airplane to obtain sideways lift in knife-flight or during hesitation rolls. The wings have wood spars, are extensively strutted and braced, and are sharply backswept. There are ailerons on both upper and lower mainplanes, and the quite complicated aileron circuits are fully tensioned loops (to remove hysteresis and slop), aerodynamically and mass balanced for a linear-force feel. As in all the control circuits, extensive use is made of ball bearings. The tail unit is welded steel tube, fabric-covered, an airfoil in cross section, and the tail moment arm is relatively large. Jungmeisters were built with the seven-cylinder, 160-hp Siemens radial, on a very short engine mount and with characteristic blistered cowling. (Bevo Howard's airplane and one of Frank Price's have been converted to 185-hp Warner radials, Price's other machine has a 200-hp Lycoming.) The Siemens has two float carburetors, for level and inverted flight, and a system of vents, breathers, and oil and fuel lines to allow unlimited inverted flight.

In aerobatics, the Jungmeister will do every maneuver yet thought up. It is most noted for snap maneuvers. It is perhaps the fastest-snapping airplane ever built, and two or even three consecutive snaps are perfectly possible. You can do one and a half snap rolls from knife-flight to knife-flight in a Jungmeister and stop exactly in the opposite vertical bank to the one from which you started. The airplane also does miraculously precise hesitation rolls. While it will do outside maneuvers, its airfoil is not too suitable for high lift while inverted, nor is the airplane ideal for vertical maneuvers. Being a biplane, its drag is too high. And it is precisely these maneuvers—largely inverted, largely up and down the sky—that the modern school of aerobatics, led by the Czechs, favors. For this reason, the Jungmeister has fallen out of favor for international competition, yielding place to low-drag monoplanes like the Zlin. One reason for this, perhaps, is that Jose L. Aresti, the Spanish pilot who invented the Aerocryptographic system of noting and scoring aerobatic contests, was himself a Jungmeister pilot, and in consequence rated snap maneuvers rather low, and outside and vertical maneuvers very high. But, as in hem lengths, there are fashions in aerobatics, and they may well change back.

An ambitious plan for putting the Jungmeister back into production was conceived by Jack D. Canary, a former North American Aviation sales engineer. It might have seemed an impossible venture, were it not for two lucky breaks: his discovery in Sweden of a warehouse filled to the rafters with brand-new, unused Siemens 160-hp radials; and the fact that CASA, the original Spanish licensees, still had a full set of Jungmeister blueprints and engineering data. (All those in the old Bücker factory near Berlin had disappeared in 1945.) Despite Canary's death in a plane crash, the project is being continued. The new Jungmeister, however, is still largely hand built, and it is certainly a rich man's airplane: $18,000 at the factory, $20,000 delivered and duty paid in New York.

129

Mr. Piper's Cub

She was conceived in bankruptcy and nurtured in penury, a true child of the Depression, but she grew up to be a star and to make a fortune for her backer, if not her designer. When war came the soldiers loved her, too. She initiated more gauche young men into the joys of flight than any other airplane ever; and now, as a sprightly old lady, she is still much loved. With more power to her elbow, and a fashionable "Super" to her name, she still seems young and fascinating to her swains.

The Cub was sired by the brothers Taylor—C. G. and Gordon—as the Roaring Twenties drew to a close. These brothers had begun fabricating airplanes in upstate New York several years earlier with a design called the Chummy. With a name like that it was,  of course, a two-seater. It also had a 90-hp radial engine and was offered to the public at $4,000, which was rather too much for the aviating public then. The Chummy became an early victim of the Depression.

In 1928 brother Gordon died. The two Taylor brothers had been very close: They'd always worked on their airplanes together, and together they'd gone out barnstorming whenever they had no customers for a Chummy, which was very often. C. G. Taylor felt he couldn't stand to live in Rochester after his brother's death, so he began casting around for somewhere else to build airplanes. He chose Bradford, Pennsylvania, an oil city with money to spend on new industries. The good citizens of Bradford put up $50,000 to persuade Taylor to set up shop there. Of that sum $800 came out of the pocket of one William T. Piper, a highly successful oil man of forty-eight years, a man who had never had aught to do with avia-

tion before, but who found himself suddenly the holder of a seat on the board of the Taylor Aircraft Corporation. But Piper, if a novice in aviation, was no beginner in business. He could see at once that what aviation lacked was a cheap little airplane, cheap both to buy and to operate. He persuaded Taylor to design such a machine, a kind of scaled-down Chummy. It was named the E-2, and the first one was put together within a month, in late 1930.

The first E-2 was powered by an engine with the lovely name of Brownbach Kitten. It wasn't much of an engine, but it did serve to inspire the name of Cub for the E-2. Various other engines were tried. "The first engines were so bad we always had to travel double—with an automobile to bring the pilot home!" said Mr. Piper, who until his death in 1970 kept up with the affairs of his corporation. Eventually they settled on Continental Motors' A-40 with 37 horsepower.

They also went bankrupt. After bankruptcy proceedings, Piper bought the entire assets of the company for around $600. No doubt it hardly looked a bargain at the time. The new Taylor Aircraft Corporation had C. G. Taylor as president and Piper as treasurer. But on June 15, 1931, a date Mr. Piper remembered proudly and with clarity, they got the Cub licensed. They sold twenty-two that year, at a price of $1,325 each.

Business was hardly brisk. Sales dropped to seventeen aircraft in 1933, then climbed to seventy-one the next year, two hundred in 1935, and five hundred in 1936. This was the improved J-2 model, with, for the first time, an enclosed cockpit. In the spring of 1936 Piper bought Taylor out. "Just like anybody else, we got thinking along different lines," Mr. Piper told me on one occasion. "He wanted to do one thing, I wanted to do another. I had all the money in the thing; he had all the know-how. He couldn't get anybody to buy me out, so I bought him out."

Then came a holocaust: The entire works burned to the ground. Piper was in Hollywood on a selling trip; he was told by telephone that his new business was a smoking heap of ashes.

"We began looking around for someplace to go," he told me, not adding that only five percent of the company's value was covered by insurance. And so Piper came to Lock Haven, Pennsylvania. "Here was a town that was financially sick," he said. "Here was an old silk mill that could be bought for a fraction of what it cost. And an airport right next door. It was a very good move for us."

It was an even better move for Lock Haven, an old lumber town that had settled into decline. That silk mill was a little large for Piper at first, so the second floor was rented out. But not for long. Sales mounted to 687 in 1937, and in 1938 the new, improved J-3 was introduced. This offered the choice of Franklin and Lycoming engines, as well as the Continental—all of them 40 hp, all to be developed over the years till they gave 65 hp. Then, with the Civilian Pilot Training Program, the Cub really started to go: 1,806 were sold in 1939; 3,017 in 1940, and 3,197 in 1941.

The scene now changes to Tennessee, midsummer 1941. The U. S. Army is on maneuvers and it has asked the Air Corps for some planes for observation purposes. The Air Corps is sorry, it can't help. It has nothing suitable. So Piper, along with Aeronca and Taylorcraft (Taylor had started up again by himself), supply a dozen light planes and their crews.

A Cub brings a message to Major General Innes P. Swift, commander of the U. S.

1st Cavalry Brigade. Apparently the old warrior could understand horses and even tanks in a pinch, but what the hell, he thought, is the U. S. Army doing messing around with airplanes, and pretty flimsy-looking ones at that? So to the pilot he growled: "You looked just like a damn grasshopper when you landed that thing out there in those boondocks."

"Grasshoppers" they remained to him from then on, and eventually the U. S. Army capitulated and called them Grasshoppers, too. The Army bought 5,673 from Piper between December 7 and V-J Day. (Even so Grasshoppers weren't Piper's chief contribution to the war effort. Steel radar masts were.)

In the collapse of the postwar flying boom, Piper Aircraft failed once again, and then was refinanced and reopened with 250 people instead of the 2,700 employed before the shutdown. But the Cub went on—now in a variety of models, such as the PA-11 Cub Special with 90 hp, the Vagabond, the Family Cruiser and the Clipper, the Pacer and the Tri-Pacer, and the Colt. They were getting further and further away from the basic Cub, but still were recognizably its children.

But the Super Cub, introduced in 1949, is a real Cub, even though you can now get it with all of 150 hp. It's still being manufactured in dribs and drabs, as orders trickle in from prospectors in Alaska and wildlifers in Kenya and anybody else who needs an airplane but has only the boondocks for an airport.

Is there a pilot in America who has not flown a Cub?

It's a strangely modern-looking airplane when you remember that its genesis was back in the days when the biplane was still king and the last words in modernity were such period pieces as the Ford Tri-Motor and the Lockheed Vega.

The shape is instantly familiar to every fledgling aviator, however, because it's

133

also the shape of everybody's first model airplane: high wing for stability, slab-sided fuselage for ease of construction, gear well forward to bounce her back into the air again.

Getting into it is everyone's biggest problem with the Cub. Each evolves his own technique, but they all are variations on the basic necessity to bend yourself double and twist through 180 degrees at the same time. If you have lumbago, better fly something else. Once in, things get easier. The engine fires at once. Taxiing is easy enough, but it takes a bit of practice before your heels stop slipping off the little brake pedals that rise, mushroom-like, from the cockpit floor. You must swing from side to side to see around the engine. Check the switches and carb heat, and, if you're solo, reach a long, long way forward from the back seat to reset the altimeter. Taxiing in a circle is the only way to ensure there is nobody about to land.

The takeoff is the first surprise. You leave the ground almost before you've got the throttle fully open. After that you creep upward at barely 400 fpm, with 55 mph and 2,150 rpm on the dials. Several of those sixty-five horses seem to be expended in sheer noise. From the rear seat the visibility is not of the best. I guess the sky wasn't so crowded back in 1930. Watch the oil temperature; on a hot day it may be nudging the limit by the time you reach circuit height. Full bore gives about 87 mph and a hot cooking smell from the engine. A realistic cruise is 75 mph at 2,150 rpm. With any sort of breeze on your nose the cars on the thruway will leave you behind.

The aileron drag is remarkable. It's a blessing that a rudder is good and powerful. It's when you try slow flight that the Cub begins really to impress you. Power off, the stall comes up at about 35 mph, gentle, with a slight left wing drop if you keep the stick hard back.

The nose falls away before the wing, so that you tend to be picking up speed again before the wing really has much chance to go down. The center-of-pressure travel must be considerable. Fierce and prolonged back pressure on the stick is required to reach the stall, and if you release the stick at the moment of stall, the ship will pitch sixty degrees nose-down. The Cub (Mach 0.17) preceded the F-86 Sabre by about eighteen years with the variable incidence tail, though it's a slow and finger-aching game trimming the thing.

Stalls with power on in turns are even more impressive. Try a climbing turn, with full power, top rudder, and the airspeed dropping. First a good warning buffet—and just about nothing else happens. The airspeed disappears into that region of uncertainty at the bottom of the dial, but she will not snap on you. If you really force it and go on forcing it, she may very gently shudder into level flight.

What a marvelously safe airplane for military observation purposes the Cub must have been! Its stalling characteristics must be as safe as any airplane ever made.

The approach in a Cub is best done at higher-than-necessary speed. There is no aerodynamic reason for this, just the fact that if you try gliding in at the Cub's natural speed you are likely to have other airplanes weaving and dodging and backing up and overshooting behind you.

You can't see very much straight ahead if you're in the back seat. A crosswind helps. You can then peer around the side of the nose. If you are going to side-slip in, close the window first, or you will arrive in a billowing cloud of cockpit dust and papers. And you know what they say: If you can land a Cub smoothly, you can land anything.

You can aerobat the Cub. The Cub I flew was an old one with wooden spars, and I was asked not to do more than spins and wing overs in case the wood had become a little

creaky with age.

That big door makes the Cub series probably the best-ever light plane for air-to-air photography. That huge window-door gives you a magnificent field of view, with only the wing strut to get in the way, and more often than not, it is the wing strut that makes the picture.

What does it cost to operate a J-3? One owner told me it costs him no more than $3.78 an hour! Here is how that figure is made up, based on 200 hours' flying a year: fuel, 900 gallons, $396; oil, 36 quarts, $18; engine maintenance, $40 (own labor); airframe maintenance, $125 (own labor); tiedown, $180 ($15 a month). That's a total of $759, over 200 hours, or $3.78 an hour.

Notice that no depreciation is included. The airplane is simply no longer depre-

ciating. It may even be appreciating. Another Cub owner gives these figures for operating his J-3 for 250 hours in a year: initial purchase price, $1,100; fuel, $495; oil, $50; charts, computers, landing fees, and the like, $35; tiedown and hangar, $180; liability insurance, $150; maintenance, $75; annual inspection, $100; and initial registration fee, $4. So his costs were $1,100 down and $1,089 for the year, which works out to $4.34 an hour (excluding purchase price). In the second year he flew 300 hours for $3 an hour, and in the third year about the same. He then sold the plane for only $100 less than he had paid for it, so his flying over those three years averaged $3.60 an hour.

I talked also to Walter Jamouneau, Piper's chief engineer. He was, in fact, the first qualified engineer they hired (old C. G. Taylor was self-taught), and the first job he was given

Above: Piper J-5 Cruiser was a fat postwar Cub with seats for three, 75-hp engine, and cruising speed of 85 mph.
Opposite: Very first Cub—model E-2 of 1930—was manufactured with Continental A-40 engine of 37 hp. Price was a modest $1,325.

was to design a cockpit for the early Cub. I asked him why he thought the Cub has been such a phenomenal success.

"An airfoil that is very reluctant to stall," he said. "It has a broad peak to the lift curve. Undoubtedly more people learned to fly in this airplane than any other single type. Flying schools found you couldn't break them. And repairs were easy to make. The airplane is a little tricky to land—it porpoises. It does put the student on his guard." It does, indeed.

The oddest thing about the Cub is how heavy the controls are. You might almost be flying a bomber instead of the lightest of light planes. "The principal reason is that it has a high degree of lateral stability. It just doesn't like being rolled." Its slow cruising speed? "It's terribly dirty. There's really been no effort made to fair the intersections of any of the various

parts. It's not the wing. A great many of us in this company have a great love and respect for that wing. It put us in business. And it's still used on the Aztec. I think that airfoil was a happy choice."

And the future of the Super Cub? "When it becomes our last fabric-covered airplane"—the other is the Pawnee—"I don't think there'll be any qualms about cutting it off unceremoniously."

Piper was still at the height of its success with the 65-horse J-3 Cub when it began developing bigger and better things out of the basic Cub airframe. First came the J-4, the side-by-side Cub—a smooth airplane, if you can find one. Not many more than a hundred are still flying. Then the J-5 Cruiser, a fat Cub with seats for three, cruising 85 mph on 75 hp, which is not half bad.

Those were the days just before Pearl Harbor, and by peacetime the Cruiser had become the J-5C Super Cruiser, with 100 hp, an electrical system, and redesigned landing gear. About this time, Piper abandoned the J nomenclature and started the PA series; the Super Cruiser is also known as the PA-12.

The last of the Cruisers was the PA-14 Family Cruiser, with seats for four, 115 hp, and a devastating 110-mph cruise. The Super Cruiser is far more abundant than its two brothers, for upward of a thousand Supers are still active, while less than a hundred PA-14's and maybe two hundred 75-horse J-5's are still about. They were all, in their day, extraordinary value; you could get a J-5 new for $1,995 in 1940 and a PA-12 for $2,995 in 1945.

The Cruiser made its tiny mark on history, too, for in 1947 two PA-12's flew around the world, their two pilots spending four months battling headwinds, ice, desert heat, and every possible kind of foul-up. But they proved the superior dependability of the Piper airframes. The worst mechanical problem in five hundred hours of flying thirty percent over gross was a cracked tailwheel.

If you think the Cub is a real fun airplane, you should try the Super Cub, while you've still got a chance. For a start, you fly it solo from the front rather than the rear seat, which is a big improvement. You run it up to full power against the brakes, lift the tail on the slipstream, let go of the brakes, lurch forward a few yards, lower full flap, and haul back viciously on the stick. Surprise! You get airborne.

You can climb a Super Cub at 1,000 fpm. You can climb at an angle of forty-five degrees to the horizontal. In a wind you can fly slowly backward relative to the ground.

You can reach well over 20,000 feet quite quickly, and with the arctic heater Piper installs, you can gently roast yourself at the same time. You can land in almost as short a distance as needed for takeoff, but not quite, so that you can be sure of getting out of any field you've gotten into. The technique is to approach with full flaps, a little power, and the airspeed way off the bottom of the dial. At the moment of touchdown, cut the power, raise the flaps, and stand on the brakes. With practice you can achieve a most impressively sudden arrival.

We once paced out what a real expert could achieve in the way of a short landing run. Against a reasonable breeze it was thirty-seven yards. But have a care, for the Super Cub is heavier than the old J-3, and it can stall on you.

The load you could carry for the horsepower has always been one of the Cub's notable qualities. The early ones with only 37 hp would take 400 pounds disposable load; with 50 hp, 500 pounds; with 65 hp, 540 pounds.

The big 150 Super Cub will carry 820 pounds. Nor is it very critical, for you can get away with fair overloads, and the allowable center of gravity range is generous. In consequence, all the Cub series have always been favorites for any kind of flying job, be it at work, air shows, endurance flights, or mountain landings. Truly, a universal airplane.

Let the late Mr. Piper have the last word in this story, about his old partner C. G. Taylor. "Taylor designed a good airplane," he said. "Have to give the devil his due." And what did old devil Taylor do? He went away and designed the Taylorcraft. It wasn't really anything like the Cub: It had side-by-side seats and a very different airfoil. C. G. Taylor moved to Alliance, Ohio, and set up the Taylorcraft Aviation Corporation to build his new bird. At first it had a 40-hp Continental, and a cruising speed of less than 90 mph, but soon the Taylorcraft moved up to 65 hp—Lycoming, Franklin, or Continental, according to the customer's choice, though by far the largest number chose the Continental.

The owner of one Taylorcraft acquired his bird, a 1940 B-12 Continental-powered model, as a wreck from someone's chicken coop. He then rebuilt it himself. Introducing us to his machine, he said, "I think it's an excellent airplane. It's efficient. You can cruise nicely at 2,050 rpm, where the engine's real smooth, and you're making 90 to 95 mph."

He went on: "I paid $200 for it as a bag of bones. I guess I've put about $1,600 into it since, rebuilding. And we've flown some five hundred hours in it. It's a little faster, perhaps a little more maneuverable than a J-3. It's a nice cross-country airplane. I've only got one wing tank in mine, but I've heard they used to have four, as well as a fuselage tank.

"In turbulence she does have a tendency to bounce around a lot, but she's a gentle and forgiving old machine—though if you stall with a bit of rudder you'll go right into a spin."

We climbed aboard and it's cozy inside. Don't take anyone with sharp elbows into a T'craft. The airplane has enormous round control wheels, like something out of a 1930's cloth bomber. How cockpit styles have changed! The airplane's owner has painted a yellow mark on his wheels to show where top dead center lies. And he shows us the trim lever, under his seat, and makes us open the door to peer back and see the trim tab, a separate vane mounted underneath the stabilizer.

Fired up, we bounce and hop across the stones to the takeoff point, which at Old Rhinebeck in this wind is at one side of a big pit. You hurtle down one side of the pit, and stagger up the other, waiting for the right combination of bump and gust to get airborne. In the T'craft this moment seems to come very smartly, for the takeoff is quite short. We climb out indicating 1,100 fpm, which means the VSI is lying in its teeth, but even so, the climb-out is right smart.

At 2,000 feet we level off. It's a real wintry day, and while the cabin heat is good around the feet there's a Force Eight gale coming in the door onto your face. Visibility is better than expected, except in a turn.

Stability in pitch is good, but the T'craft lacks positive stability in yaw. Sideslip and let go, and she stays sideslipping, with only a slow return to straight flight. You must keep on the rudder all the time, or the ball in the slip indicator will be all over the place. The ailerons on this airplane are very big and sensitive, and quite uncompensated, which doesn't help.

Before starting the approach, we are told that the airplane tends to float, due to the curved undersurface of its wing. The best glide is 60 to 65; the sink rate goes up at lower speeds, and if you slow it up too soon you can find yourself sinking onto the ground with rather an untidy thump. We find we need to keep pushing on the rudder to keep things straight on final. But there's perfectly adequate control on the roll-out.

Taylorcraft went on building the 65-hp Model B for many years. During World War II it produced a tandem trainer that looked very much like the old Cub, and also considerable numbers of the L-2B—called Grasshopper, as was the military Cub—in which an observer sat behind the pilot. Production of the BC-12-D, basically the same as the old prewar B-12, resumed after the war, reaching at one time a level of fifty a day in 1946. Taylor designed a four-seater Model 15 with a 150-hp Franklin, but what with a fire in the plant and overproduction of the 65-hp model, Taylorcraft was soon bankrupt again. The corporation was revived in 1947 and lingered on into the mid-fifties, experimenting with molded fiberglass coverings and models with up to 225 hp. C. G. Taylor, though he designed splendid airplanes, was never the world's best businessman, whereas perhaps his old partner W. T. Piper was.

139

The Imperishable DC-3

"Okay, son," he'd say, settling lumpily into the left seat. "You got much heavy time?" And you'd say, no, not much, and hope he wouldn't ask you what you *did* have time in. (Piper Cubs, mostly.) He'd have a skin like leather, and those deep crow's feet around the eyes that old pilots get from twenty years of screwing up their faces against the glare. And then he'd slowly light up a foul cigar and blow a great cloud of blue fumes against the windshield. After inspecting the glowing tip of his stogie, he'd peer at valves and selectors and taps behind you and above and between the seats, touching and turning one or two here and there with the firm delicacy of a surgeon. "You'll soon get the hang of it," he'd say, hopefully, and then, "Are we clear your side?" And you'd say, yes, sir, and he'd say "Don't call me sir," and there'd be a whirring and grinding and puffs of smoke from the right engine fit to match his cigar, and then the big Pratt & Whitney would rumble to life. Then the left one, but the whole thing was done so mesmerically that you had no real idea at all what he'd been doing.

When he'd begin taxiing you knew you were out of your depth. For a start, the nose was so high off the ground it was like driving a barn from the dormer window. The angle of the fuselage to the ground was so acute that you might have been reclining in a dentist's chair. He'd steer the DC-3 across the concrete mainly with huge blasts of differential throttle, while the instrument panel danced madly on its rubber mounts and you were deafened by a whole Spike Jones cacophony of sounds: creaks, groans, squeals and shrieks from the brakes, and a variety of trash-can rattles from everywhere. The crazy airplane had to be falling apart! But if it was, *he* didn't seem to care.

He'd let the old Gooney grind to a halt short of the runway, and run up the engines with the same deftness he'd shown when starting them. Then he'd pull out on the runway and wiggle the throttle forward. Motors roared, the nose went down as the tail came up, and the back end of the airplane swayed. The old captain would puff on his cigar till he vanished in the smoke and when he dimly reappeared you realized that the DC-3 had somehow contrived to become airborne, and that the gear was coming up.

"You'll soon get the hang of it," he'd repeat, and soon he would be showing you cruise-power settings, and stalls that got you almost on your back, and single-engined flight during which one giant propeller (always the one on *your* side) would sit motionless, its blades edge-on to the air like three twisted knives. On one engine the DC-3 felt as though it was about to give up and roll over dead, but he'd assure you that it was really well under control, and would turn toward the live engine to prove it. When he'd relent and start up the feathered engine, you'd realize with an astonished glance at the altimeter that you were actually a thousand feet higher than when he'd shut it down.

The approach seemed to take as long as an old lady preparing for bed, with a slow descent and much fiddling with power settings and other cranks and levers. But he obviously knew just how high off the ground the barn was, because there would be no bounce.

In truth, you did learn all you needed quickly; perhaps because a copilot's duties and responsibilities were severely limited. All the brains were in the left seat. You were there to work the gear and flaps and keep an eye on things if the old man felt like a nap, and that was about all. "I am a copilot, I sit on the right," began the famous rhyme:
"It's up to me to be quick and bright;
I never talk back, for I have regrets,
But I have to remember what the captain forgets.
I make out the flight plan and study the weather,
Pull up the gear, and stand by to feather;
Make out the mail forms and do the reporting,

142

And fly the old crate while the captain is courting."

The last verse ran:
"All in all, I'm a general stooge,
As I sit on the right of the man I call Scrooge;
I guess you think that it's past understanding,
But maybe some day he will give me a landing!"

Captains weren't all bad. That historic doggerel actually was written by one—Keith Murray of Colonial (later Eastern) Airlines.

With your increasing experience as a copilot came an amazed understanding of just what that old bucket of bolts was worth. "The DC-3 groaned," said one copilot named Len Morgan who loved the airplane so much he wrote a book about her, "it protested, it rattled, it leaked oil, it ran hot, it ran cold, it ran rough, it staggered along on hot days and scared you half to death, its wings flexed and twisted in a horrifying manner, it sank back to earth with a great sigh of relief—but it flew and flew and flew. It took us and ten thousand crews around the globe to where we had to go and brought us home again, honest, faithful and magnificent machine that it was." The birth of the DC-3 can be pinned down to one precise moment in time: the instant on August 2, 1932, that Jack Frye, twenty-nine-year-old boy wonder vice president of TWA, attached his name to a letter to several airplane manufacturers, announcing that TWA was interested in purchasing ten or more twelve-passenger tri-motored planes. Donald Douglas got one of the letters, and immediately saw in it the chance he had been long awaiting to break into manufacturing airliners, most of his previous work having been for the military. Douglas read the specifications that came with the letter, and decided to have a go. Only he would better them. And not with a tri-motor. The death of Notre Dame's Knute Rockne in a disintegrating TWA-Fokker tri-motor had given the breed a bad name and prompted Frye's search for something better. Douglas thought that the big new radial engines coming along from Wright and Pratt & Whitney would allow him to meet the TWA specifications with a twin-engined airplane.

The Douglas company put all it had into winning the contract, and as winner it was awarded $125,000 to build a test airplane. Douglas spent twice that in doing the job, but the prototype—called the DC-1—beat Frye's performance demands handsomely, to such an extent that the production airplane (the DC-2) was able to carry two extra passengers in a longer cabin—two more revenue seats for the same operating costs, a thought to make any airline executive happy. But Douglas spent so much on developing the airplane that although he received $1,625,000 on TWA's eventual order for twenty-five airplanes, he was still a quarter-million out of pocket. The designers had been extraordinarily thoughtful and thorough. Much wind-tunnel work had gone into getting stability just right and drag as low as possible. The basic design—with its thin, tapered and backswept wing, retractable gear, big wing flaps, and neat engine cowlings—was most ambitious

143

Above: DC-1 prototype of 1933 was Douglas entry in competition for TWA order for ten 12-passenger airliners.

Left: DC-2, the first production model, had longer cabin, could carry fourteen passengers. Basic design was considered ambitious and advanced for its day, but airplane proved to be fast, comfortable, efficient, and attractive to passengers. Some two hundred DC-2's eventually were built. Below: Li-2, a DC-3 built by Soviets under license. Opposite: Oddball DC-2½ of China National Airways Corp. was wartime improvisation. When replacement for DC-3's damaged starboard wing was unavailable, mechanics jury-rigged a workable DC-2 wing.

for its day. Immense pains were taken to make the cabin a quiet and comfortable place to ride in. Engineers spent days in a wooden mock-up of the cockpit devising the best layout for instruments and controls. The design also employed a multicellular construction devised by Jack Northrop, in which a thick skin sat on numerous ribs and longitudinal members, forming a honeycomb of many small boxes, very strong in torsion and rigidity but light in weight.

The DC-2 came perhaps just in time, for U.S. airlines in 1933 were floundering in poverty. Air travel hitherto had been an ordeal of endurance and discomfort, mingled with occasional moments of stark terror. Only the brave, or the extremely impatient, flew the airlines before the DC-2. Not only was it fast enough and quiet and comfortable enough to attract new passengers, but its efficiency enabled its operators to turn a profit. The DC airplanes really rescued the airlines from the poorhouse.

Donald Douglas finally got his money back. In all, he sold almost two hundred DC-2's. He was so busy for so long keeping up with orders for them that when C. R. Smith of American Airlines asked if Douglas could make a Pullman "sleeper" version, he was at first reluctant. But Smith kept pestering him, offering to buy twenty, sight unseen, if Douglas would try it. "So, they buy twenty of our ships," grumbled Douglas. "We'll be lucky if we break even!" He grumbled some more, as the new DST sleeper transport went through eleven wind-tunnel models and half a million dollars of the DC-2's precious profits. Douglas was right about the short life of the sleeper plane, but altogether wrong about the DST, for this essentially was the first DC-3. Before production of that model ceased in 1945, 803 had been sold to the airlines and 10,000 to the military. As for getting his money back, Douglas probably grossed more than $1,000,000,000 on this exemplary aircraft.

Its success was total. By 1938, DC-3's were carrying ninety-five percent of all airline traffic in the U. S. and were being operated with equal success by thirty foreign airlines. Before the war in Europe stopped civil air operations in much of the world, ninety percent of the world's entire airline business was flown with DC-3's.

In military use, the DC-3 was perhaps the only airplane to be operated by every major combatant on both sides. The Japanese and the Soviets had begun building them under license before war began, and the Germans operated a motley fleet captured from various airlines in their rampage across Europe. In Allied service, DC-3's—now designated as C-47's—carried anything that could be fitted into them, and much that could not—such as wings for other airplanes which were strapped to the belly. The airlines taught the Army how to fly them, it used to be said, and the Army showed the airlines how to overload them. The DC-3 in which General Jimmy Doolittle fled from China over the Hump to India after his Tokyo raid carried seventy-two people. Even this was not the ultimate record. I know of one that carried ninety-eight people.

Today the DC-3 is half as old as aviation; at twice her age the Wright brothers had not yet flown. Yet it seems that Jack Northrop's lightly stressed, multicellular structure might last forever, for this aerial mule simply refuses to retire. A 1966 survey disclosed that a third of the world's transport airplanes still were DC-3's. In Vietnam, the DC-3 continues in the forefront of combat as a Gatling gunship designated AC-47. Most of today's DC-3's are military surplus which sold in 1945 for as little as $1,200. One or two still exist that are as old as the breed and have flown nearly 90,000 hours —a total ten of their thirty-five years spent aloft. I believe that many aviators yet to be born will still get the chance to sit in the copilot's seat of the admirable and immortal DC-3.

Walter Beech & the Staggerwing

Ever hear of the "Wichita Fokker"? It was one name for the old OX5-powered Travel Air biplane, and in truth it did look like the 1918 Fokker D-VII, having the same overhanging elephant-ear ailerons and rudder, and much the same general configuration. I'm sure the resemblance was unintentional, but it was excellent for sales, what with the movies like *Hell's Angels* that Hollywood was cranking out in the late twenties. A producer would buy six Travel Airs and deck them out in black crosses, and half a dozen U. S. war-surplus Tommie Morse Scouts with huge RFC roundels (they were the "Sopwith Camels," you see), and have himself a battle right there, high above the war-torn trenches of Southern California.

The Travel Air Manufacturing Company, as formed in February, 1925, was in essence Walter Beech, Lloyd Stearman, and Clyde Cessna (*the* Beech, *the* Stearman, and *the* Cessna), all backed by a wise old moneyman named Walter P. Innes. Travel Air built fine sturdy biplanes; many survive. It built some efficient monoplanes, including the Woolaroc—that obvious imitation of Lindbergh's Ryan with which Art Goebel won the doleful Dole Derby race to Honolulu. But rarely do powerfully creative men get along for long, and in 1926 Stearman quit to go it alone. Cessna followed a year later. Cessna's bone of contention was that he thought the monoplane was the way to go, while Walter Beech felt there was life left yet in the biplane. Both really were right.

In August, 1929, stock changed hands, and the Curtiss-Wright Corporation became the controlling power in Travel Air. Travel Air's production had been one tenth of the total U. S. output of commercial airplanes, so it must have looked like a good buy to Curtiss-Wright. That same year was the year of the highly successful Mystery Ship racers, which added further brief luster to the reputations of both Travel Air and Walter Beech. As the De-

pression hit, Beech found himself with a pocketful of cash from the sale of his stock in the Travel Air corporation and a tedious job as sales boss of the Curtiss-Wright headquarters in New York. It seemed a good time to quit, and he did.

Remember 1932? Crude oil was ten cents a barrel, wheat went for a quarter a bushel, and GM stock was less than ten bucks a share, with no takers. It was a good time to hoard cash, you might think, but Beech thought otherwise. He hankered after one last biplane. Back in Wichita he founded the Beech Aircraft Company, and set about designing a luxury, five-place biplane with a high speed of 200 mph, a touchdown not above 60, a range of one thousand miles at a filling, and the comfort and *grande luxe* you might expect from the rarest and most elaborate sedan. Now, in 1932, even military pursuit ships—as fighters were called—didn't go 200 mph, so Beech's ambition was the equal of sitting down to lay out a Mach Three business jet today.

Beech's first Beechcraft flew on November 4, 1932, and it did everything he had dreamed it would. It was also a bear to land. It would even ground-loop on takeoff. Its official name was Model 17, simply because Beech's last project with Travel Air had been Model 16. The name Staggerwing was coined at the 1933 Miami Air Maneuvers when an exuberant announcer exclaimed, as the first Model 17 crossed the finish-line in a race, "Gee, look at that negative stagger wing Beech go!" He was right. It did go, and it did have a negative stagger. Stagger in a biplane means that one wing is placed ahead of the other. Negative stagger means that the *lower* wing is ahead. It is a rare layout. But "negative" was hardly a selling word, so the Model 17 became the "Staggerwing."

On test this first Staggerwing was timed at 201.2 mph, with a rate of climb of 1,600 fpm and a ceiling of 21,500 feet—nearly impossible performance for its day. The only problem was, no one was buying. In its first two years the Beech Aircraft Company sold just one airplane. The customer was a Tulsa oil-drilling outfit, whose pilot perhaps gave a clue as to why sales were so slow. For his first hundred hours in the airplane, he reported laconically, he had had very little idea where it was going during takeoff or landing.

Walter Beech wasn't desperate. He still had money left. But he began to be quietly worried. The airplane would have to be improved. As a first step—just to see what would happen—he advertised the plane, which already had 420 hp, as available also with the gigantic 700-hp Wright Cyclone engine. What happened was an order for one such model from a worsted mill in Maine. Beech built the airplane, but just running up the engine shook the airframe so badly that it continually broke weld joints. In the air it was smoother, and could hit 250 mph, which was faster than any fighter of the time. The pilot who flew it for the customer was given one hundred days to live by his friends, but he confounded them by flying it safely for a year. Thereafter it was sold to Howard Hughes in whose service it was cracked up on takeoff in the 1937 Bendix Race. It was ugly; if most Staggerwings look like graceful dragonflies, this Cyclone-powered monster looked like a fat-headed bug. Meanwhile, Walter Beech reversed direction, and designed a lightweight, low-powered Staggerwing—the B model. One huge improvement was a retractable landing gear, so that with a modest 225 hp the airplane could still cruise at 150 mph. This machine was much more accurately tuned to the market in

those still-depressed times, and Beech at last began to sell Staggerwings: eighteen in 1934 and twice that in 1935 when business began to pick up, as it did for everyone. The Staggerwing had finally achieved commercial success.

Structurally the Staggerwing uses an odd mixture of materials and methods. The fuselage has a basic framework of welded steel tube over which is a web of wooden formers and stringers to shape the fabric covering. The wings are all wood: wood spars, wood truss ribs, and, again, fabric skin. The landing gear employs big metal springs instead of oleos, and is electrically operated. The whole airplane is quite beautifully built. It quickly established the reputation for quality and care that modern Beech airplanes still enjoy today. The Staggerwing's structure has proved lastingly strong, except for an ugly era of flutter failures of the top wing, which Beech cured by aileron balancing and plywood stiffening for the wing tips.

In 1935 a Staggerwing was successfully flown clear around the world, by a splendid English diplomat named Captain Harold Farquhar, late of His Majesty's Coldstream Guards, who took along with him a German, Fritz Beiler, as if to show that bygones could be just that. They had many adventures, but little trouble, except with the authorities in those parts of the world that were still subject to British bureaucracy. Walter Beech immediately coined the slogan, "The world is small when you fly Beechcraft," a pardonable exaggeration. Captain Farquhar's jaunt did the Staggerwing's reputation a power of good.

More improvements to the breed followed. The C-model Staggerwing gained a shorter landing gear and had the flaps on the lower wing to improve ground handling, which was still a little hairy. Then came the D model,

151

From top: Early Beech Travel Air
(here restored) preceded Staggerwing design.
First of the line, model 17R of 1932,
did 210 mph with 420-hp Wright engine. Head-on
view of D17S. Bottom left: G17S.
Bottom right: A17F-5 of 1934-1935 had huge 700-hp
Wright Cyclone. Only two were built.

with a longer rear fuselage, and ailerons moved to the top mainplane, all to the same end—better control on the ground. Most Staggerwings still flying today are the D17S model, which was built in some quantity as the UC-43 light transport for the Air Corps, and later sold as surplus when peace again broke out. (The Navy also had a few, and called them GB-1s and 2s.) An old 1940 price list shows that an E17B went for $12,380, while the higher-powered D17S listed at $18,870. No Beechcraft was ever cheap.

A ride in a Staggerwing is a wondrous thing. First of all, you enter by the rear fuselage, as though it were an airliner, and you must clamber uphill to the pilots' seats. You begin to feel at once that immensely soft, but solidly luxurious feel of all Beech aircraft. The plane overwhelms you with space, and power, and luxury. To one more used to modern airplanes, the engine levers, flap control, and such seem scattered oddly all over the panel, almost at random. And you have wind-up windows, as though you were in an automobile, a curiously rare feature in an airplane; the only other type I know that has them is the old Model 24 Fairchild. You can't see directly forward on the ground, but with a little straining and stretching you can peer around that big Pratt & Whitney R-985 sufficiently well to taxi.

The takeoff is a moment of simple, glorious joy. There is this gigantic thundering, clattering roar as you push the power lever forward, a brief moment of directional uncertainty, an overwhelming aroma of warm oil, and then she leaps, bounds, into the air and starts upward as though all the wolves in Siberia were baying at her heels. That climb! It's more like a jet! In level flight the forward view is excellent, and the engine's thunder is almost drowned out by the roar and hiss of airflow. You are exquisitely aware of those beautiful Spitfire-elliptical wings, one pair at your shoulders, the other at your heels, as though

you were Mercury. The controls are lithe, alert, quick—almost an extension of your own thoughts, rather than a mere mechanical system you must move with your hands. You also have a feeling of pure efficiency about the airplane that belies its biplane layout, and you are right: a Staggerwing, engine off, has a glide ratio of fully fifteen to one.

Landing begins with power reduction, and again you are reminded of the Spitfire, for there is that same crackling backfire from the Pratt & Whitney that you get with a Merlin, and when the gear is down, there is again that aroma of overwrought oil. You do not land three-point, but rather a little tail-low, and some light but delicate footwork is required during the roll-out. It is better if people do not bother you with questions at this time. As you lower the tail, the whole airplane bounds up and down briefly, like an eager St. Bernard. A flight in a Staggerwing is a joyous experience!

The final Staggerwing was the postwar G17S, embodying a number of improvements that had been hanging fire during the war years: a cleaned-up cowl line, windshield, and gear doors; bigger tail controls; a still more luxurious interior. Only twenty G17's were built, and maybe ten survive—the most highly prized Staggerwings of all. They seldom change owners and then at ridiculous prices.

I suppose maybe two hundred Staggerwings in all still exist. Fewer than that are still flying. They are among the most enduringly beautiful airplanes ever made. Even on the ground, standing clumsily on its gear, a Staggerwing will invariably attract a crowd of admirers at any airport. But no Staggerwing, for all Beech's many improvements, is happy on the ground. One must be seen in the air to be completely enjoyed. A Staggerwing aloft cleaves its way through the sky as a shark idles through the water, unconscious of any effort. Truly it is a design for all time.

153

Messerschmitt 109

Willy Messerschmitt was a precocious and ambitious youth. He founded his own airplane company before he was out of technical high school, and was the first student there to be allowed to build a glider as his thesis. Gliders were all that a German was allowed to build under the terms of the infamous Versailles Treaty, but before long Germany decided the hell with the Versailles Treaty, and Willy Messerschmitt progressed to powered designs, mostly undistinguished models with the bathtub fuselages then in style. He was a somewhat cold-blooded individual. German aviators had a saying that each new Messerschmitt model killed at least one good test pilot. But Willy was a convert to National Socialism at the right moment, and a close chum of Rudolf Hess and Hermann Goering. His first great success was in 1934 with a sports plane, the 108 Taifun, a beautifully sleek, long-winged design that bears a striking resemblance to his famous fighter. With four seats and a 240-hp engine, the wooden Taifun carried a useful load of over a thousand pounds and cruised at 165 mph, a performance that Cessna, Piper, and Beech are hard put to better thirty-six years later. Messerschmitt's basic 108 design was still being manufactured in France in the fifties as the Nord Noralpha.

Messerschmitt's airplanes were seldom overstrong, and the 108 was no exception. The first production batch was noted for failures, at excessive speeds, of the skinning where the wing joined the fuselage. Everybody knew this, it seems, except Hess, who took one up at an air show and proceeded to do aerobatics in it. Knowledgeable spectators expected every maneuver to be his last, but he was lucky, very lucky, as he realized when afterwards they showed him where the wing and fuselage had begun to part. Later 180's had a covering of heavier gauge metal.

The Luftwaffe liked the Taifun and used it as a trainer. Messerschmitt, who had never designed a combat plane, was one of four manufacturers invited to take part in a contest to choose a new monoplane fighter. He sat down to re-engineer his basic 108 design in metal, further slimming and refining its lines until he had absolutely the smallest, lightest, sleekest airframe possible behind the biggest engine he could get, which in those days was a Rolls-Royce Kestrel V. The 109 prototype took to the air in mid-September, 1935, and impressed all who watched with its flying qualities. It also impressed the pilot with its handling qualities on the ground, which were terrible. Messerschmitt had chosen to make the gear retract outward into the wings, which allowed a lighter spar since it did not have to take the landing loads. The disadvantage was that you were stuck with a very narrow-track main gear, and Messerschmitt's first design was altogether *too* narrow. The airplane rolled and wallowed as it taxied over rough grass; it swung badly on takeoff and tried to ground-loop on landing. Messerschmitt widened the track of the wheels even before the contest, but difficult ground handling and collapsing landing gears remained the Me-109's greatest weaknesses throughout its life. One historian has estimated that perhaps five percent of the total production of 109's was eventually written off in landing or taxiing accidents.

Despite its problems, the 109 won the contest. Its competitors, with the possible exception of the Heinkel, were terrible old tubs. The world first saw the 109 at the Berlin Olympic Games in 1936, when one flashed by in a demonstration of what the new Germany could do. The world first recognized the potential of the 109 when five were entered in one of those wonderful prewar European aviation meetings—the 1937 International Flying Meeting at Zurich. Three were standard Luftwaffe B-2 models, with a proper German engine, a

640-hp Junkers Jumo, instead of the Rolls-Royce. They also had a variable-pitch metal propeller instead of the clumsy wooden oar on the prototype, and there was nothing German about it, for it was an American Hamilton Standard built under license. The other two 109's were hot ones with almost 1,000 hp—too hot, perhaps, for one had engine trouble and was wrecked, though its pilot, the great Ernst Udet, was unhurt. The other 109 walked off with the climb-and-dive contest, snarling its way up to 9,800 feet and back down to the airfield (situated at 1,000 feet altitude) in two minutes, five seconds. The standard B-2 models won all the other important events.

Meanwhile, a few 109's were being flown in combat in the Spanish Civil War. While most of the biplanes they were up against could turn inside them, the 109's were so fast they could accept or refuse combat at will, and proved most successful. They also taught the Luftwaffe much about how air combat had changed since 1918.

When Britain declared war on Germany after the invasion of Poland, the Luftwaffe had 1,085 Me-109's, of which 850 were the latest E model. This was the Battle-of-Britain 109, nicknamed "Emil" by the Germans. In general the 109's had made mincemeat of the Hurricanes, Battles, and assorted French fighters they encountered in the fighting in France. Not until Spitfires appeared over Dunkirk were the odds evened.

The Emil was undoubtedly as formidable a weapon as could then be achieved. With a 1,150-hp inverted-V Daimler-Benz engine, the 109E could hit 357 mph at its best altitude of about 12,000 feet, had an initial rate of climb of better than 3,000 feet per minute, and had a service ceiling of about 36,000 feet. Its armament was two machine guns mounted on top of the engine crankcase, firing through the propeller arc, plus two 20mm cannon in the wings—probably a fairly even match for the Spitfire's eight .303 Brownings. The two airplanes were remarkably similar in design philosophy, with the exception of wing configuration. The designer of the Spitfire, R. J. Mitchell, had chosen a large wing of elliptical plan form with simple split flaps, while Messerschmitt had given the 109 a much smaller, straight-tapered wing with high lift devices— automatic leading-edge slats (originally a British invention), slotted flaps and slotted ailerons that drooped with the flaps. The 109 had a much higher wing loading (thirty-two pounds per square foot against the Spitfire's twenty-five), but the Messerschmitt pilot did have an indication that he was getting near the stall when the slats began to pop out, while the Spitfire pilot didn't. Both airplanes had similar cockpits, though the 109 had no artificial horizon, and its propeller pitch control was rather oddly mounted in the center of the panel.

The Emil's greatest weakness in the Battle of Britain was its limited fuel capacity, which allowed a maximum of twenty minutes' full-throttle combat over England. Of course, 109 pilots sometimes got carried away in the excitement of battle and overstayed. Not a few force-landed with dry tanks on the beaches of northern France on the way home, while some did not even make it that far. (The Spit-

Evolution of Messerschmitt 109.
From top: 1939 Battle of Britain "Emil"; one
of several prototypes developed
in late 1930's; pair of 109 F's of 1944.
Opposite: Front end of early
Me-109 battle-tested by Franco forces
during Spanish Civil War.

fire was little better, but the Spitfire was fighting over home ground.) Bomber escort was almost certainly a role for which the 109 was not designed, but even so it is odd no one thought of drop tanks till much later in the war. The 109E could perhaps have done with more armor plate, particularly as the pilot's seat was right over the fuel tank. A Spitfire pilot had much better rearward visibility, and could also see better when taxiing, since the 109 had to have an acute ground angle because of the low thrust line and long propeller.

An RAF test pilot who flew a captured Emil liked the way trim and flap wheels were situated alongside each other, so that they could be operated together with one hand. He thought the cockpit rather cramped and narrow, and felt uncomfortable in the semi-reclining position imposed by the seat. He was astonished by the perfect pickup of the fuel-injection engine when he pushed the throttle open, and was convinced that Emil climbed faster than the Spitfire. He felt the airplane needed rudder trim, and noted that at high speeds his leg muscles began to ache with the strain of holding the machine straight. He found the 109's controls considerably heavier than a Spitfire's, and judged the 109 to be more stable longitudinally—perhaps too stable. He thought the elevators quite ineffective at high speeds and found that even at 400 mph he could not pull enough G to get anywhere near blacking himself out. He thought that if you could tempt a 109 pilot into a half-roll and pull-through at low alti-

Top: Another Merlin Me-109. Nazi
Germany's principal World War II fighter,
the 109 was developed from
Willy Messerschmitt's first successful
design, the 108 Taifun (above). Me-109's
first appeared in late 1935,
and all told some 30,000 were produced.

tude he might go straight into the ground. He noticed that the ailerons snatched as he approached the stall, owing to one slat popping open a moment before the other, and thought this would upset gun sighting for a moment. He wondered whether this had not saved many an Allied fighter pilot.

Halfway through his test flight he found himself being stalked by a Spitfire, whose pilot saw the RAF roundels on the captured 109 and came alongside. For a few moments they fought a mock battle. The test pilot in the 109 found he could steeply outclimb the Spitfire, and could also lose his pursuer by abruptly pushing the nose down, but he found the Messerschmitt's heavy controls quite exhausting. He summed up his impressions of the two airplanes with a subjective evaluation: "The Me-109 flew as though on rails, but the Spitfire was as sensitive as a fiery horse."

Yet the Me-109 must be judged one of the most successful fighters ever. Certainly it was built in the largest quantities ever, for well over thirty thousand were turned out in factories all over Germany, in Czechoslovakia, and in Spain. No other design ever shot down so many aircraft. Like the Spitfire, it was continually developed and improved, up to the final K

version with 1,500 hp and a top speed of around 450 mph. Every high-scoring German ace of the Second World War flew 109's at some time in his career, and most of the really gigantic scores were built up on 109's. (Fifteen German pilots shot down more than two hundred aircraft each, while two shot down more than three hundred—a record the Allies never even approached.)

Air combat's all-time ace-of-aces, Erich Hartmann, who shot down 352 aircraft and was himself shot down sixteen times, always flew Me-109's. He survived the war and imprisonment by the Russians, and is today a colonel in the new Luftwaffe. Hartmann flies F-104 Starfighters today, but still hankers after the Messerschmitt.

Curiously, the 109 finished its operational life as it began, with a Rolls-Royce engine: Until very recently, the Spanish air force continued to operate a few squadrons of 109's powered by Rolls-Royce Merlins. The whole lot was then sold to United Artists for use in a movie about the Battle of Britain. Painted in 1940 Luftwaffe colors, the 109 did finally get to fly from an RAF airfield, twenty-eight years after the battle that had been its first and greatest defeat.

The Spitfire

The war was almost a year old, though it felt older. Huddled winter and wet spring had given way to a strangely glorious summer, with the dog roses shining pink from every hedgerow and the ripening wheat changing from green to gold across the land. Yet France had fallen, Belgium and Holland had gone the same quick and bloody way as Norway and Denmark, Poland and Czechoslovakia. England, the world knew, was next; and while no one had taken England for nine hundred years, no one had yet stopped Hitler either.

It was a time of great danger and of intoxicating, messianic speeches by Winston Churchill, all delivered in a fruity, boozy voice that might have been God Himself speaking. "The battle of France is over," he acknowledged heavily, adding: "I expect the Battle of Britain is about to begin. Upon this battle depends the survival of Christian civilization. Upon it depends our own British way of life, and the long continuity of our institutions and our Empire. The whole fury and might of the enemy must very soon be turned on us. Hitler knows that he will have to break us in this island or lose the war. If we can stand up to him all Europe may be free. . . . But if we fail, then the whole world, including the United States, including all that we have known and cared for, will sink into the abyss of a new Dark Age made more sinister, and perhaps more protracted, by the lights of perverted science." Then came the sentence that made you know you were more than just some human ant crawling over the paving stones of history: "Let us therefore brace ourselves to our duties, and so bear ourselves that, if the British Empire and its Commonwealth last for a thousand years, men will still say, 'This was their finest hour.' "

Three secret weapons won the Battle of Britain: radar (but more particularly the resourceful organization that went with it); that old Churchillian oratory, scattered by the BBC across a land that had always dearly loved words; and the Supermarine Spitfire.

If you were a British fighter pilot in 1940, as that strange summer was turning to an unnatural, golden, Valhalla-like autumn, your fighting days began and ended in a wooden hut called Dispersal. Dispersal was untidily decorated with rude pinned-up pictures of nearly naked pin-ups, models of airplanes—theirs and ours—for recognition purposes, parachutes, helmets, boisterous dogs, an iron stove, a table, chairs, and decks of cards, and more powerful than any oracle of Delphi, a telephone. That telephone! "Whatever memory I have of those days, a telephone rings urgently and insistently in the background," one pilot remembers. "That was the Operations telephone in our dispersal hut, and its note meant more to us than any human voice. Often it interrupted a sentence that was never finished. . . ."

Scramble! was the shout you waited to hear, and it sent you running to your aircraft, where you fought and struggled to clip your parachute harness over your "Mae West," while humble happy airmen helped and stumbled, and got your starter turning and your engine coughing and smoking and choking and, finally, running. Over the bungalow roofs you flew and formed up, as a squadron, while into your ears there came, like another, different voice of God, the half-coded instructions of the controller. *Vector* was the course to steer, and *Angels* the height to struggle up to, while *Bandits* were the Hun, and *Tally ho!* your leader's excited shout when he first caught sight of the enemy. At first glance the formation of black-crossed enemy bombers would seem to fill the entire sky from horizon to horizon. You'd pick yours, and start down behind him, when the anguished shout *Break! For God's sake, break!* would scream in your helmet's earphones, and you knew the Messerschmitts had started down in turn after you. The dogfights began, whirl-

166

ing twisting death-dances of G forces and juddering machine guns, insane shouting and curses over the radio, with black funereal smoke and greedy yellow flames consuming the falling, dying airplanes. It was a weird battle. One moment the sky around you would be filled with dueling machinery. The next instant it could be miraculously empty of action, and you were alone in sudden peace as the fight drifted off elsewhere to lower levels. Or you might be dead, or worse, alive but fast burning to an evil-smelling crisp, struggling to open a jammed canopy. With luck you might leap, trusting to your parachute. If you fought in the Battle of Britain, you were a hero, like it or not.

But it was an odd battle. The contrasts were so extraordinary. You rose from and returned to your homeland, a peaceful and familiar world quite untouched as yet by the war, an ancient rural landscape still at peace with the sky. While you had put your life on the line, had dared death, and had returned, still very young but growing suddenly old, others had done nothing more dramatic than bring in the harvest, while staring up in awe at the distant contrails and listening to the high faint howl of engines and the childlike rattle of the guns. You might rise from this earthly paradise into Armageddon and drop down gently again three times in one short day.

The reason for the Battle of Britain was that, before they could invade England, the Germans had to destroy the RAF. Their invasion barges were too vulnerable to stand air attack. The attempt quite failed; Britain was effectively able to manufacture pilots and aircraft to match her losses, while the Luftwaffe's strength slowly declined. Each side badly overestimated its own victories. The Germans claimed 3,058 British airplanes, but actually got only 915, while the RAF claimed 2,698 Huns, although German records after the war showed that only 1,753 went down. The battle was short (six weeks), and utterly decisive; it surely determined the course of subsequent history. It was an almost gladiatorial combat, for at the apex of the vast pyramid of fighter manufacturing and supply was a mere handful of men actually in the line of fire. At the battle's start Fighter Command had 1,434 pilots, most of them barely trained. "Never," rumbled Churchill, with his genius for putting powerfully into words the half-formed thought of every Briton, "in the field of human conflict was so much owed by so many to so few." Few, indeed! On almost any day during the battle many fewer than a thousand British fighter pilots fought at all, and when it was over, and Fighter Command had time to mourn its dead heroes, there were fewer than five hundred in number. (Actually 449, of whom 402 were British, 5 were Belgian, 7 Czech, 29 Polish, 3 Canadian, and 3 New Zealander.) Yet it was, like an earlier battle

in Britain's illustrious history, a "damned close-run thing." One fine September Sunday morning, at its height, Churchill, on his way to his country home, stopped to visit Fighter Command's No. 11 Group Operations Room at Uxbridge, where in a cool, concrete underground control room Air Vice Marshal Keith Park was waiting to direct the day's operations. W.A.A.F. girl plotters, armed with telephone headsets and long croupier's wands, waited around a gridded table-map to display the formation's positions, Theirs and Ours, while on one wall was a display in colored lights of the disposition of 11 Group's squadrons. At first, quiet. "Not so many today," someone

167

ventured. The plots began, first some labeled in waspish yellow-and-black "H" for "hostile," and moments later, as Park scrambled his forces, others in their path labeled "F" for "fighter." The Germans came in three gargantuan waves, and one by one the "readiness" lights on the "Tote" display of Park's squadrons went out, and one by one they came on again as squadrons "pancaked," that is, landed briefly to refuel and rearm. Churchill watched in thoughtful silence, only breaking it to ask Park, quietly, "What other reserves have we?" Said Air Vice Marshal Park, simply and respectfully, "There are none." Words for all time. And, indeed, that Uxbridge operations room is preserved today, with the plots, Hostile and Fighter, still on the table as at the height of that day's battle, and in the ash tray on the balcony the butt of Churchill's cigar still remains.

Nor were all these squadrons equipped with Spitfires. Would they had been! At the start of the battle only nineteen of Park's units had Spitfires. The other twenty-nine had Hurricanes, excellent airplanes, solid and easy to manufacture, but no real match for the German Messerschmitt 109's. The idea was that the Hurricanes would go for the lumbering German bombers, leaving the Spits to cope with the 109's, but in the melee that always followed interception, it did not often work out so tidily. So as far as aircraft were concerned, then, the battle's honors are evenly divided.

Credit for fathering the Spitfire is firmly given to R. J. Mitchell, a quiet, pipe-smoking sort of chap in baggy tweeds. He joined the fledgling firm of Supermarine in 1916 as an engineer, and began to cut his teeth as an aircraft designer on entries for the famous Schneider Trophy seaplane races in the 1920's. Over a decade he struggled with monoplane structural stressing, control-surface flutter, minimum-drag configurations, the heartbreaking anxieties of the enormously powerful and terribly short-lived liquid-cooled racing engines of the day—all with such success that in 1931 one of his S.6B's retired the trophy (with a third consecutive win for Britain) at a carefully timed 340.08 mph, and later set a world speed record of 407.5 mph. These racers, with their impossible handling characteristics, were by no means Spitfires, but they did make Mitchell's reputation to such an extent that when Vickers bought up Supermarine it insisted that Mitchell be included in the deal, and they did give him a unique fund of experience in messing about with high-speed flight. (Racing really does improve the breed!)

It may be that Mitchell knew as much as anyone in the world about designing for high speeds, and when in 1934 the Air Ministry issued its specification F37/34 for an eight-gun fighter capable of 275 mph and 33,000 feet, Mitchell's design, called simply Type Number 300, was eagerly accepted as a tender. Type 300 was as sleek and slippery a speedster as you could ever hope to see. Its narrow undercarriage retracted in flight into a knife-thin wing of elegant elliptical shape, and the lines of the fuselage seemed to flow like liquid from the compact V-12 Rolls-Royce engine back past the all-enclosed cockpit to the tiny tail surfaces. When Vickers' chief test pilot Mutt Summers trundled out the prototype, a tiny sky-blue airplane hiding behind an enormous propeller, for its first flight, on March 5, 1936, he started his takeoff run across wind, as you had had to with Schneider Trophy racers, but the torque, impressive though it was, proved containable by a bootful of rudder. She was airborne in a trice, and the handful of spectators watched entranced as the undercarriage legs disappeared into the wings. The Spitfire was on its way. Mitchell himself was there that day, but he would not be for many more, for he was dying of cancer. A stomach operation the year before had been only partly successful; the disease was progressing inexorably.

Soon came the first production con-

169

tract, for 310 airplanes, and it set Supermarine in a real tizzy, for it was a small firm and the Spitfire was simply not designed for mass production. Its all-metal, stressed-skin structure demanded elaborate and costly jigs and tools, and all the complex curves inherent in its beautiful elliptical wing and graceful lines cannot have helped. So the great octopus organization of subcontractors that would later churn out Spitfires by the thousands was begun. Even so, one estimate is that it took 330,000 man-hours, the equivalent of the entire working lives of three men, to build one Spitfire.

For brave Mitchell the end was very near. Another operation served only to reveal how far advanced was his disease, and he was given but three months to live. Courageously he set his affairs in order and headed for an American clinic in Vienna, for which miracles were claimed. However, it was too late

even for miracles, and a month later he returned home. On June 11, 1937, the Spitfire's designer, aged forty-two, died. But he had found time to hand over his job to Joseph Smith, hitherto Supermarine's chief draftsman. While Smith's part in the initial creation of the airplane had perhaps been small, under his leadership began the long and tireless development program that kept the Spitfire in the forefront of fighter performance right up to 1945. Some changes came soon: a tailwheel instead of a skid; replacement of fixed-pitch mahogany airscrews, with, first two-position, then metal constant-speed propellers. A slab of bulletproof glass was bolted to the outside of the windshield after Hugh "Stuffy" Dowding, commander-in-chief of Fighter Command, had grumbled, "If Chicago gangsters can ride behind bullet-proof glass I see no reason why my pilots should not do so, too." Thank you, Al

172

Preceding pages: Final Griffon-engined Spitfire had 2,500 hp, top speed of 500 mph. Above left: Designer R. J. Mitchell did not live to see Spitfire in production. Top: Prototype Spitfire of 1937. Above: 1938 Mk I recalls Schneider Trophy racers. Opposite: No. 19, first Spitfire squadron, 1938.

Capone. Other innovations were less immediately successful and appreciated: A plan to replace or supplement the Spitfire's eight .303 machine guns (designed by the Colt Automatic Weapon Corporation of Hartford, Connecticut, by the way) with 20mm cannon went sour because of the cannon's persistent jamming.

By the outbreak of war nine RAF squadrons had Spits, and more were "converting" to the type. By the beginning of the battle proper, there were twenty such squadrons, and production had reached the heady figure of around five a day, about half the rate of manufacture of the easier-to-build Hurricane. Manufacturing Spitfire pilots was more of a problem. Trained initially on light aircraft with fixed undercarriages, they found the leap forward to something as sleek and slippery and powerful as the Spit awesome. Fines for poor performance helped them remember: five shillings for

taxiing with the flaps down, for boiling the engine coolant, for bending the propeller; up to five pounds for landing with the wheels still snugly tucked into the wings. (The fines were shared among the ground crews; they grew rich.) But raw pilots sent to operational squadrons were at first terrifyingly undertrained. They either survived and learned, or they didn't. One of the more persistent problems was that new pilots were pitifully poor marksmen, and right through the battle it was a tiny majority of aces who did all the scoring, while many fighter pilots never did hit anything at all.

What was the Spitfire like to fly? Under your smelly rubber "Mae West" you wore a blue uniform of heavy, itchy serge, with a sweater under that; you wore a silk neck scarf if you felt particularly dashing, and a brown leather helmet from which dangled a rubber oxygen mask and self-contained microphone, a

173

pipe for the oxygen, and a long, far too long, electrical umbilical. You strapped on your seat parachute, then clambered like a pregnant spider up on the wing and into the cockpit, whose floor was thickly covered with mud from the boots of many others of the Few. There was always a strong smell of glycol coolant. You fastened the four X-straps of the Sutton harness, and plugged in the heavy R/T lead. One of the ground crew opened a flap on the side of the engine cowling and plugged in a battery of electrical accumulators from a nearby trolley. A few strokes of the hand-primer, and you hit the starter. Reluctantly the propeller three yards in front of you turned, coughed, spat blue smoke, and began to run with a hideous roar. The starting batteries were disconnected, you released the brakes with a catch on the stick, and began to taxi, bumping and rocking on your narrow main gear over the rough grass. Your "office," the cockpit, which had looked so small before you got in, was roomy enough once you were strapped in and tidy. The stick had a ring at its top, with the gun button nestling under your thumb. In the center of the panel were the six basic flight instruments—airspeed, horizon, vertical speed, altimeter, gyrocompass, and turn-and-bank—in an arrangement very similar to that which obtains in modern airplanes to this day. Above was the gunsight. To the right was a cluster of engine instruments, and beneath the panel an enormous magnetic compass. The flap lever was way up in the panel's left-hand corner, oddly placed by today's standards. To the right was the undercarriage position selector and, if you were unlucky, an enormous handle by which you yourself pumped the wheels up and down. (Seventeen full strokes to raise them after takeoff.) If you were lucky, and got one of the newer Spits, an engine-driven pump did the work for you.

The takeoff took some care. You had to open the throttle slowly, and you had to be ready with the rudder to hold the yaw when you applied power. You kept the stick fairly well back, so as not to ding the prop in the mud. You were airborne very quickly, and at once set about raising the undercarriage. An immediate delight was the lightness and quickness of the controls, and the rate of climb—better than 2,500 fpm. Soon you were sliding the open bubble-hood closed and picking up speed. With just over 1,000 hp, the Mks I and II Spitfires would do 360 to 370 mph at best altitude, burning more than a gallon of eighty octane a minute at full throttle. The design's gloriously sleek lines were something you could almost feel when you flew one, for she seemed to go on forever slowly accelerating, and was in no hurry to slow down when you reduced power. At high speeds you found the controls not nearly so light. The ailerons in particular became very heavy to move.

After the slow trainers you were used to, it was miraculously easy to rack up enormous G loads that sent the blood draining from your brain, so that the sky around you turned gray and then black if you continued to pull on the stick. Had they warned you about *negative* G? Early Spits had old-fashioned float carburetors, and if you pushed the plane sharply forward into a dive the engine quit instantly, a jet of fuel from a vent poured all over the windscreen, and of course you got a faceful of dried mud from the cockpit floor and only your straps held you in the seat. The engine came back to life again in the end, but by that time the Messerschmitt you were chasing, blessed with fuel injection, was far ahead.

Which brings us to the old question: Which was better, Spitfire or 109? It seems they were most evenly matched. The German ace Adolf Galland has written that he thought his 109 to be 10 or 15 mph faster, while the Spitfire, with its greater wing area,

Altogether there were twenty-four Spitfire marks, an evolutionary course which saw plane raise speed by 100 mph and ceiling by 11,000 feet. Left: Low-level Mk XII of April, 1944, had blunt wing tips. Below left: High-altitude model with extended tips. Below: Mk XIV profile shows Spitfire as a new design, rather than new stage of old. Right: Mk XXII of 1945 leads two Mk XXI's at around 450 mph.

could turn steeper and tighter. Even the British conceded that the 109 had the advantage at altitudes above 20,000 feet. Yet there is a popular story that Galland once improvidently told Reichsmarschall Hermann Goering that he would prefer a wing of Spitfires to his 109's. The truth of it was that under most circumstances the fighting skill of the individual pilot made the real difference in combat.

The Battle of Britain, though it was the moment the Spitfire achieved its principal glory, was only the beginning of the air-plane's battle history. Spitfires were built throughout the war, the total being some twenty thousand airframes, in the course of which the basic design went from a 1,000-hp, 350-mph airplane to something with a completely new wing and a 2,500-hp Griffon engine that would nudge 500 mph. There were twenty-four marks of Spitfire, though the later few were really a new type of airplane. It was the Mks I and II that fought the Battle of Britain; many pilots considered the Mark V the quintessential Spit-fire in its handling qualities. There were vari-

ants with cropped superchargers and clipped wing tips specially for low-altitude combat, and pressurized-cabin Spitfires with extended wings for operation at above 40,000 feet. There were unarmed photoreconnaissance Spitfires, and armed reconnaissance Spitfires, and Seafires with arrester hooks for carrier operation. Spitfires flew under many colors, including those of the United States, which obtained six hundred of them. Spitfires even fought Spitfires, briefly, when in 1948 an Egyptian Squadron tangled with two RAF units withdrawing from the newly formed state of Israel. How many still fly today? The film company making "The Battle of Britain" in 1968 was able to assemble a dozen in the air at one time, and maybe as many more that could be taxied but were not fit to fly. So shall we say twenty Spitfires are still airworthy? They are almost all later marks, for I know of only one that fought in the Battle itself and still flies. Many more exist, half-derelict, as exhibition and museum airframes. Somewhere, somehow, I think there will be a handful of Spitfires in this world forever.

P-51: the Wide-ranging Mustang

Tank selector to *left main*, flaps *up*, battery *on*, fuel booster *on*. Crack the throttle, two shots of prime, and hit the starter switch. Let four prop blades slide by, then turn the magnetos to *on*, still cranking. There's a shudder violent enough to make you believe the engine is coming off its mounts, and great belches of blue smoke go drifting back past your canopy. Then the engine begins to run smoothly, with a great grumbling roar that even at idle makes the whole airframe tremble mightily.

Chocks away, parking brake *off*. With the stick aft of neutral the tailwheel is locked and can swivel only six degrees to each side, but to get out of the parking place you need more than that, so you heave the pole forward to get free swivel and use a touch of brake to swing you round. You taxi in a drunken weave, because you must to see where you're going.

The run-up has you busier than a one-handed handclapper. No more than forty inches of power or you'll lift the tail, and you must lean right forward to reach the mag switch between your knees. You check the mags at 2,300 rpm, at which the Merlin bellows like a bull in pain. (Whatever else this bird is going to be in flight, it won't be quiet, you begin to realize.) Check the prop governor, then the supercharger by momentarily selecting *high*. Then check coolant and oil switches on *automatic,* mixture *auto-rich,* prop *full forward,* friction locks *tight,* fuel boost *on*, canopy locked, harness tight, full and free on the controls. Call the tower for takeoff clearance, taxi out on the runway. Hold the stick well back, then slowly advance the power to wow! sixty-one inches. Long before you get there, the thing has started down the runway in a blast of sound that paralyzes your brain. The nose comes down of its own accord, affording you a fine head-on view of the trees at the side of the runway. You feed in rudder, and the Mustang straightens up. Now you know why she's called Mustang: the takeoff is exactly like trying to hold onto a runaway horse! In a trice you are a mile from the airport, ascending at a furious rate, the altimeter spinning round like clock hands gone crazy. Gear *up,* and come back to forty-six inches and 2,700 rpm. At 16,000 feet the engine switches itself automatically to *high blower,* with a wrench that feels as though plane and engine were about to separate.

You level off at twenty grand, and try the controls. They're light, really light. But the Fifty-one simply isn't stable; you can trim her out all you will, but she's never going to fly hands-off. Stuff the nose down a hair, and in no time the ASI is climbing up near 500 mph, and the bird is coming downhill like a dropped bomb. Ease back on the stick, and the G plasters you flat down against your parachute pack. It's no trick to get a Fifty-one into compressibility, so clean is her airframe. You'll know when you're there all right, because the controls will stiffen and the airplane will begin shuddering uncontrollably, and maybe yawing and pitching, too. Roll into a vertical dive from 250 mph at 15,000 feet, and you'll need to start your recovery before you are down to 10,000. And nobody ever just leveled out from a dive in a Fifty-one; no, you pulled some more and did a vertical climbing roll going back up, or an Immelmann, or some such nonsense. The Mustang just begged to be allowed to do aerobatics, but woe betide you if you got chicken and tried to pull through from halfway around a slow roll: you'd better have miles of height and no fear of G or high indicated airspeeds before you tried that.

The moment of truth, as with any high-performance airplane, came when you first tried to land the thing. However hard you tried, it seemed you were always going 200 mph too fast when you entered the traffic pattern. "I at once made known my intention to land," remembers one author, Len Morgan, describing his first ride in a Mustang, "in order to allay any suspicion the tower might entertain that the field was under sudden air attack. With power off and engine backfiring like a machine gun and apparently trying to vibrate itself off the mounts, the airspeed reluctantly dipped to 170." You lowered the gear, selected half-flap, and she at last began to slow down. You crossed the fence at 130 mph, and eased her onto the runway. She had slowed to a walk before half the runway had rolled away under your wheels.

In truth, the Mustang was not a difficult airplane to fly, if you knew the Pilot Training Manual by heart, and had any kind of feel for flying. She had only one vice: The torque from those 1,400 horses was entirely capable of rolling you clear on your back at low airspeeds. At some point in your early days in the beast you would be instructed to climb up to a goodly altitude, drop the flaps and gear, slow down to 125 mph, then suddenly pour on sixty-one inches. One such demonstration was enough: With everything in the right-hand corner of the cockpit you still fell over to the left quite out of control. At low airspeeds, then, power could be applied only with great care.

Your other criticism of the bird would be that, no matter how hard you tried, you could never get really comfortable in the cockpit. The noise from the engine was absolutely shattering; your head rang for hours after you landed. And always the cockpit seemed too hot.

The P-51D was a concept long thought to be impossible: a high-performance single-seat fighter with the range of a bomber. It was the first fighter that could escort American day bombers all the way to Berlin. The Mustang was surely the best American fighter of World War II, and it perhaps changed the course of the war, for before it came along, early in 1944, the Luftwaffe had fought the unescorted Fortresses of the Eighth Air Force to a complete standstill. The Mustang allowed the Eighth to resume pounding Germany to rubble. One man who understood the airplane's importance right from the start was Goering. When the first Mustang was reported deep inside Germany during a raid on Hanover he is supposed to have raged at the Luftwaffe reporting center that they had to be mistaken. When finally convinced that there were indeed American fighters over Hanover, he muttered, "We have lost the war."

Yet for an airplane destined for such greatness, the Mustang had an oddly undistinguished birth. We must go back to the spring of 1940, almost two years before America was in the war at all, when a British Air Purchasing Commission set up shop in a New York City hotel, to buy U.S. airplanes for the RAF. The gigantic production capability of the U.S. aircraft industry was something the beleaguered British could not afford to ignore, though in general they were singularly unimpressed by the fighting abilities of American airplanes. One U.S. design they did like (perhaps mistakenly) was the Curtiss P-40. But the Curtiss factory was snowed under with orders, so the British sought out other manufacturers who might build the Curtiss design under license. One firm they approached was North American, whose president, James "Dutch" Kindelberger, had read every account of air combat over Eu-

181

P-51A (below), armed with four
20mm cannon, was first of Mustang family
accepted by USAAF. Plane also was
first with belly racks for bombs or
long-range fuel tanks. Opposite (from top):
Mustang I prototype, the NA-73, was
turned out for British in 117
days. Capt. Don Gentile, American ace, in
P-51B "Shangri-la." RAF Mustang III's
got Malcolm hoods to
improve rearward visibility.

Above: P-51D. More than half of the 16,000 Mustangs built were Ds. Long-range missions were made possible by tanks carrying ton and a half of fuel. Left: P-51H appeared in 1945, was ultimate Mustang. It served in Korean War and equipped many Air National Guard units.

rope that he could lay his hands on, and who thought he had an idea for a better plane than the chubby P-40. Jolly good, said the British, but could he build a prototype inside 120 days? For that's how desperate for fighters they were. North American rolled their NA-73 prototype out of the hangar just 117 days later. Only very close examination would show that it didn't as yet have an engine, and that the wheels were borrowed from an AT-6 trainer. Six weeks later the NA-73 made its first flight, and a week or

two after that the test pilot became the first of many Mustang pilots to discover that if the engine quit you should belly it in. *He* put it down in a plowed field with the gear down, and over-turned and wrecked it.

The RAF got its first Mustangs late in 1941, and quickly discovered them to be much the best American fighters it had seen, and, at 380 mph, faster even than its own Spitfires. These early Mustangs had Allison engines, and the RAF soon found out that they were no use at all at altitude, since the Allison had only a low-speed supercharger, and simply ran out of puff above about 20,000 feet.

Then someone (I'm not sure who) had the brilliant, if rather obvious, idea of mating this lovely fighter airframe with the Rolls-Royce Merlin engine. Five Mustangs were quickly given to Rolls-Royce to be re-engined, and when the first Merlin Mustang flew in October, 1942, it was immediately evident to all that here was the best fighter yet built. It would do 432 mph at 22,000 feet, for the Merlin had a fabulous two-stage, two-speed supercharger that gave the Mustang all the altitude performance it had so sadly lacked with the Allison. North American quickly switched to building Mustangs with Packard-built Merlin engines, and within a month General "Hap" Arnold was reporting to President Roosevelt that the USAAF, which hitherto had seen little virtue in the Mustang, now had more than two thousand on order. The Eighth got its first Merlin Mustangs on December 1, 1942, and two weeks later flew its first long-range escort mission, taking the Fortresses to Kiel and back, an impressive jaunt of almost five hundred miles roundtrip.

One weakness remained: poor rearward visibility. The RAF had tried to cure this by junking the close-fitting hoods their early Mustangs came with and replacing them with bulged "Malcolm" hoods, but the problem was not entirely taken care of till the D model appeared with the teardrop bubble hood. The D model is the famous and familiar one. More than half of the sixteen-thousand-odd Mustangs built were Ds. The P-51D could hit 437 mph at 15,000 feet, and could do it more than a thousand miles from base. With its ton and a half of gas, the Mustang had seven-league boots.

That bold, brave handful of Americans who fought with the RAF in the Battle of Britain later so increased in number that there eventually were three Eagle Squadrons entirely staffed by such antifascist volunteers. In 1942 they were transferred to the USAAF's Eighth, robbed of their beloved Spitfires and given Thunderbolts instead. Their pay multiplied four times, but they weren't happy. "It ought to dive. It certainly won't climb," grumbled 133 Squadron's commander Don Blakeslee of his Thunderbolt, on being congratulated for his destruction of a Focke-Wulf after a chase among the treetops. Blakeslee and his merry men wanted Mustangs. "That's okay, General, sir," he answered when his boss argued there was no time for them to retrain on the new fighter. "We can learn to fly them on the way to the target!" And so they did.

Blakeslee led his Fourth Fighter Group in their Mustangs on escort duty all the way to Berlin, fully 1,100 miles from home base. These were gigantic air battles—the biggest in the history of air warfare—for Blakeslee would be leading as many as eight hundred Mustangs and Thunderbolts in support of thirteen hundred bombers, and they might meet a thousand Luftwaffe defenders. It was straight battle, with little subterfuge: How can you seek to disguise the approach of two thousand airplanes?

Blakeslee's boys were the arch-exponents of team work. Two of them who habitually fought together—Captains Don S. Gentile (twenty-three air victories) and John T. Godfrey (eighteen)—were in the opinion of British fighter chief Johnnie Johnson "the best pair ever to fight over Germany." Goering is alleged to have said he would gladly give two of his best squadrons for their capture, while Churchill called them "the Damon and Pythias of the twentieth century." If you have forgotten who Damon and Pythias were, so have I, but they must have been fabulous warriors to have been the Godfrey and Gentile of their day.

Fully 150 Mustangs (almost every one a D-model) are still airworthy today. About the only battles they still wage are with Bearcats for first prize in the Reno Air Races.

185

The Flying Fortress

The flashlight came stabbing through your troubled dreams, a lightning bolt of awakening. "Roll, boy," growled a voice. "Breakfast at two, briefing at three." A yawn came and departed, yielding to a shiver. The Nissen hut, even when you managed to steal midnight coal from the sergeants for the ineffectual stove, was bitter. The barest of bulbs made ghosts of the figures you had taped to the wall—ikons of the two most spiritual visions of your soul: Betty Grable and the P-51. The atmosphere held the familiar rankness of massed socks and white-wash and acrid Army blankets. In the latrine there was water that never ran hot, and a mirror that by trickery showed an old man's leathery features where yours should have been. An old man of twenty-two. You shaved carefully; the merest stubble itched irritably under the grasp of your oxygen mask.

Breakfast was oily bacon and the curds of powdered eggs, oozing water. When you gathered for briefing you made a raunchy congregation, coughing, still bad-tempered from sleep, sick beyond weariness of the whole bloody mess of total war. The mission map would be covered up at first, but the bobbin of twine that reached from your home base to the target was an indication of the horrors the day would throw at you. A fat bobbin meant a short mission—maybe a "milk run" to the submarine pens of Lorient or Saint-Nazaire. A lean bobbin meant a long lunge deep into Germany and hours of murderous battling with the enraged and desperate Luftwaffe. Above all you prayed to God and the Eighth Air Force it wouldn't be somewhere like Schweinfurt. That killer town! Of three hundred Fortresses that formed up and set out for Schweinfurt on October 14, 1943, sixty-five—more than twenty percent—went down. Almost six hundred men were gone with them and the planes that crawled home brought fifty more dead or injured. One little unit, the 305th Bomb Group at Chelveston, dispatched fifteen Fortresses on this mission, and got back two.

The black cloth was lifted, and the briefing officer's pointer darted about the map, busy with tracks and diversions, known hornets' nests of flak and fighters. Stormy, the weather guy, would read off his litany of clouds and winds, and the Old Man would call a time check, and then you'd ride out to the flight lines, where the ghostly Fortresses waited in the lingering dawn mists, like gigantic insects. From a distance every Seventeen seemed the same, the drab multiparous khaki offspring of mass production. But to you each bird had its own soul and personality. Some planes were given to mulish malfunctions; others would carry their crews blithely through a hundred hellish missions with never a drop of blood spilled. You had done your best to enliven your own Fortress by having a neat row of bombs painted on the nose—one for each mission—plus an optimistic row of swastikas, one for every German fighter your gunners were convinced they'd got. And you had dignified her with a name, and alongside the name you'd caused the group's artist to paint the most lascivious-looking babe he could devise, for you were young and horny; all ten of you were probably under twenty-five.

And then you dressed up fatter than fall bears in electrically-heated long johns —and a flying suit over that, and fur boots and triple-layered gloves, an armored flak jacket and a parachute harness; then a leather helmet and its dangling rubber cupped-hand of an oxygen mask, with umbilicals for oxygen and intercom. The ground crew told you they'd changed the plugs on number three. They were sure she'd be okay now. The gunners climbed in and lovingly caressed and examined their big fifties. And while you waited, stomping about in the dew-bejewelled grass or lying stretched out on an engine tarpaulin, "sweating it out," the bombardiers screwed fuses into thousand-pounders. Bombardiers did blunder, but nobody ever knew how, for nothing was left to tell of it; in the searing flash of a detonated bomb the entire airplane was vaporized—an inkling of the effect when dropped on a city.

A flare rocketing up from Control signified "start engines," and your fears began to yield in the relief of having something to do at last. You all taxied away, nose to tail, in a deafening rumble of motors and squealing brakes. One by one, at sixty-second intervals, you thundered down the runway and clambered up into the clammy overcast. You climbed through gray blankets of stratus, through lacy curled curtains of cirrus, following the twitching finger of your radio compass as it pointed to the "splasher" beacon where you were to assemble. Here you joined a lazy, hour-long maelstrom of circling Fortresses, struggling to form up in the huge pyramid-shaped formations in which you had to meet the enemy if your massed guns were to provide mutual protection. (More than once Fortresses collided while undertaking this maneuver; then sixteen tons of high explosives, several thousand gallons of high-octane, half a million dollars, and twenty men would vanish in a puff of white fire.)

Formed up, the aerial armada set sail for Germany. You flew at an inconsiderable speed—about 160 mph—but at a very fair altitude of twenty to twenty-five thousand feet: high enough for your exhausts to stream great trails of vapor in which German fighters would sometimes hide till they had crept up on top of you. If the air were moist enough, curlicues of vapor also spiraled back from your propeller tips, and even your wing tips might draw a chalk mark of condensation. You flew in a "combat box," a close but irregular arrowhead of perhaps eighteen planes.

The Fortress was a sturdy bird whose extensively convoluted construction often allowed one structural member to assume the stresses ordinarily borne by a neighboring member if that piece happened to be shot away. The Fortress could take a tremendous amount of battle damage and stay flying. Spanning just over a hundred feet and grossing more than thirty tons, she was a large bird for her day. In the very nose lived the bombardier, behind a conical dome of plexiglass that had a lozenge-shaped panel of optically flat glass underneath through which he scanned the target with the Norden bombsight, which, it was said, could "hit a pickle barrel from twenty thousand feet." So it could, when things were easy; but when the flak formed a black and greasy carpet so thick you could have gotten out and walked on it, or when the fighters came at you in a swarm, you might not bomb within miles of the target. The bombardier had switches to open the bomb-bay doors, and switches to drop the bombs singly or severally, and in later Seventeens he had an electronic link-up with the autopilot so he could effectively fly the plane through the Norden sight on the bombing run. The bombardier doubled as a gunner, with a hand-held fifty aimed forward and left, more for his morale than anything else. He might also have rigged up a *second* fifty

Early B-17's were truly "peacetime" bombers. Advanced for 1935, they were outmoded by time World War II began, proved almost defenseless against fighter attacks. RAF B-17C (bottom) was particularly disappointing to British, who assigned it to maritime reconnaissance work where combat risk was slight. Overhaul of design, increase of armament eventually improved **Fortresses'** performance.

Forts at Work: B-17F's
(opposite, top) on raid. Vapor
trails are being made by
"Little Friends" (escort
fighters). Mid-air collision
with Me-109 over Tunis
nearly severed Fort's fuselage,
but it landed at base before
cracking up. Doomed Fort at
bottom has lost wing to
cannon fire. A third
of all Fortresses built
went down. Left: Starboard
waist gunner, dressed and masked
for altitude, fires 50-caliber
machine gun at attacker
coming from one o'clock low.
Below: Bombs away. Sticks drop
somewhere in Germany. One
B-17, trailing smoke, is dying.

pointing straight ahead through that glass bubble, or even a cluster of them, for German fighter chief Adolf Galland had examined a captured Fort and noticed that though it bristled with guns, it was open to head-on attack, since most of its armor plate was necessarily behind the crew. This encouraged the Luftwaffe to try straight-ahead fighter tactics with cannon and, later in the war, rockets. (The G-model Seventeen gained a power chin turret, to fill this chink in the airplane's defense.)

Behind the bombardier was the navigator, who also had a gun, on the right of the nose. The two pilots were seated on high, deeply embedded in instruments and levers. The engineer sat behind them and also worked the big power turret on top of the airplane; behind his twin fifties, he had the best view of all. To get farther back you traversed a narrow catwalk through the bomb bay to the radioman's compartment. He, too, had a gun; he could fire straight up when the Luftwaffe decided to attack straight down in a vertical dive. Behind him were the two waist gunners, staggered to give each other room; even electrically-heated suits couldn't keep them warm against forty-below air blasting in through their open gun ports. There were two more power-turret gunners: the ball man, a little guy always, who hung hunched up like an embryo, firing between his spread legs from an eyeball-like turret under the airplane's belly; and the tail gunner, perched in the rearmost wedge of the airplane, astride an oversized bicycle seat, firing twin fifties that operated on cables and pulleys.

You fired at everything that ap-

B-29 Superfortress (top right
& middle) was enlarged and pressurized
redesign of B-17 (top left).
With four 2,200-hp engines giving it twice
the power of B-17, B-29 could hit
400 mph, had service ceiling of 30,000 feet
plus. Crew numbered eleven men.

proached and grew elated when you scored, which, sad to say, was not so often as you believed. (The Eighth Air Force claimed 177 German fighters after an earlier Schweinfurt raid: Luftwaffe records later showed only fourteen destroyed, nine damaged.) In the early days there was no shortage of targets: You saw Me-109's, cannon-firing FW-190's, Me-110's and 410's, Dornier-215's and 217's, Ju-88's, even Stukas, and, near the end, weird and terrifying jet and rocket interceptors. Machine-gun fire the Seventeen could stand, but heavy cannon shells and rockets went through like a knife through butter. When the fighters came in, Fortresses close around you would start to go down. A Fortress had many ways of dying: pitching slowly forward into a steepening dive; spinning down with one wing blown clean away; in a long, obscene trail of smoke or fire; or even in one quick gigantic flash that left nothing but smoldering debris. And always you watched and prayed for parachutes: *C'mon, baby. Get out, baby. Bail out before she goes up.* In the bad days toward the end of 1943, when the Germans had pulled back their fighters to defend the Fatherland and could put up a *thousand* at once, and had got fighter production up to a *thousand* every month, USAAF losses hit 120 percent of full complement inside four months. A bomber crew's tour was twenty-five missions, and with one in ten Seventeens going down every mission, you were on borrowed time if you lasted beyond your first ten.

What saved the Seventeens, early in 1944, was the sudden abundance of escorting long-range P-51's—the "Little Friends." With the lead bomber more often making it to the target, bombing accuracy went up. And since prime targets were fighter factories and oil refineries, there began to be ever fewer German fighters coming up to intercept. Even so, one third of all the 12,731 B-17's ever built went down, and the Eighth and Fifteenth Air Forces'

losses in killed, wounded, taken prisoner, or simply missing, totaled nearly one hundred thousand men. As for how many Germans died in the flaming holocausts of rubble to which the USAAF by day and the RAF by night reduced their cities, no one will ever know. But up to its time the B-17 Flying Fortress, like the B-29 Superfortress which similarly incinerated Japan, was surely the most terrible weapon of war ever unsheathed.

Carnage had even attended the birth of both planes. The prototype B-17 crashed on an early flight (after takeoff with elevators locked) and burned its two pilots to death. The second prototype B-29 developed an inextinguishable engine fire and dived into an office building, starting a conflagration that killed nineteen in the building as well as all of its crew of eleven. The third B-29 also crashed.

Losses during the B-29 raids on Japan, while they never matched those sustained by the B-17's in 1943, were sufficient to persuade General Curtis LeMay finally to abandon day bombing in favor of low-altitude incendiary attacks after dark. Japan's wood and paper cities took fire like tinder, till finally there were few targets left. They also were able to offer so little defense that B-29 combat losses were hardly more than on training missions. (Engine fires remained a scourge.) The atomic bomb was no more than the *coup de grâce,* an excuse for a Japanese surrender without loss of face.

The B-29 was a pressurized Fortress, with remotely controlled power gun turrets that pressurization necessitated. It was one-third larger, twice as powerful and nearly twice as heavy as the B-17. Almost four thousand—costing $639,188 each—were built. The final Superfortress was the postwar B-50, with gigantic 3,500-hp, 28-cylinder, four-row Pratt & Whitneys. In 1949, a B-50, sustained by in-flight refueling, became the first airplane to circumnavigate the world nonstop.

Grumman's Cats

58

"The enemy plane was a new type I had never seen before," remembers Lieutenant Saburo Sakai, whose sixty-four kills made him the leading Japanese ace to survive the war. "Probably a Grumman F4F Wildcat, a type we were told was in the area. The enemy pilot was very skilled in combat. As we fought, twisting and turning, I realized also that the Grumman's fighting performance far exceeded that of any other American, Dutch or Chinese fighter planes I had encountered.

"I had full confidence in my ability to destroy the Grumman, and decided to finish off the enemy fighter with only my 7.7mm machine guns." (The Zero also carried two 20mm slow-firing cannons.) "For some strange reason, even after I had poured about five or six hundred rounds of ammunition directly into the Grumman, the airplane did not fall but kept on flying. I thought this very odd—it had never happened before—and closed the distance between the two airplanes until I could almost reach out and touch the Grumman. To my surprise, his rudder and tail were ripped to shreds, looking like an old torn piece of rag.

"My Zero pulled ahead of the enemy fighter. I slid open the canopy and turned to look back at the enemy pilot. He was a big man, with an oval face and a fair complexion. We stared at each other for countless seconds; I would never forget the strange feeling when our eyes met. He was seriously wounded. Changing his hand holding the control stick from his right to his left hand, he acted as though he were praying, 'Save me!' with his right."

But there's little place for pity in war. "The time had come to destroy the enemy fighter," Sakai decided. "Switching the cannon switch to 'on' I closed in again and pushed the trigger. The Grumman went to pieces in the air, and plunged earthwards. Far below I saw a parachute open."

The Zero had been a very nasty surprise to Americans, long used to dismissing the products of Japanese industry as cheap, shoddy, and imitative. Combat quickly proved that of U.S. Navy fighters the Wildcat alone was fit to be sent up against the Zero, and at that the Grumman was outclassed in speed, climb, range, and maneuverability. Yet it made a fearsome combat weapon once pilots learned how to use it. The Grumman F4F was almost unbelievably rugged. Designed to have an 8G structure, it proved capable of withstanding better than twelve. Its abundant armor plate and self-sealing gas tanks enabled it to absorb a hail of enemy fire and still fly, and its six Browning fifties were a far better weapon system than the Zero's combination of rifle-caliber machine guns and low-muzzle-velocity cannon.

You couldn't stay around to mess with the Zeros in a Wildcat. You got as high above the Nips as you could and dove like hell, right through their formation, firing as you came, continuing your dive until you could safely zoom back up to altitude and repeat the maneuver. And you didn't cruise along in neat formations as they did, but flew in pairs in a "Thach weave," forever corkscrewing across each other's tail lest you be jumped while daydreaming.

The Wildcat was the U. S. Navy's principal, indeed, *only* fighter for the entire first half of the Pacific campaign, throughout those grim months when the Japanese pounded southeastward across the islands of the tropical Pacific, until the tide was turned and the fighting began to crawl back westward. Twelve Wildcats, a very gallant few, defended Wake Island just after Pearl Harbor, and Wildcats fought valiantly in the Battle of the Coral Sea, that foretaste of the future, the first naval battle in history in which ship never fired at ship. To our eyes today the Wildcat may look tubby and undistinguished aerodynamically, but it was absolutely the first successful Allied shipboard fighter, and also the first fighter ever to enter service with two-stage supercharging. LeRoy Grumman began his career working on seaplanes for Grover Loening. In 1930 he left and set up on his own in a Long Island garage. The Navy's enduring love affair with the Grumman Aircraft Engineering Corporation began with "Fifi," the FF-1, which pioneered the enclosed cockpit and retractable landing gear for naval biplane fighters. More FFs followed: the FF-2, the F2F, and the F3F, all following the same general scheme of things. They were "pilots' airplanes," and they were rugged, for those were the days when the terminal velocity dive was the final acceptance test.

The F4F was first conceived as a biplane, and as such lost out in a Navy design contest to the useless Brewster Buffalo. But as a monoplane the F4F did arouse the Navy's interest and they kept up with its development. Thank heaven! For the Wildcat saved the U. S. Pacific fleet from destruction in the six months after Pearl Harbor. Eight thousand Wildcats were built in all. Some served with the British Fleet Air Arm, which commandeered shipments of them going to France and Greece after those countries had collapsed; the English liked them so much they ordered more.

And if the Wildcat, when excellently flown, was a fair match for the Zero, then its successor, the F6F Hellcat, was the Zero's nemesis. The Hellcat began as a redesign of the Wildcat to take the enormous Pratt & Whitney Double Wasp, but it was very much more than that. It was the first Grumman fighter to be wholly designed after the war had begun, incorporating the lessons learned from combat not only in the Pacific but in Europe as well. (During its development the U. S. also managed to resurrect and fly a crashed Zero found in the Aleutians. Much that was learned about that design's strengths and weaknesses went into the Hellcat.)

"The F6F," wrote Japanese staff officer Masatake Okumiya, "had a higher maximum speed than the Zero, could outclimb and outdive and outgun it, and retained the benefits of high structural strength, armor plating, and self-sealing fuel tanks. In fact, with the exception of turning radius and range, the Hellcat completely outperformed the Zero . . . it was twice as powerful as the Zero."

More than twelve thousand Hellcats were built and delivered in three years. They are credited with five thousand Japanese airplanes shot down in air combat, which is four-fifths of carrier aviation's total score. The zenith of the destruction they wreaked was a mission by the U. S. Navy's highest-scoring ace, David McCampbell, in which he and a wingman accounted for fifteen Japanese aircraft definitely destroyed, out of an incoming force numbering more than a hundred.

There were other Grumman Cats of lesser fame: the F7F Tigercat, with two Twin Wasps, intended first as a ground-attack machine and then as a night fighter, and getting nowhere as either, like most airplanes whose role is changed in mid-development. And there was the F8F Bearcat, too late for combat but my candidate for that much-debated title, the ultimate piston-engined fighter. A Bearcat-owning friend

F8F Bearcat—shown here in contemporary racing colors—was produced too late for World War II combat, but was perhaps the ultimate piston-engined fighter. It can go 503 mph at 13,000 feet, and has a higher initial rate of climb than any other fighter, including jets. Dozen which survive are privately owned and are flown in pylon races against P-51D Mustangs.

Grumman's close relationship with U.S. Navy began with "Fifi"—the FF-1, which pioneered enclosed cockpit and retractable landing gear for Navy biplane fighters. FF-2 (right) and F3F-1 (below) followed. Experimental XF4F-3 (opposite, top) was third version of Wildcat, Navy's main fighter for first half of Pacific campaign. Bottom: Production version of F4F-3. Landing gear—as in early biplane Grummans—retracted in fuselage, rather than wings.

of mine—a *late* friend, for he eventually flew it into the side of a mountain—removed all his F8F's armor, and timed himself from standstill to 10,000 feet in eighty-one seconds, and had himself measured over a five-mile run at 13,000 feet at 503 mph. A dozen Bearcats fly today in private hands, extravagantly prized as private aviation's ultimate hot rods. One, owned by a Lockheed test pilot named Darryl Greenamyer and equipped with a DC-6 engine, a Skyraider propeller, and other goodies, managed in August, 1969, to wrest the thirty-year-old piston-engined world air speed record from a Messerschmitt

test pilot, Fritz Wendel. Greenamyer, flying near sea level across the California desert, enveloped in an incandescent cloud of nitro fuel, averaged 483.041 mph over four runs.

In forty years Gruman has gone from a garage to the moon (they built the Apollo lunar modules), but the Navy remains their favorite customer. There have been other fighters—jets—with feline titles: Cougar, Panther, and Tiger. When their newest, the F14, was announced, it was undignified by any name. Tomcat, perhaps? But any Grumman fighter is a tomcat in a battle.

F6F Hellcat on carrier
flight deck (left) began as
redesign of Wildcat to
take huge Pratt & Whitney
Double Wasp. Eventually 12,000
were built. F7F Tigercat
(right) was powered
by two Twin Wasps, but failed
both at ground attack
and as night fighter. Below:
Greenamyer Bearcat Special
set world's speed record
for piston-engined
airplanes in 1969: 483.041
mph. It has DC-6 engine,
Skyraider prop, and
is one of private
aviation's hottest hot rods.

Yak: Hero of the Soviet Union

A Russian was the first man to fly. You didn't know that? Every Russian schoolboy does. Just for the record he was I. N. Golubev, and the airplane was a batwinged monoplane designed by Alexander Mozhaiski, with two 30-hp steam engines and three propellers, and the date was July, 1882. And if you don't believe it, all I can say is, there's no vinism like chauvinism. There's a model of the airplane in the Moscow aviation museum to this day, and it's certainly a neater design than the Wrights' birdcages. The Russians also claim to have invented the helicopter. You and I think another Russian named Igor Sikorsky was the first to construct a practical helicopter, but that was in another country, and to the Russians, anything achieved by Russians who dare to leave Mother Russia doesn't count, and even less when done in the United States of America. Certainly Sikorsky started work gloriously enough in his native land; in 1913 he flew a gigantic machine called the Illya Mourometz, with four 100-hp engines and ropes stretched back along the fuselage top decking, so you could take a windy stroll in flight. A photograph survives of the machine's first flight (see page 210.) There are two Russian officers standing up halfway to the tail; one of them isn't even bothering to hold on. Sikorsky went on to build about seventy-five four-engined bombers whose span (this was in 1917, mind you) was a bare twenty-one inches less than that of the Boeing B-17. The gigantic has always appealed to the Russian soul. In 1934 Russians flew an eight-engined giant named the Maxim Gorki, which required a crew of twenty, could carry up to seventy passengers, and was fitted with loudspeakers and a printing press in its left

wing that could turn out the socialist message in flight, in two colors and at the rate of 12,000 leaflets an hour. Bravado, however, was the downfall of the Maxim Gorki. A fighter performing aerobatics alongside it for the edification of its forty-nine passengers crashed into it, and all perished.

Another aspect of the Russian soul is an indubitable inferiority complex concerning Soviet achievements as compared with those of decadent Western nations. Perhaps this (along with their sporting instincts) is the reason they place such store by world records, battling neck and neck with the U.S.A. for speed, altitude, and distance. It began in the thirties, when the Russians made some prodigious flights of up to three days without refueling, in single-engined ANT-25's, usually over the Arctic to North America. They were not always totally successful. In 1939 a handsome young Russian named Vladimir Kokkinaki set off from Moscow for New York five thousand miles away, only to make a forced landing in a New Brunswick bog, just seven hundred miles short of his destination. I met Kokkinaki in Moscow ·in 1966—General Kokkinaki now, every kind of Hero of the Soviet Union, a splendid old warrior with a splendid limp from some crash, still test-flying Ilyushin jets, still a notable figure in Soviet sport flying.

Russian airplanes do have enormous character. I once flew from Vilnius to Moscow and back in an Antonov An-2, and was richly entertained. It is an airplane difficult not to love—a monstrous fat mother of a biplane, its wings a busy tangle of slats and flaps and bracing wires, impelled by a single clattering 1,000-hp radial engine. There seems to be a union problem in Russian aviation, for I noticed that neither of the two pilots was allowed to start the engine, an engineer being carried for this express purpose. In addition there was a fourth crew member, a small, well-rounded Russian aviator of enormous authority and magnificent golden teeth, who served as airplane commander. Communications between crew members and by radio with the outside world were always at fever pitch. Here, I felt, were people who were still very much alive to the inherent drama of flight.

Soviet aviation, like every other field of Soviet technology, has made giant strides since 1945, and is today very far from the backward confusion that Lindbergh found on his tour of inspection in the late thirties. Though traditionally serving the twin gods of war and transportation, it was very clear when Russia played host to the fifth World Aerobatic Contest in 1966 that Russian aviation is now extremely keen on sporting flying, too. Of course, it is all highly socialized. No one is actually allowed to own his own airplane. But Russia obviously does have a thriving network of flying clubs, mostly sponsored by trade unions. During the contest the ancient and deeply ingrained Russian xenophobia and love of secrecy were thrust aside to allow visiting sporting pilots a tantalizing glimpse of a most professional amateur flying organization. And the one Soviet design bureau to have concentrated with success on sporting airplane designs was revealed to be that of Yakovlev.

Alexander Sergeivitch Yakovlev was born in Moscow on March 19, 1906. He first saw an airplane when he was six; it was a Blériot that ran about the field a lot but quite failed to become airborne. Alexander was unimpressed; he wanted to be a railroad engineer when he grew up. He ruthlessly gutted all his toys to see how they worked. He tried to make a perpetual motion machine. He built a wireless receiver that worked. He read Rudyard Kipling, Mark Twain, and Jules Verne. He was sometimes good in school, sometimes not, but always, at all times, insatiably curious.

One day he came across a book that contained a diagram and a description of a glider. From that moment on, young Yakovlev forgot about trains and lived in a jumble of wood shavings, paper scraps, and glue. Some of his school friends caught his aviation fever, too, and joined him in making model gliders and pestering the grownup aviators at the local flying field. They found there a dump for wrecked airplanes, and acquired something practical to work with—the remains of an old Nieuport that had been captured by the Red Army from the Interventionists in the revolution.

In 1922 young Yakovlev read of a Soviet national glider contest to be held in the sunny Crimea the next winter, and he sought out the man in charge, who made him assistant to one of the entrants, Anoshchenko. A hopeless entrant was Anoshchenko, his machine a simple hang-glider with no stability and no controls; it rose ten feet in the air and fell in a heap. Yakovlev didn't mind a bit, for the crack-up left him free to watch the other gliders for the remainder of the contest. The next year he was back with a glider of his own design (with some help from an engineering student named Sergei Ilyushin) and won a prize of 200 rubles.

Yakovlev now dreamed of entering the Soviet Air Force Academy as an engineering cadet, like Ilyushin, but to be eligible he needed prior military service. Lacking this, he became a hand in the academy's workshops and after two years was promoted to airfield crew. Yet he still burned to build airplanes, and with more help from Ilyushin and the assistance of his line-crew colleagues Yakovlev designed and built a little 60-hp biplane that was successfully flown nonstop from Sevastopol to Moscow (880 miles) in fifteen and a half hours, gaining two world records for sport planes. Yakovlev's talent could no longer be ignored and he was finally made a cadet at the

209

Air Force Academy.

Yakovlev graduated in August, 1931 (even while studying he found some time to design two new airplanes) and was sent to join Polikarpov's Moscow design bureau, where everyone was working on a new biplane fighter. This was old hat to Yakovlev, who thought the monoplane was the way to go and said so, which did not help his popularity. But his own design somehow got built and proved to be 31 mph faster than Polikarpov's. Yakovlev became even less popular. When this early Yak lost an aileron owing to flutter and had to force-land in a timber yard, the commission of investigation gave as its verdict that Yakovlev should not design any more airplanes.

Thus thwarted, Yakovlev went right to the top and appealed to the Kremlin. A high party official heard him out, then took a ride in an earlier cabin design of Yakovlev's to see for himself how the boy's airplanes flew.

Soon Yakovlev had a design bureau of his own, set up in an old bed factory in Moscow.

In 1935, Yakovlev's UT-2, a two-seat sports trainer, won the all-Soviet Union trial for such machines, and that summer, in an impromptu race arranged on Toushino Aviation Day, it was an easy winner. Stalin was watching (and others, including an eager young official named Khrushchev). Afterwards Stalin came over to inspect the machine and to question its designer.

It is a mark of special favor in the Soviet Union if officialdom allows you to travel abroad. Yakovlev was allowed to make a tour of the aircraft industries of all Europe. He was unimpressed, although perhaps piqued by the Nazis' boastfulness. Back home he designed a new single-seat version of the UT-2, the UT-1 (it is unclear why the UT-1 came *after* the UT-2) powered by a five-cylinder, 160-hp radial engine. This gained a world record in its class

by flying at 160-mph—one mph per horse-power, which would be a creditable effort even today. Like Messerschmitt in Germany at around that time, Yakovlev found himself invited to enter a design contest for a new fighter for the air force; he drew heavily on his sporting designs to produce the I-26 fighter, which was named winner. At the young age of thirty-two, he was summoned to the Kremlin to receive his rewards from the hands of Josef Stalin himself: a 100,000 ruble prize, the Order of Lenin, and (favor of favors) an automobile. But Yakovlev's greatest moment was when he saw three of his new fighters fly by as the culmination of the next May Day celebrations in Red Square. More honors came to Yakovlev later: first the title of "Doctor of Technical Science," and then the ultimate, "Hero of Socialist Labor."

As events in the West were leading inevitably toward war, some heroic socialist labor went on around Yakovlev's design bureau. The translation of his I-26 prototype into the production Yak-1 fighter had its full share of headaches, notably from engine vibration which cracked the oil and gas pipes and led to nasty fires. In fact, his famous fighter was almost not ready for the fight; what with development problems and the headaches of setting up a production line staffed by inexperienced workers, not one operational Yak had been delivered by the time the Germans invaded Russia. Yakovlev's factory was just outside Moscow, right in the path of the Germans' steamroller advance. The Russians had long considered moving their armaments industry east of the Urals. But the German invasion had taken them by surprise; they were not ready. The Yak factory was transported east of the Urals in freight trains of forty boxcars each, machine tools and all, with workers riding right along together with their wives and children. The first fighter rolled from the production line in the new Yakovlev

From top: UT-1, single-seat sport trainer of mid-1930's, was one of early designs which called Yakovlev to Kremlin attention. Five-cylinder, 160-hp engine gave efficient one mph per horsepower. Yak-1, World War II fighter, was similar to Spit and Me-109. Yak-9 DD was long-range escort for Allied shuttle-bombing raids. Right: Yak-3 of 1943 (top) was ultralight fighter which went 40 mph faster than Yak-1 with same engine. Yak-18 A's of 1951 were primary trainer for Soviet and satellite air forces.

factory just three weeks after the jigs and tools arrived from Moscow, and within three months the production rate had passed that of the old factory. How was it done? Well, for one thing, if workers failed to complete their task in the production line within the scheduled time, the aircraft was removed from the line and put on display, along with cards bearing the names of the slackers for all to see.

The Yak-1 was in every way very like its foreign contemporaries, the Spitfire and the Me-109, except in structure. The Russians had no light alloys, so the Yak-1 had a steel-tube fuselage and two-spar wooden wings covered with a shell of plywood and fabric. With a 1,000-hp, twelve-cylinder, liquid-cooled engine evolved by Yakovlev's friend Klimov from a Hispano-Suiza design, the Yak-1 had a maximum speed of 363 mph at its best altitude of around 15,000 feet. Maximum range was about 500 miles. Armament was one 20mm cannon firing through the propeller shaft, and two 7.62mm wing-mounted machine guns firing through the propeller arc.

Yakovlev's fighters were the mainstay of the Soviet fighter force throughout the war and were built in enormous quantities. They underwent the same kind of continuing development as Allied and German designs and could more than hold their own with the enemy throughout the war. The Yak-1 first evolved into the Yak-7 two-seat trainer, which was also built as a single-seater. Then came the Yak-9, with the cockpit moved aft and a new metal-spar wing structure that enabled more fuel to be carried. The Yak-9D was a long-range (900-mile) version, while the Yak-9DD was a 1,300-mile ultralong-range version built to escort American bombers flying shuttle raids between England, Russia, and Italy. There were some splendid Yaks mounting gigantic cannons: the Yak-9T carried a 37mm weapon. When this proved ineffective against German Tiger and Panther tanks, Yakovlev came out with the Yak-9K carrying a 45mm gun and he was prepared to go even larger.

The neatest wartime Yak was the Yak-3, a very successful ultralight fighter that proved to be 40 mph faster than Yak-1's with the same engine. The Yak-3 was smaller and ten percent lighter than the -1, yet it contrived to carry the same 20mm cannon and two ma-

chine guns of even heavier caliber (12.7mm). There was a fine Free-French unit, the Normandy-Niemen Fighter Regiment, operating with the Soviets. First they flew Yak-1's, then Yak-9's. Finally they were offered a free choice of any airplane the Russians had, including U.S. and British lend-lease types. They chose the Yak-3, and liked the type so much they took forty-one of them back to France in 1945.

All Yak fighters were stable airplanes with delightful handling qualities—always better below 15,000 feet than above it. They remained highly controllable even when being hawked around tight turns in combat. They were light enough that even women could fly them. The 585th Fighter Regiment was an all-woman squadron, unique in history and distinguished in combat.

The final piston-engined Yaks were the -9U and -9P, completely engineered in metal, machines that were capable of around 420 mph at 16,000 feet. They survived the war only to be turned against the Soviet Union's former allies, for American Mustangs met Yak-9's in combat in the early days of the Korean war. One was even captured and evaluated by the USAF, which found it comparable to the P-51 in performance.

Since the Great Patriotic War ended in 1945, the Yakovlev design bureau has broadened its scope most adventurously. There have been twin-jet night-fighter Yaks, and helicopter Yaks, a supersonic strike aircraft, a little jet airliner modestly content with grass airfields (of which Russia has no shortage), and even a kind of Yak U-2 spy plane. But Yakovlev's greatest postwar successes have been in the realm in which he began more than thirty years ago—training and sporting designs. There was the Yak-11 (the Russian AT-6 if you like), and the Yak-12, which was perhaps the Soviet Bird-Dog. Yakovlev's real ruble-raiser has been the Yak-18, which has been made in enormous quantity and joyously bought for every air force and every flying club in every country behind the Iron Curtain. The Yak-18 is a primary trainer and a very good one. Yuri Gagarin was one Soviet pilot who learned to fly on Yak-18's. But the really fabulous Yaks are the special contest aerobatic models, which have been increasingly improving their scores in international competitions;

in fact, at Toushino in the 1966 World Aerobatic Contest—at last on home ground—the latest Yak-18PM won every prize there was. Of course, the home team does have huge advantages, not least a feeling in the government that, having spent all that money to play host, it might as well spend a hair more on their aircraft and take the honors too. Even so, we all could see that the Russian pilots were fabulously good and so were their Yaks.

And while other modern Soviet designs could well have more influence on the troubled course of history, I'll wager none are more interesting to a red-blooded pilot than the Yak-18PM, which is why I've chosen to describe it here. The airplane is oddly and powerfully beautiful. A long, long fuselage tapers away from the red apple-round engine cowling to a curved question mark of a fin. It sits on a huge flat wing and a narrow, bunched-up, tricycle landing gear. The airplane also has considerable power. Its nine-cylinder radial engine produces 300 hp as a matter of course, and there were rumors that the contest airplanes were putting out over 400. The engine drives a slow-turning paddle-bladed propeller that makes most efficient use of all that urge. In fact, the Yak has such an abundance of power it can start a contest routine at its lower height limit and work upwards—maintaining height throughout an aerobatic sequence seems to be absolutely no problem. The fuselage is sturdily constructed of indifferently welded steel tubing, mostly fabric-covered, while the wings are of metal two-spar construction with metal-covered leading edges and the rest fabric-covered. The engine has an odd venetian-blind arrangement of flaps for variable cooling, which is operated by a valve from the cockpit. Landing gear, wheel brakes, and a board-type air brake under the center section are all operated by pneumatics, something that has hardly been used in the West since the days of the Spitfire. The cockpit has a very long joystick (to give the pilot a good mechanical advantage) and push-rod controls, despite which the controls are rather stiff. There are adjustable straps to hold your feet on the rudder pedals while inverted. The instruments, even with Russian lettering, seem very familiar. The airplane boasts a non-tumbling attitude indicator, something only military airplanes aspire to in the United States, and two accelerometers, one of which is mounted upside down. (It seems the Russians have not yet developed a meter that shows both positive and negative G on the same dial.)

Despite its performance the Yak is an easy airplane to fly, which is no doubt why Russians have generously allowed so many western aerobatic pilots to have a go in it. Most of these report its handling to be conventional enough, though on the heavy side, and one told me he had gained an altogether new respect for the Russian pilots and the way they could throw the Yak around. If it has one fault for contest flying it is that it does a very poor snap roll. The Yak's great virtue is in its power-weight ratio. The sturdily constructed airframe weighs only around 2,000 pounds.

Yakovlev, seemingly alone among the world's aircraft designers, has also built two sporting jets: the single-seat Yak-32 and the tandem-seat Yak-30, both neat, straight-winged light planes with a tiny jet engine under the tail. The little Yak-30 even set two world records in its weight class, of about 53,000 feet and 477 mph. They seem to have been built just for record attempts and air-show flying—for contest work the international rules specify piston engines only. One wonders what the real cost of manufacturing a light sporting jet might be. Soviet accounting procedures being what they are, it is unlikely that the Russians really know. Perhaps it's better that way, for the idea of a sports jet is original and intriguing, indeed, and a real "first" for the Russians.

217

The Howl of the Zlin

Catch an unexpected glimpse of a Zlin in full and fearless flight and you may wonder if you have taken leave of your senses, for surely no mere airplane can be made to dance in the air, as though it were a piece of paper flung in the wind, climbing and twisting and fluttering, tumbling end over end about axes no airplane ever tumbled about before and survived. Can the Zlin be real? Does every Zlin have some private arrangement with the force of gravity that allows it to run up and down the sky like a monkey, to growl its way—more often downside up than vice versa—through a circus tumbler's full repertoire of tricks? Maybe. For the Zlin is the magical machine from Czechoslovakia that has rewritten the rule book for the most splendid of sports: aerobatics. The Zlin is the apocalypse of stunt flying. Zlins have scored highest in five out of six World Aerobatic Contests, and won seven out of nine times in the British Lockheed International Aerobatic Trophy.

Seen close to, a Zlin looks like nothing so much as the progeny from a night of joy between an Me-109 and a North American AT-6. Great long wings angle back from the slenderest and most streamlined of fuselages, while the longest and biggest nose you ever saw Pinocchios out from the narrow, knock-kneed landing gear. The engine seems to hide inside the cowling like a shrunken walnut in its shell, but the noise the thing makes at full power would wake the dead.

The Zlin first burst upon us startled British aerobatic enthusiasts in the mid-1950's. There used to be a marvelous event every year called the Lockheed Trophy, for which every aerobatic expert from anywhere in Europe would gather at some dewy British aerodrome on a magnificent May morning to undergo two or three days of gentle contest. Each entrant was allowed five minutes of absolutely free-style flying—anything he could, or thought he could, do—before a panel of judges, senior gentlemen from the early days of British aviation who were made welcome and comfortable, and allowed a little gin but never too much. There were no endless set routines, or four-dimensional scoring, no complex aerocryptographics that puff the World Aerobatic Contest into a two-week orgy of protest and argument; just five minutes before the judges to demonstrate the best you and your machine could do. It was the friendliest fun and no matter if you could not understand Hungarian or Serbo-Croatian or whatever, someone could always be found to translate via German or French, for we were all comrades in the sport. The Czechs with their Zlins were a revelation. Aerobatics had till then been a matter of performing up and down along the front of the crowd, from one end of the aerodrome to the other and back, always struggling to conserve your altitude. But these Czechs in their growling, howling Zlins had choreographed the sky. They could perform in two vertical planes or in a tall narrow box, or even from below upwards. And the things they did! "What in God's name is THAT?" we asked, as one made his Zlin rotate first completely flat, then in an end-over-end tumble. "Lomcóvak," one of his colleagues answered, but we never could get a decent translation of what *lomcóvak* meant. (The best we ever managed was: "I have had too much plum brandy and my gyros have toppled." You could believe it.)

One glorious day I caught Jiri Blaha, twice Czech national champion, at Oxford aerodrome delivering a brand-new Zlin 326 to the British agent, and persuaded him to give me a demonstration. It was one of the more fantastic experiences of my young life. *Up* and *down* seemed to lose their meaning, and even though I'd tightened my double harness till it hurt I still seemed to be two inches off my seat for the whole flight, since it was almost all conducted under prolonged negative G. The maneuvers were so violent and followed each other with such effortless and breathless speed that it was difficult to be sure what exactly was happening. I do remember there seemed to be at least three different ways of entering a *lomcóvak,* each as nasty as the next. It was an insane ride.

Aerobatics seem to have been long a hallowed tradition in Czechoslovakia, for Adolphe Pégoud, the Frenchman who invented the loop (and also persuaded my great-aunt Edith to take an airplane ride, an equally formidable achievement), put on a display for the citizens of Prague before the First World War. No sooner had peace set in than Czech aviators were themselves taking to flip-flops with enthusiasm and gusto. It is a matter of record that in 1920, one Josef Novak (with his airplane's strong-stomached designer as passenger) performed 255 loops in 44 minutes 52.7 seconds. By 1927, another Czech pilot, Captain Frantisek Malkovsky, was competing with Germany's great Gerhard Fieseler and France's fantastic Marcel Doré, though not successfully, for his wings came off. In the Berlin Olympics Czech pilots were second, third, and eighth, being beaten only by the legendary Graf Otto von Hagenburg.

The Zlin company itself was founded in 1935 as a subsidiary of the famous Bata shoe company. Can there ever have been another aircraft company that sprang from boots and shoes? Maybe after prolonged preoccupation with feet it is only natural that your thoughts should turn to the sky. In any event,

the first Zlin was a little two-seater not unlike the modern Zlin, but very low-powered. The second was a beautiful racer. Then the Germans walked in, and there were no more Zlins until 1945. Czechoslovakia fell into the communist way of life, and the little Zlin Letecka A.S. was nationalized. State ownership is usually the kiss of death to any commercial enterprise, but not in this case. The first Zlin Trener was the Z-26 of 1947, with mixed wood and steel-tube construction and a 105-hp motor. Then followed the Z-126 in 1953, the first with a metal wing structure, and in 1954 the Z-226, which began the wild success of the species. The retractable-gear Z-326 first droned into the sky in 1957. The latest mark is the Z-526, with a strange, self-contained, automatic propeller. Any Zlin with the single-seat competition canopy is known as an Akrobat, while earlier types with the Avia propeller are called Specials.

Walk round a Zlin. The wing has a strange, thick airfoil with a very rounded entry, and it has small dihedral but quite marked sweepback—a way of obtaining roll-yaw stability that works as well inverted as right way up. The airplane's structure is all-metal, though parts of it are fabric-covered, and it is so strong that to my knowledge none has ever been broken by overstressing. The worst that happens is that a fuselage cross-member that mounts the rear seat tends to crack. If so, you simply weld it again. The airplane is aerodynamically as clean as a shark, and the control surfaces are huge.

Climb aboard. The seats are extraordinarily comfortable, the harness simple but strong. Ground handling is easier than that narrow-track gear might lead you to believe.

Airborne, all controls are extraordinarily powerful and harmoniously balanced. Stability borders on neutral, though the airplane is no strain to fly cross-country. I once

221

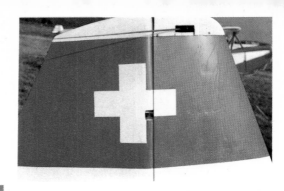

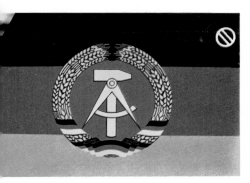

Bright heraldry of international assembly of Zlins includes Swiss crosses, Czech tricolors, and East German symbol. Below is Z-326 Trener, which first appeared in 1957. Airplane is all metal (though partially fabric-covered) and so strongly constructed that none seems ever to have been broken by overstressing. Current Zlins are powered by six-cylinder 160-hp Walter Minor engine.

Extraordinarily agile gymnasts, Zlins
are said to be happy any way except right side
up. Z-326 (left) can climb nearly
1,000 feet/minute. Z-526 on edge in
knife-flight and inverted can do stunts
a Jungmeister would find impossible—though
not with a Jungmeister's ease.

flew a 326 from Vitebsk to Smolensk in formation with the greatest ease. However, the Zlin is by no means the easiest airplane to fly in aerobatics. For one thing there is a marked yaw with the application of aileron, which makes accurate rolls a deal of hard work, and there are powerful changes in trim both with speed and from level to inverted. Most Zlins now have a fixed anti-tab on the elevator (a modification the Hungarians devised). This trim tab lightens stick loads by working in the opposite direction of the elevator. Even so you need muscle to handle a Zlin. Stalls are a revelation. With the stick held hard back the airplane simply mushes straight ahead, with all controls still powerfully effective. This explains how recovery from vertical maneuvers can happily be made well below the one-G stalling speed with no danger of the airplane starting to spin or wander. (If you watch the Czech pilots at work it seems they spend much of their time at zero airspeed, using the propeller slipstream over the elevator and rudder to move the airplane.) Spins are started and stopped with miraculous precision. The only one that needs watching is the inverted power-on spin, where she tends to go flat with only a very slow recovery. Snap

rolls are best entered at around 100 mph, and you will need both hands on the stick. Recovery can be left very late. A full 360-degree aileron roll takes but six seconds either way, and the ailerons are the lightest of the controls. For a vertical upward roll you need 180 mph (redline is 200). Both loops and hammerheads require care; the Zlin must be, as they say "flown around"—with always a sensitive hand on the stick. Aerobatics in a Zlin are never the consummate joy they are in a Jungmeister. On the other hand, a Jungmeister simply will not do half the things that are possible in a Zlin.

The Zlin has been a considerable financial success for Czechoslovakia. Not only has every Eastern European country bought large numbers for their aero clubs, but many have been sold in the West for valuable hard currency in spite of a price of almost $20,000. For competition flying the Zlin simply has no rival. Much of the credit for the airplane's success must go to Ladislav Bezak, the chief Zlin test pilot and first world aerobatic champion, and his colleagues, whose insatiable demands for ever better performance have been the spur for the design's continuing development. Superb machinery can never be made overnight.

Frati: Design for Speed

The first reference I can find to Signor Stelio Frati is as the assistant designer of the Assalto Radioguidato flying bomb of World War II, which is a singularly appropriate beginning for a man who has been designing real go-like-a-bomb airplanes ever since. Frati is a freelance designer whose elegant designs are built—hand-built—in tiny quantities by several Italian manufacturers.

All of Frati's designs are variations on a single theme; they all resemble each other, and each is instantly recognizable at a glance as "a Frati." They are finished as smoothly as mirrors, as though needless drag were more evil than the devil. They have the feel of tiny fighters, for you sit under a fighter pilot's sliding teardrop canopy, gripping a fighter pilot's stick, and the thing will be halfway round an aileron roll even before you've entirely made up your mind to do one. There is no superabundance of room in a Frati airplane, and they are all extremely noisy, but you will come down from your first flight in one with an unbelieving stare. It is much like the first time you ever drove a Ferrari; a damnation of all lesser vehicles for eternity. For the controls are so light, so delicate, the visibility so like falling free through space, and the airplane's stability even in turbulence so arrow-straight and intransmutable that you feel a fool for not knowing that light airplanes could be like this.

Frati's finest plane so far is the SF.260, an all-metal three-seater that was briefly merchandised in the United States as the "Waco Meteor." Out of a production run of one hundred, many have gone to the Belgian Air Force, Air France, and Sabena for use as trainers. With a 260-hp Lycoming, the SF.260 will hit 235 mph, all-out at sea level, and throttled back to cruise power at altitude it will still better 210 mph. (One holds an FAI class speed record gained in flying from Las Vegas to Los Angeles at 214.08 mph.) Initial rate of climb approaches

two thousand feet per minute. Perhaps the most surprising thing about the SF.260, considering its slipperiness at speed, is the airplane's gentleness and tractability at low speeds. The stalling speed is only 70 mph, and thanks to a strange stubby vane that projects from the inside of the tip tanks to correct the airflow at high angles of attack, you never run out of aileron control. And the SF.260 will get on or off inside a thousand feet of ground run. The handling qualities, at all speeds, are sublime.

Wooden airplanes, unjustly despised in the United States, are highly appreciated in Europe, and many of Frati's designs have used wood extensively in their structure. The 1955 two-seater Falco was all wood, as was its offspring, the Nibbio, while the 1959 Procaer Picchio employs a wooden structure covered with plywood panels and an outer skin of aluminum. Frati even designed an all-wood jet, a very ugly and forgettable 1952 two-seater named the Caproni Trento F.5. Frati has had little luck with jets. His 1960 Cobra 400, also of mixed wood and metal construction, was never built in quantity, and even the prototype eventually crashed. Re-engineered in metal as the Cobra F.480, it is still making only slow progress.

The most beautiful of Frati's designs is perhaps the F.8.L Super Falco, a tiny machine whose span is only 26 feet, and which weighs empty a mere 1,212 lbs. The little Super Falco is immensely strong, being designed, when in aerobatic trim, to an ultimate load of 9.4 Gs. It is so sleek that with only 160 hp it can still hit 200 mph. The entire airplane has a finish that shines like polished glass. It is certainly the masterwork among Frati designs.

Yet even when parked all Fratis look as though they are going two hundred miles an hour. For they are the most exquisitely streamlined, curved, and tapered machines you ever saw. They are the epitome of the Italian designer's style.

228

Opening pages & above: SF.260 is Frati's finest design. An all-metal three-seater with 260-hp Lycoming engine, it will go 235 mph at sea level, 210-plus at cruising altitude. It has climb rate of nearly 2,000 feet/minute. Left: Falco of 1955 was all-wood two-seater. Below: Cobra 400 jet of 1960 had mixed wood and metal construction. It never was built in quantity. Prototype eventually crashed, was re-engineered as Cobra F.480.

Lear: the 500-mph Limousine

The stories that are told about Bill Lear—best by Lear himself! How once, seeing some Air Force jets coming to investigate his plane, he set it on autopilot, sat his three-year-old son in the pilot's seat, and went and hid in the back. How, on being written up for his latest infraction of the FARs in his own Lear Jet, he wrote a long screed to President Nixon proposing that the FAA be done away with. How, on being refused permission to land at Los Angeles because of a dense fog, he was asked for his position, and gave it: Landed, directly in front of the control tower.

It would be hard to take such a man seriously, were he not the undoubted inventor of the automobile radio, the airplane transceiver, the airborne direction finder, and the lightweight autopilot. Lear, a high school dropout, self-educated, sustained and fortified by the precepts of Horatio Alger, has always delighted in seeing himself as the technological David slinging pebbles at the Goliaths of industry and government. He went into the manufacture of jet airplanes "like a gladiator entering a tournament," to quote his official biography.

The idea of the Lear Jet first came to Lear back in 1959, when even jet airliners were still a novelty. The idea: an economy-sized businessman's jet, costing half a million or so. Lear was then resident in Switzerland, and there was a Swiss jet fighter named the P-16 that he liked the look of. (No one else did; P-16's kept crashing.) Lear hired the P-16's designer, who drew up the Model 23, with the P-16's wing and tail surfaces mated to a new cabin fuselage. But they've never heard of Horatio Alger in Switzerland, and Lear soon found the pace of life and labor there far too leisurely for his needs, so he upped and moved the whole project to Wichita. Lear is a colossal gambler, and this venture was a gamble with every penny he had, not least on the eventual size of the bizjet market. (Early in the sixties, the FAA thought two hundred airplanes by 1970, *total*. Lear thought eight

hundred worldwide, and perhaps two to three thousand more for military use. Today more than two hundred Learjets alone have been sold, not one to the military.) His bet on the business jet was to pay off handsomely, however, for he eventually sold the Lear Jet Corporation to Gates Rubber for $28 million (whereupon the plane became the Gates Learjet).

The economics of these *barouches* is still turning corporation comptrollers gray. The littlest Lear today lists for $698,000 complete, and costs over $300 an hour to fly. Learjets are tiny, with room for only six or eight passengers, and their endurance is pitiful, for they cannot even fly coast-to-coast nonstop. But just ride in one once and it's enough to convince you forever that no other way of travel will ever do again. A Learjet on takeoff accelerates like a bolt from a crossbow, rotates into a climb of 6,300 feet per minute, which is faster than an F-100, and reaches 41,000 feet in eighteen minutes. (A laden 707 takes twice that.) Learjets go about the land at 45,000 feet, which is higher than most airliners are certificated for. True, you can't stand up in the thing, but neither can you, Bill Lear is quick to point out, in your Cadillac.

Passengers are pampered in a Learjet: sat on supple and soft leathers; lulled by curved walls in green or mustard or cream, and eight-track stereo and cool drinks conjured from behind walnut veneer. "Practical, working comfort for efficient business travel," the manufacturers call it. For pilots, the Learjet has as smooth and light a set of controls as any bizjet, and is rock-steady at cruise, even on the roof of the sky. Truth is, the cathedral quietness and meteor speed of the bird, allied with the joy of not being harried by any airline's passenger-handling system, is reason enough to tell your comptroller to go hang. There are qualities of living that supersede mere economics, and the rich comforts and velocities of bizjet travel are among them.

Opening pages: Model 23 is creator Bill
Lear's private 500-mph jet. Upper two planes on
this page also are 23's—an early model on
test (top) and production design. Bottom one is
Model 25, whose improvements include
more room, more range, and bird-proof windshield.
Left: Circular section of Model 25 interior.

F-86 Sabrejet

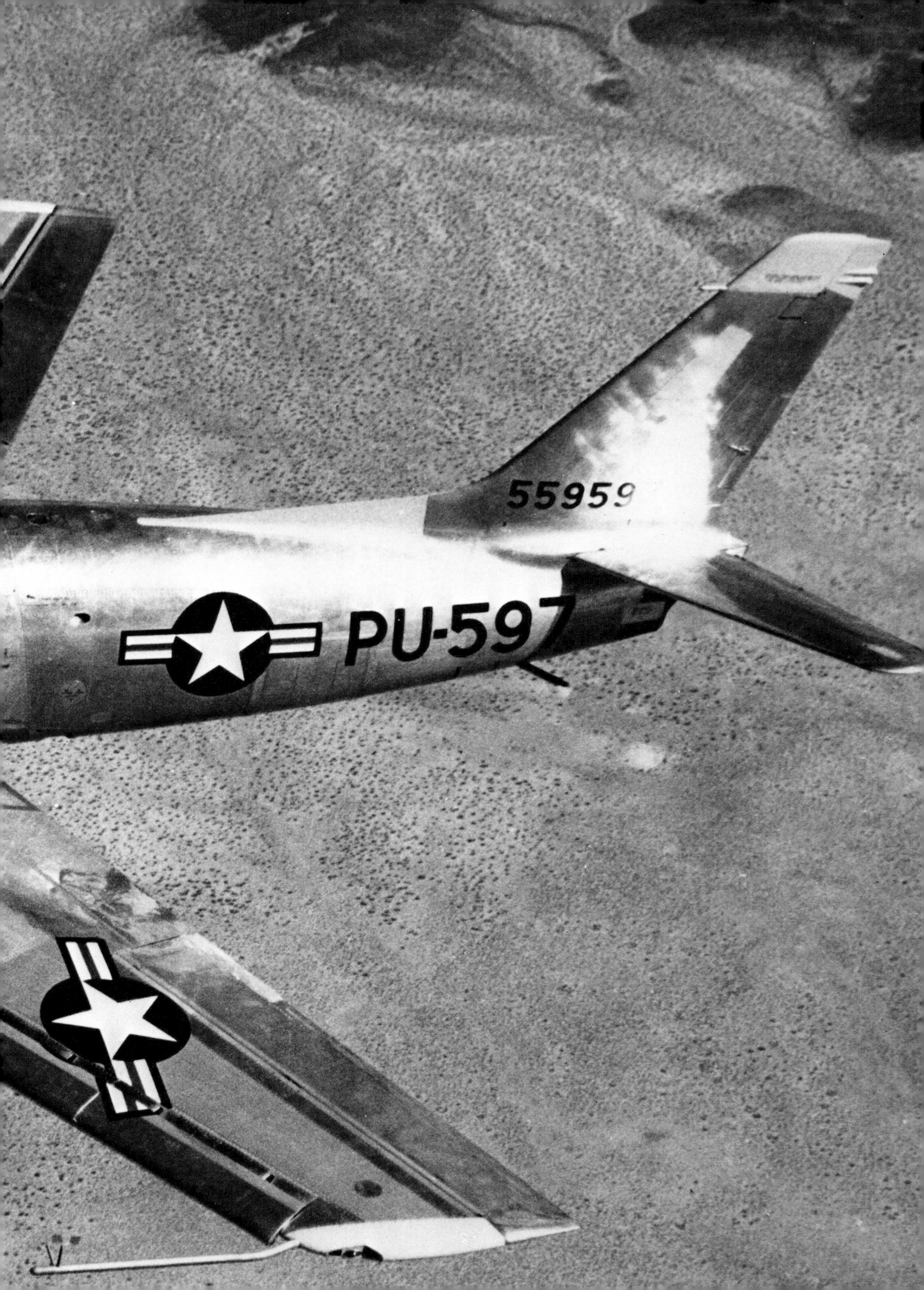

55959
PU-597

"I did plenty of flying from Langley Field, Virginia," the RAF's Group Captain Johnnie Johnson remembers, "and when the fighter group there got the finest interceptor of those times, the F-86A made by North American Aviation Inc., I lost no opportunity in checking out in this splendid aeroplane. The Sabre handled as beautifully as the Spitfire; at height, its 5,000 pounds of thrust pushed it along at a top speed approaching that of sound, it was supersonic in a very steep dive, and had a good radius of action." With thirty-eight confirmed kills, Johnnie Johnson was the Allies' highest-scoring ace in World War II, and his opinions on new fighter types were sought out. After a year with the Canadians he had been sent to Tactical Air Command headquarters in Virginia.

Those were the days when the Cold War reached its peak chill and then turned hot, as the North Koreans exploded over the border into South Korea. At first neither side was equipped to do aerial battle. The few poorly flown piston-engined Yaks the North Koreans could muster were soon driven from the skies by the F-80 Shooting Stars. Once or twice American pilots saw sleek, swept-wing jets in the distance over Manchuria, but that was forbidden territory, and it was not until November, 1950, when the war was six months old, that these Russian-built MiG-15's came over for a battle. It was at once obvious that they could outclimb, outaccelerate and outturn the F-80's. But what bothered Johnson, who had by now wangled himself a posting to Korea, was who could be flying the MiGs? Some of them, in their use of the sun as a hiding place, and finger-four formations, and line-astern defensive maneuvering, reminded him strangely of the lately vanquished Luftwaffe. It came out later that these more skilled MiG pilots were Russians. (A MiG pilot who proved himself a worthy opponent was a "hondo" to Americans, from a Japanese word for "boss.")

Only one American fighter was in the MiG's class, the F-86 Sabrejet, and squadrons of them were rushed to Korea. Even this magnificent fighter had no clear advantage. In the opinion of Colonel James Jabara, who became the world's first jet ace, and who shot down fifteen enemy planes in all over Korea, "the MiG was a better airplane than our F-86 above 30,000 feet, which was where most of the fighting was. The MiG could outperform us; it was lighter and had as much thrust as we did. But we had better gun sights, and our airplanes were sturdier-built. And we had better training, more discipline, more aggressiveness, and the desire to get the job done. That's why we shot down some 850 airplanes, and lost only fifty-six of our own."

In a way it was a repeat of the Pacific campaign against the Japanese: better training, tougher airframes, and stronger will matched against lighter and more maneuverable fighters. For a while the MiGs had things pretty much their own way, being matched only against much slower planes: B-26's, B-29's, F-80's, and Meteor 8's. The advent of nuclear weapons and no one's desire to use them had introduced the strange artificial concepts of "limited war." The MiGs could simply withdraw over the border to China and be in sanctuary. And they were controlled by radar, while the Sabres weren't, and were two hundred miles from their home base, at that.

The Sabres went into battle in fours, in finger-tip aligned "finger-four" formations not unlike those introduced by Oswald Boelcke in 1916, at the dawn of air battle. A favorite altitude was 27,000 to 33,000 feet, just low enough not to leave contrails, but high enough to see those made by the waiting MiGs above. Sometimes the Sabres would come up on the Yalu as high as 45,000 feet, though still five thousand below the waiting MiGs. The Sabre pilots strove to maintain high Mach, where their power-boosted controls and anti-G pressure suits gave them a slight advantage. A dog-fight between jets was a different kind of battle; the enormous speeds, wide, lazy turning circles at altitude, and high control forces made it hard to draw a bead on the enemy. Planes went from finger-four to pairs for combat, where the leader was the gun and his wing man the eyes; that way you had a friend to guard your tail while you were busy shooting down the enemy. Closing speeds could be as high as 1,200 mph in a head-on pass. Yet there was still scope for an ace's battle cunning, as Colonel Harrison R. Thyng described in his book *Air Power*. "You 'sucker' the MiG into a position where the outstanding advantage of your aircraft will give you a chance to outmaneuver him. . . . Suddenly you go into a steep turn. Your Mach drops off. The MiG turns with you, and you let him gradually creep up and outturn you. At the critical moment you reverse your turn. The hydraulic controls work beautifully. The MiG cannot turn as quickly as you and is slung out to the side. When you pop the speed brakes, the MiG flashes by you. Quickly closing the brakes, you slide on his tail and hammer him with your fifties. Pieces fly off the MiG, but he won't burn or explode at that high altitude. He twists and turns and attempts to dive away, but you will not be denied. Your fifties have hit him in the engine and slowed him up enough so he cannot get away from you. His canopy suddenly blows and the pilot catapults out, barely missing your airplane." A dog-

fight might quickly work its way down to ground level, or might suddenly disintegrate; a pilot could then find himself cruising serenely along in an empty sky, with neither friend nor foe in sight. The end usually came when somebody called, "Bingo," which meant he had only 1,500 pounds of fuel remaining. Then the F-86's would start for home. (There were those who miscalculated, and finished the mission as gliders.) Towards the end of the Korean War the Communists were putting up almost a hundred MiGs at once, and many of their pilots were ill-trained, nervous, and easily panicked. The MiG pilots were told not to exceed 0.92 Mach. Their instructions were never to spin their airplanes, but sometimes a pilot could be tricked into a spin accidentally. Such a fight could end without a shot being fired, the MiG pilot ejecting or spinning to earth with his plane. The Sabre pilots' tally of some eight hundred MiGs for fifty-six Sabres was confirmed shortly after the truce, when Project Moolah was announced—a $100,000 prize for any Communist pilot who cared to defect and bring his MiG-15 along with him. The first man across was a lieutenant of the North Korean Air Force, who allowed that his side had lost more than eight hundred MiGs, including two Soviet units entirely wiped out. The Chinese, he said, had been unable to train pilots fast enough.

Like that earlier fabulous fighter from North American, the Mustang, the Sabre had a distinctly low-key birth. In the fall of 1944 North American had been designing its first jet, named the XFJ-1 Fury, when the USAAF called

for a 600-mph day fighter that could double as a dive-bomber. North American quickly redrew the Fury without all its naval equipment and rechristened it in Air Force nomenclature the XP-86. But to no avail; the design was not about to do 600 mph.

After the German surrender, the Allies discovered that German scientists had been doing fine work with transsonic wind tunnels and had tumbled onto the astonishing fact that most of the effects of "compressibility" (drag rise and loss of control through shifting pressure waves), which an airplane experienced as it approached the speed of sound, might be delayed to still higher Mach numbers if the wings were angled backward. Returning to the drawing board (and to their own wind tunnels), the North American designers found to their joy that swept wings and tail would indeed do wonders for the performance of their own XP-86. At *high* speeds. At low speeds swept wings wanted to fall out of the sky.

The North American engineers got hold of a "liberated" Me-262, which was blessed with slightly-swept wings, and noticed that Messerschmitt had employed leading-edge slats on the 262's wings (as they had on the 109's). They tinkered with automatic slats of one kind or another on the XP-86 till the airplane had very pleasant low-speed handling, too.

The prototype XP-86, with test pilot George Welch at the controls, made its maiden flight on October 1, 1947. We, who have grown so accustomed to the angled wings of every jet we see, cannot appreciate how odd that first Sabre must have looked, with its ever-gaping mouth and aluminum skin gleaming like a fish's scales. But it was fast; even early production Sabres hit 680 mph at sea level. It had an initial rate of climb of 7,500 fpm and could touch 50,000 feet. Six months after that first flight George Welch put the XP-86 through the sound barrier in a shallow dive—some feat when you

remember that this scary trick had been done only once before, and then in a highly special rocket ship.

The first Sabres in Korea were of the A model (when the airplane became operational and the Air Force dropped "pursuit" for "fighter," the XP-86 became the F-86A). But the real MiG killer was the F-86E, blessed with a radar-ranging gunsight neatly installed in the upper lip of the air intake, and an all-flying tail, whereby the entire horizontal stabilizer moved, instead of just the hinged elevator.

Like most of the world's great fighters, the Sabre needed flying. In the words of one test pilot: "You hear how nice the controls were; well, yes, they were light, but the plane flew right on the edge of instability, and very nearly needed the yaw dampers it didn't have."

After the Korean War a multitude of Sabres were given away under the Mutual Defense Assistance Program—so many that, what with MDAP and license production abroad, the Sabre came to serve in the colors of almost thirty countries. (Other marks of note were the D, a long-nosed all-weather fighter which fired a passel of rockets from its belly; the F, which had an extended slatless wing, and was hotter than a MiG-15 at any altitude; and the H, which was a low-level fighter-bomber.) The final Sabre was first named the Sabre 45, and later became the F-100 Super Sabre. Like the F-86, the F-100 held the world air speed record more than once. That same George Welch was charged with seeing the F-100 through its test program, and he began boldly enough by flying the airplane faster than sound on its maiden flight. Not long after, the F-100 ran into a stability problem called "roll-yaw coupling," something that was to become depressingly familiar with supersonic jets. Sadly, grappling with it took Welch's life.

So let the F-86 be his memorial: the world's first successful swept-wing jet, and the only jet to distinguish itself in air combat.

239

Boeing

Jetliners

The decor is coffee-shop plastic done in those sickly, dessert-pastel shades that women choose, and if you expect to be comfortable you had better be no larger or longer than the Average Man. But it's a superior way to go: that lovely, long, sling-shot acceleration to the almost 200 mph speed needed for flight; that effortless, towering climb as the familiar world disappears below; the comfort of the cruise, as you sit, seemingly motionless, poised on a pinhead of smooth silence, swimming through the thin, icy calm of the stratosphere. Principally the jet airliner is swift. It has shrunk the round world for mankind. The Atlantic, for example, is no longer eleven or thirteen hours of propeller-driven pounding through the bouncy clouds, but seven or eight quiet hours of smoothness.

And these bountiful birds are beautiful to watch. One will sit at the start of the runway and wind itself up in a thunderclap of black smoke before starting out down the two miles of concrete run it needs for its ballet-dancer's leap into the air, poised on four black pillars of smoke. A cruising jet is too high to be noticed, except when sometimes it spearheads a contrailing column of white steam, at the tip of which we can just pick out the tiny silver arrow-head that is the airplane. The jet's passage from horizon to horizon will take but a few minutes, and if its contrail persists, it will be quite clearly arced, reflecting the curvature of the earth seven or eight miles below.

Sometimes, if you sit by the window in a jet, you may see another jet go by at a different altitude. If headed in the opposite direction, it will pass in a flash. If you should overtake another jet headed the way you're going, it will seem like a great friendly silver dolphin gliding slowly along.

There are many breeds of jet airliners—DC-8's and -9's, Convairs, Soviet Ilyushins, and British One-Elevens and VC-10's—but first, most numerous, and incomparably the greatest is the Boeing family: the 707, 727, 737, and big 747. The story of their making is a matchless industrial saga.

The primordial glimmerings of the 707 came in the early 1950's, when Boeing was building the very large B-52 jet bombers for the Air Force, and had lately finished a run of KC-97 piston-engined aerial refueling tankers for the same customer. It seemed poor thinking to Boeing to ask a B-52 to descend from the stratosphere and slow up sufficiently to keep pace with a lumbering prop-driven tanker while it gulped kerosene. So in 1951 Boeing proposed a jet-powered KC-97 to the Air Force, and was turned down flat! But its sales department had a suspicion that airline interest in jets was burgeoning, for those were the days when the British were introducing their first Comets. It tried the Air Force again, and was again refused. Maybe, Boeing thought, a simple jet conversion of the old 97 was too unambitious; maybe the project should be slicked up a lot. Maybe it did not need the built-in headwinds of an old design, but should simply ask, "What will make the best airplane?"

The Comet had been first, but something of a venture onto thin ice, for the low power and indifferent efficiency of those early jet engines dictated a small, barely economic, and lightly constructed airframe. The Comet's fragility was to be its undoing. But better engines were coming along.

By the early fifties Boeing had built more heavy military aircraft and more multi-engined jet aircraft than all other manufacturers together. But Boeing had not made money on a commercial plane in twenty years. It had lost $4.2 million on the prewar 307 Stratoliner and Clipper models, and $13.5 million on the postwar Stratocruiser, though this loss had been made up by the C-97 and KC-97 versions of it sold to the Air Force. The Stratocruiser had been liked by passengers, but dogged throughout its career by engine and propeller problems (inherited from the B-29, whose entire wing had been grafted to it without modifications); also, its operating costs were high. Did Boeing want to gamble on another airliner? Even building a prototype would cost easily $14 million. Would the Air Force have a change of heart and buy a tanker version? Would Pratt & Whitney's new J-57 engine turn out as well as it promised? The Boeing people did their sums, and studied the wind-tunnel figures, and estimated, and had meetings and more meetings, and on April 22, 1952, one bare week after the first B-52 had made its maiden flight, Boeing decided to build the 707. Only at first it was called the 367-80, to fool any rival manufacturer into thinking it would be just a re-engined Model 367, or Strato-cruiser.

Fourteen million dollars grew to sixteen million and two years passed before the "Dash Eighty" was rolled out, on May 15, 1954. It was a poignant moment. "Employees were given time off for the event," remembers Harold Mansfield in his history of the Boeing Company, *Vision*. "There was a band, and a speakers' stand on the front apron. William E. Boeing was honor guest, and Mrs. Boeing would christen the airplane. At 3:53 P.M. Superintendent Joe Donnelly signaled 'Ready.' The big doors started climbing, folding into canopy position overhead. Out of the shadow the jet transport moved into the sun, swept-winged and gleaming, freshly painted, rich yellow on top with copper-brown trim—a great beauty queen of metal. It rated a champion's applause. 'I christen thee—the airplane of tomorrow—the Boeing Jet Stratoliner and Stratotanker,' said Bertha Boeing, shattering a bottle of champagne over the plane. William E. Boeing, 72, watched

with moist eyes." Then they rolled her back in again, for at this point Dash Eighty was but an empty shell.

Two months later the completed Dash Eighty made her maiden flight, and six weeks after that came a nibble from a customer: The Air Force ordered twenty-nine jet tankers for Strategic Air Command. Soon Boeing salesmen were knocking on the door of every airline executive up and down the land—and beginning to meet Douglas salesmen coming out. For Douglas had decided to go ahead with its rival DC-8. But neither team came home with any orders. The airlines were unsure that jets would be profitable, and still had financial indigestion from the last round of piston-engined equipment they had bought. They were in no mood for still more huge cash outlays. In any case, they were not sure they shouldn't buy turboprops first, and they found it peculiarly hard to choose between Boeing, which had more experience building big jets, and Douglas, whose piston planes they were then flying.

It was Pan Am that finally broke the stalemate, although it hedged its move. In October, 1955, it announced an order for twenty 707's, but also for twenty-five DC-8's. The sales scramble began in earnest. It was an altogether new game for Boeing, and at first it lacked the polish of the Douglas people. "A bunch of hicks," was how one airline executive unkindly described the first Boeing salesmen he saw, adding, "They seemed like boys in the selling business." But their very inexperience could be an asset. When teams from both corporations were in London trying to sell jets to BOAC (surreptitiously, for Britain was seething with "Buy British" sentiment), the Douglas people already knew the right British government officials from earlier sales successes, and swiftly made their own appointments with the powers of Whitehall. But the Boeing boys knew nobody, and had to ask BOAC for introductions to government officials, making it appear to the latter

that BOAC already favored the Boeing airplane.

Meanwhile, at the factory at Renton, Washington, the Dash Eighty prototype was busy with flight testing. It had its scary moments. Even before the airplane's first flight, on a taxi run, there'd been some brake chatter and one landing gear had collapsed. On one test flight the brakes quit cold, and after landing the aircraft had to be swung off the runway onto the grass, which caused the nose gear to collapse. On one high-Mach test, in test pilot Tex Johnston's own expressive words, "Instantaneous severe rudder flutter was encountered. Even though no external damage to the airplane was experienced, I can assure you the resulting vibration was appreciable . . . . The flight engineer's panel was ripped from its mounting." On another test, "at approximately 20,000 feet there was a terrific explosion—a sound similar to someone shooting both barrels of a twelve-gauge shotgun in the cockpit—and the chase plane reported

black streaks in the vicinity of the wheel wells. The gear was immediately extended and sure enough some of the tires were on fire and obviously blown out." But the fire went out and a safe landing was made, though Johnston noted, "No brakes were required as we rolled to a stop."

But there were no real disasters and the first production 707 was duly certificated for passenger service and delivered to Pan Am in August, 1958. By this time Boeing's investment in the 707 had risen to a horrendous $185 million—$36 million more than the corporation's net worth! As Boeing chairman William T. Allen was to explain it years later, "The really big financial risk comes when the manufacturer commits himself to build production airplanes. He sells the first airplanes at far below actual costs. If the number sold turns out to be much smaller than hoped for, or if the costs turn out to much higher than anticipated, the difference is a direct loss." So you do your sums and

plot your graphs, and still end up faced with a colossal gamble, and in the words of *Fortune* magazine, "Colossal gambles are an Allen trademark." For Boeing the gamble paid off. Ten years after Pan Am's inaugural 707 flight from New York to Paris in October, 1958, orders for Boeing jetliners totaled nearly two thousand. Nearly one thousand had been sold to the military alone. The secret, then, is sales—and the tightest possible control over costs. Other manufacturers were less lucky, or less skillful. Runaway costs on the DC-8 and -9 program brought down Douglas and brought about a merger with McDonnell. The Convair division of General Dynamics had, by the end of 1961, written off $425 million on its jetliner project—the biggest production loss ever sustained by any corporation ever, and almost one-quarter of General Dynamics' net worth!

Boeing's salesmen quickly found that no two customers seemed to want the same

Boeing family of jetliners represents half of free world jet transport total. Opposite: 707 (top) and 727. This page: 737 (top) and 747. Like 727, the 737 is designed for short runways. Jumbojet 747 began service with Pan Am in early 1970, seats up to 400, is 2½ times longer than 737.

airplane, so the 707 evolved into a family of airplanes. As engines improved in performance, the fuselage was "stretched" to carry more passengers and the wings to carry more fuel. There was, for example, a special high-powered 707 for Braniff to use out of high-altitude South American airports; a version with extraordinary communications capabilities for the President of the United States; and a Rolls-Royce powered version for BOAC and its friends. This latter introduced the wholesale switch to fanjet engines which has further enhanced the 707's performance. (A fanjet 707 is faster, while burning four tons less fuel on a transcontinental trip, which permits four tons more revenue load.)

For the airlines, too, the 707 has proved to be a gamble that paid off. While the jet engine's thirst for fuel had been in no way exaggerated, other costs came tumbling down. The jets seemed to need much less maintenance. The engines ran almost forever, and the lack of vibration gave every other part of the structure a longer life. Training pilots to fly the big bent-wing birds was easier than expected, and to everyone's astonishment (in view of their much higher takeoff and approach speeds) they turned out twice as safe as any previous airliner. This was owing to enormous power (for getting up out of trouble), very strong structures, and a wing specially designed to cope with the (very rare) engine problems. But principally it was the jets' prodigious capacity for work that made them pay off. In one hour of flight they carried a third more paying passengers twice as far as the noisy piston machinery they had replaced. And they kept on working. More than ten hours a day average, every day of the year, was not unusual.

Among the busiest of Boeings, still, is that venerable prototype 707, the Dash Eighty. She has proved out the flying-boom refueling system for the Air Force's tankers, and has accommodated to numerous engines. She has flown with a fifth engine mounted on the rear fuselage, 727-fashion, and with three different types of engine installed at one time. She has flown with a variety of quite overpowering wing-flap systems, including the 727's triple-slotted barn doors, and a power-driven blown-flap system that enabled her to land at a mere 80 mph. Dash Eighty has flown off mud and sand on a special landing gear with twice the normal number of wheels. With a fifteen-foot-long Pinocchio extension to her nose, and a horrible Walt Disney face dreamed up by someone in the paint shop, she has served with computer help to assay the low-speed handling qualities of Boeing's SST designs.

"We have to win," Bill Allen had said at an early stage in the game, "by technical excellence." And Boeing did. The game was closely run. Just how close it could be is shown by the figures for the 727, the short-range tri-motored jet that Boeing evolved to meet Eastern Airlines' insistence on a jet that could use La Guardia's 4,980-foot instrument runway. Boeing found on flight-testing the prototype 727 that its drag was a tiny 3.5 percent less than expected; that its engines burned just under three percent less fuel than Pratt & Whitney had promised; and that its structure was ten percent stronger than they had calculated. The net effect was an increase in payload capability worth $2 million over ten years to each operator of every $4.2-million 727 built.

Boeing's jetliner family has grown to include the little 737 short-range transport, as well as the 707 and its 720 derivative, and the 727. Newest is the 747 jumbo, with Boeing's investment in that program touching $750 million, some ninety-eight percent of the company's net worth. Yet already Boeing is looking ahead to the supersonic airliner program. That is a financial gamble so stupendous as to be, finally, beyond the limits of private enterprise. The SST is a *government*-sized program.

246

Picture Credits

The Wrights Fly
8–9: USAF. 10–11: National Air & Space Museum, Smithsonian Institution. 12–17: USAF.

Blériot Crosses the Channel
20–21: IWM. 22: JG. 24–25: MA; poster, page 24, Science Museum, London. 27: Flight International (top left & bottom right); MA (top right); IWM (middle); Science Museum, London (bottom left). 28: Hawker Siddeley (top); IWM (middle); MA (bottom).

The Fokker Scourge
30–31: JG. 32: IWM. 33: JG. 34–35 (color): JG. 35 (b&w): IWM. 36: IWM. 39: IWM. 40–41: JG.

Tommy Sopwith's Scouts
44–46: JG. 49: Hawker Siddeley (top & middle); IWM (bottom). 50–51 (color): JG. 50 (b&w): IWM. 52: Hawker Siddeley. 53: JG. 55–56: Hawker Siddeley; IWM (bottom, page 56).

SPAD: the Favorite of Aces
58–61: JG. 63: MA (top right & left, middle left); JG (middle right); Bev Griffith/Eastern Air Lines (bottom). 64: JG. 65: IWM.

Barnstorming in the Jenny
All pictures JG.

Lindbergh & the Ryans
74–75: William Wagner/Ryan Aeronautical. 78: William Wagner/Ryan Aeronautical 79: JG.

Lockheed's Plywood Bullets
80–81: Roger W. Bunce. 83–87: Lockheed Aircraft.

Ford's Tri-Motor: the Tin Goose
90: TWA. 92: USAF (bottom).

Moth: a Light Aeroplane for All
94–97: JG. 98–99 (color): JG. 98 (b&w): Hawker Siddeley (top); JG (bottom). 102: JG. 106: JG (top & middle); Flight International (bottom).

"What Waco is that, Mister?"
All pictures JG, except 113: Bruce Sifford, and 116: Waco (middle & lower middle).

The Incredibly Agile Jungmeister
All JG, except 127: United Press International (top), Joe Durham (bottom).

Mr. Piper's Cub
All JG, except 134: USAF (top left).

The Imperishable DC-3
140–141: United Air Lines. 144–145: Douglas Aircraft (top). 144: Pan American Airways. 145: Douglas Aircraft (middle); JG (bottom). 146: American Air Lines (middle).

Walter Beech & the Staggerwing
All JG, except 152: Beech Aircraft (2nd from top & bottom right).

Messerschmitt 109
154–155, 157: JG. 159: Press Association (top), IWM (bottom). 160–161: JG. 162: USAF (top), JG (middle & bottom).

The Spitfire
164–165, 168, 170–171: JG. 172: Vickers Armstrong (top right), Flight International (bottom right). 173: "Aeroplane." 175: IWM (top & middle), UPI (bottom). 177: Charles E. Brown (top), Vickers Armstrong (bottom).

P-51: the Wide-ranging Mustang
178–179: JG. 180–181: IWM. 182, 183 (top): North American. 183: IWM (middle & bottom). 184: JG.

The Flying Fortress
186–187: Hans Groenhoff/Flying. 189: Boeing. 190–191: Hans Groenhoff (top & middle). 192: USAF (top & bottom). 193: USAF (bottom).

Grumman's Cats
196–197, 200–201: JG. 202: Grumman (top), U.S. Navy (bottom). 203: Grumman (top), JG (bottom). 204: U.S. Navy (top). 205: Grumman (top). 204–205: JG (bottom).

Yak: Hero of the Soviet Union
206–207: JG. 210, 211 (top): MA. 212: John Blake (top), IWM (middle & bottom). 213: IWM (top), Sovfoto (bottom). 214–215: JG. 216: JG, except 2nd right, Sergei Yakovlev.

The Howl of the Zlin
All JG, except 224 (right) and 225: Omnipol.

Frati: Design for Speed
226–227: Richard B. Weeghman/Flying. 229: Richard B. Weeghman/Flying (top), Howard Levy (middle).

Lear: the 500-mph Limousine
233: JG, except top.

F-86 Sabrejet
234–235: North American. 237: JG. 238: North American (top), USAF (2nd from top), Department of Defense (bottom left).

Boeing Jetliners
240: JG. 241, 243, 244–245: Boeing.

Bibliography

WRIGHTS
Gibbs-Smith, Charles H., *The Invention of the Aeroplane 1799-1909*. London, Faber & Faber, 1966.
Kelly, Fred C., *Miracle at Kitty Hawk*. New York, Farrar, Straus, 1951.
————, *The Wright Brothers*. New York, Harcourt, Brace, 1943.
MacMillan, Norman, *Great Airmen*. London, Bell, 1955.
————, *Great Aircraft*. London, Bell, 1960.

BLERIOT
Turner, C. C., *The Old Flying Days*. London, Sampson Low, 1927.
Villard, Henry Serrano, *Contact! The Story of the Early Birds*. New York, Crowell, 1968.
Wheeler, Allen, *Building Aeroplanes for "Those Magnificent Men."* London, Foulis, 1965.

FOKKER
Burrows, William E., *Richthofen*. New York, Harcourt, Brace & World, 1969.
Fokker, Anthony, *Flying Dutchman*. New York, Henry Holt, 1931.
Jablonski, Edward, *The Knighted Skies*. London, Nelson, 1964.
Johnson, John, *Full Circle*. London, Chatto & Windus, 1964.
Nowarra, H. J., and Brown, Kimbrough, *Von Richthofen and the Flying Circus*. Letchworth, England, Harleyford, 1958.
Phelan, Joseph A., *Heroes and Aeroplanes of the Great War 1914-1918*. New York, Grosset & Dunlap, 1966.
Udet, Ernst, *Ace of the Black Cross*. London, Newnes, 1937.
Weyl, A. R., *Fokker: The Creative Years*. London, Putnam, 1965.

SOPWITH
Bruce, J. M., *British Aeroplanes 1914-1918*. London, Putnam, 1957.
MacMillan, Norman, *Into the Blue*. London, Duckworth, 1929.
Penrose, Harold, *British Aviation—The Pioneer Years*. London, Putnam, 1967.
————, *British Aviation—The War Years 1915-1919*. London, Putnam, 1970.

SPAD
Fonck, René, *Ace of Aces*. New York, Doubleday, 1967.
Mason, Herbert Molloy, *The Lafayette Escadrille*. New York, Random House, 1964.
Norman, Aaron, *The Great Air War*. New York, Macmillan, 1968.
Rickenbacker, Edward V., *Fighting the Flying Circus*. New York, Doubleday, 1965.
————, *Rickenbacker—an Autobiography*. Englewood Cliffs, New Jersey, Prentice-Hall, 1967.

JENNY
Caidin, Martin, *Barnstorming*. New York, Duell, Sloan & Pearce, 1965.

Dwiggins, Don, *The Barnstormers*. New York, Grosset & Dunlap, 1968.
Glines, Carroll V., *The Saga of the Air Mail*. Princeton, Van Nostrand, 1968.
Stilwell, Hart, and Rodgers, Slats, *Old Soggy No. 1*. New York, Messner, 1945.

RYAN
Lindbergh, Charles A., *The Spirit of St. Louis*. New York, Scribner's, 1953.

LOCKHEED
Allen, Richard Sanders, *Revolution in the Sky*. Brattleboro, Vermont, Stephen Green, 1967.
Post, Wiley, and Gatty, Harold, *Around the World in Eight Days*. New York, Rand McNally, 1931.
Wilkins, Sir Hubert, *Flying the Arctic*. New York, Putnam, 1928.
Of Men and Stars, March, 1957 through January, 1958. Lockheed, Burbank, California.

FORD
Stout, William B., *So Away I Went*. New York, Bobbs-Merrill, 1951.
Ingells, Douglas J., *Tin Goose*. Fallbrook, California, Aero, 1968.
Larkins, William T., *The Ford Aircraft Story*. Robert R. Longo, 1958.

MOTH
Boughton, Terence, *The Story of the British Light Aeroplane*. London, John Murray, 1963.
Bramson, Alan, and Birch, Neville, *The Tiger Moth Story*. London, Cassell, 1964.
Chichester, Francis, *Solo To Sydney*. London, John Hamilton, 1930.
————, *Ride on the Wind*. London, Hamish Hamilton, 1936.
de Havilland, Sir Geoffrey, *Sky Fever*. London, Hamish Hamilton, 1961.
Jackson, A. J., *de Havilland Aircraft Since 1915*. London, Putnam, 1968.
Sharp, Martin, *DH*. London, Faber & Faber, 1961.

WACO
Brandly, Ray, *Sport Aviation,* August through October, 1969. EAA, Hales Corners, Wisconsin.
Juptner, Joseph P., *U. S. Civil Aircraft*. In four volumes, Fallbrook, California, Aero, 1962-1967.

JUNGMEISTER
Canary, Jack D., *Shell Aviation News,* Number 353, 1967. London, Shell.
Underwood, John W., *Air Progress,* August/September, 1963. New York, Condé Nast.

CUB
Shamburger, Page, and Christie, Joe, *Command the Horizon*. New York, A. S. Barnes, 1968.
Triggs, James M., *The Piper Cub Story*. New York, Sports Car Press, 1963.

DC-3

Glines, Carroll V., and Mosely, Wendell F.,
   The DC-3. Philadelphia, Lippincott, 1966.
Ingells, Douglas J., *The Plane that Changed
   the World*. Fallbrook, California, Aero, 1966.
Maynard, Crosby, *The Douglas Story*. Santa Monica,
   California, Douglas, 1962.
Morgan, Len, *The Douglas DC-3*. New York, Arco, 1964.

STAGGERWING

McDaniel, William H., *Beech*. Wichita,
   McCormick-Armstrong, 1950.
Smith, Robert, T., *Staggerwing!*
   Media, Pennsylvania, Robert Stephen Maney, 1967.

MESSERSCHMITT

Caidin, Martin, *Me-109*. New York, Ballantine, 1969.
Constable, Trevor J., and Toliver, Raymond F.,
   Horrido!—Fighter Aces of the Luftwaffe.
   New York, Macmillan, 1968.
Galland, Adolf, *The First and the Last*. New York,
   Henry Holt, 1958.
Knoke, Hans, *I Flew for the Führer*. London, Evans, 1953.

SPITFIRE

Bishop, Edward, *The Battle of Britain*. London,
   Allen & Unwin, 1960.
Clark, Ronald W., *Battle for Britain*. New York,
   Franklin Watts, 1966.
Collier, Basil, *The Battle of Britain*. New York, Berkley, 1969.
Hillary, Richard, *The Last Enemy*. London,
   Macmillan, 1942.
Johnson, John E., *Wing Leader*. London, Chatto &
   Windus, 1956.
Mason, Francis K., *Battle over Britain*. London,
   McWhirter Twins, 1969.
Robertson, Bruce, *Spitfire*. Letchworth, England,
   Harleyford, 1961.
Wood, Derek, and Dempster, Derek, *The Narrow Margin*.
   London, Hutchinson, 1961.
Vader, John, *Spitfire*. New York, Ballantine, 1969.

MUSTANG

Green, William, *Famous Fighters of the Second
   World War*. New York, Doubleday, 1967.
Gruenhagen, Robert W., *Mustang*. New York, Arco, 1969.
Morgan, Len, *The P-51 Mustang*. New York, Arco, 1963.
Toliver, Raymond, F., and Constable, Trevor,
   Fighter Aces. New York, Macmillan, 1965.

FLYING FORTRESS

Birdsall, Steve, *The Flying Fortress*. New York, Arco, 1965.
Caidin, Martin, *Flying Forts*. New York, Ballantine, 1969.
———, *Black Thursday*. New York, Dutton, 1966.
Collison, Thomas, *Flying Fortress*. New York,
   Scribner's, 1943.
Hersey, John, *The War Lover*. New York, Knopf, 1959.
Jablonski, Edward, *Flying Fortress*. New York,
   Doubleday, 1965.

Lay, Berne, and Bartlett, Sy, *Twelve O'Clock High*.
   New York, Harper, 1948.
Stiles, Bert, *Serenade to the Big Bird*. New York,
   Norton, 1957.
Verrier, Anthony, *The Bomber Offensive*.
   London, Batsford, 1968.

GRUMMAN

Boyington, "Pappy," *Baa Baa Black Sheep*.
   New York, Putnam, 1958.
Green, William, *Famous Fighters of the Second World
   War, Second Series*. New York, Doubleday, 1968.
Okumiya, Masatake, and Horikoshi, Jiro, with
   Caidin, Martin, *Zero!* New York, Dutton, 1957.
Sakai, Samuro, with Caidin, Martin, and Saito,
   Fred, *Samurai!* New York, Dutton, 1957.
Sims, Edward H., *Greatest Fighter Missions of
   the Top Navy and Marine Aces of World War Two*.
   New York, Harper & Row, 1962.

YAK

Cain, Charles W., and Voaden, Denys J., *Military
   Aircraft of the USSR*. London, Herbert Jenkins, 1952.
Hooftman, Hugo, *Russian Aircraft*. Fallbrook,
   California, Arco, 1965.
Lee, Asher, *The Soviet Air Force*. New York, John Day, 1962.
Yakovlev, A., *Notes of an Aircraft Designer*.
   Moscow, Foreign Languages Publishing House.

ZLIN

*Aerobatics in Czechoslovakia in the Past and
   Today*. Prague, Omnipol, 1966.

LEAR

"Is Bill Lear Taking Off Again?" *Fortune* Magazine,
   July, 1965. New York, Time-Life.
Peipold, L., *William P. Lear*. Minneapolis, Denison, 1967.

SABREJET

Childerhose, R. J., *The F-86 Sabre*. New York, Arco, 1965.
Thyng, Harrison R., *Air Power: The Decisive
   Force in Korea*. Princeton, Van Nostrand, 1957.
Wagner, Ray, *The North American Sabre*. London,
   MacDonald, 1963.

BOEING

Bowers, Peter M., *Boeing Aircraft Since 1916*.
   London, Putnam, 1966.
Davies, D. P., *Handling the Big Jets*. Redhill,
   England, Air Registration Board, 1967.
Mansfield, Harold, *Vision: A Saga of the Sky*. New York,
   Duell, Sloan & Pearce, 1966.
———, *Billion Dollar Battle*. New York,
   David McKay, 1965.
Schiff, Barry, *The Boeing 707*. New York, Arco, 1967.

GENERAL

Aircraft in Profile. In several volumes, various
   authors. Doubleday, New York, 1969 on.
Jane's All the World's Aircraft, published
   annually by McGraw-Hill, New York.

Index